CAREER CONTENTMENT

Don't Settle for Anything Less

Jeffrey Garton

ASTD
PRESS

Alexandria, VA

ASTD Press is an internationally renowned source of insightful and practical information on workplace learning and performance topics, including training basics, evaluation and return-on-investment, instructional systems development, e-learning, leadership, and career development.

Ordering information: Books published by ASTD Press can be purchased by visiting our website at store.astd.org or by calling 800.628.2783 or 703.683.8100.

Library of Congress Control Number: 2007906898

ISBN-10: 1-56286-506-4
ISBN-13: 978-1-56286-506-1

ASTD Press Editorial Staff:
Director: Cat Russo
Manager, Acquisitions & Author Relations: Mark Morrow
Editorial Manager: Jacqueline Edlund-Braun
Editorial Assistant: Maureen Soyars
Retail Trade Specialist: Yelba Quinn

Copyeditor: Alfred F. Imhoff
Indexer: April Davis
Proofreader: Kris Patenaude
Interior Design and Production: Kathleen Schaner
Cover Design: Rose McLeod
Cover Illustration: David Michael Zimmerman

Printed by Victor Graphics, Baltimore, Maryland, www.victorgraphics.com

To Joe and Jeanne Garton

My father taught me: "You come into this world alone, and no one gets in your casket with you when you leave. What you do in between is all up to you."

My mother taught me: "You'll know what to do."

Contents

Preface and Acknowledgments

The idea for this book began to form during the middle 1980s, and the concepts given here have since been perfected based on my work with employees and career coaching clients, and in conversations with leading experts like Christopher Peterson, cofounder of the new positive psychology, who after our delightful conversations acknowledged that we have not only overlooked career contentment but have mistakenly confused it with job satisfaction. This book helps to explain the difference.

As with everything, there's a story behind the story, which begins in 1975 and explains why I've devoted the majority of my career to developing the idea of career contentment. My parents never went to college, and I was the first of their seven children to complete my degree and then suffer the embarrassment of being unable to find a job. This was the most depressing period of my life, and to this day, if I see a soap opera on TV, I become physically ill due to the bad memories this experience evokes.

While facing unemployment and contemplating my growing stack of rejection letters, it occurred to me that I should get a job as "rejector" instead of just remaining a "rejectee." I knew nothing about what was then called personnel, so I made a pact with God: "Help me to become a rejector, and I will devote my career to finding a solution that will help others overcome the dissatisfactions associated with looking for work so they can have and enjoy the career they desire."

Something fateful happened the moment I spoke those words. It felt as if I truly meant them, and the next things I did were to sell everything I owned and enroll in a graduate program at the University of New Mexico in organizational communication and public personnel administration. My adviser, Paul C. Feingold, introduced me to corporate America and inspired in me the desire to know more about the relations among people who work. As a result, every job I've held—all in human resources, focusing on recruiting and coaching people through transitions—has been like a human research laboratory, enabling me to develop the means to fulfill my original promise.

Along with the main narrative that follows, you're also about to read my research notes from all my career experiences, here called Recruiter's Notes. These notes illustrate the main points in the narrative through the stories of other people's and my adventures and misadventures in the world of work—seeking to convey down-home lessons enhanced by street-savvy intuition and refined by academic curiosity and practical human resources experience in a large, successful corporation.

My sincere hope is that you will be able to use this book to help you attract work that suits your purpose in life and that the book will thus empower you to enjoy your career choices for as long as you like. If you are able to achieve these goals using the book, my best hope for it will be achieved.

The largest portion of my career, from 1980 to 1996, was spent with the Miller Brewing Company. I appreciate all the wonderful people in marketing there who I was able to assist during that special time, and the opportunity to work for some of the world's finest human resources professionals, including Al Akins and Dan Masta, who hired me; Ken Aron, my first boss; and Tom Thurman, who gave me continuous support while I worked for Miller and later for Kraft Foods. I thank Paul Edmond and Jerry Misik, who taught me how to recruit, and David Brenner and John Dowell, whose friendship enabled me to endure.

I am grateful to Dave Welnetz, who has been my long-term career coach and mentor, and without whose help I would have never had the courage to pursue what has given me career contentment. I thank him for guiding my transitions from Miller to Kraft Foods and then to starting my own businesses. Similarly, I am grateful to the Career Coach Institute and Marcia Bench, who taught me the significant differences between human resources practitioner and career coach and also how to help other people find their own career contentment.

Several of the ideas in this book could not have been fully developed without the influence of numerous researchers in neurology, physics, and the behavioral sciences devoted to positive psychology, motivation, hypnotherapy, stress, resiliency, and survivor qualities. All these people and their inspirational works are listed in the further reading section.

Also benefiting this effort has been the advice and wisdom from colleagues and leaders in the human resources, recruiting, career coaching, and outplacement communities. As a result of their review of and feedback on the book, I am confident that more of these same people will agree that this information honestly represents the employment experience and, more important, provides a refreshing alternative for people to use in preparing themselves for incremental job changes and their overall career.

Thanks to my boys, Brian and Michael, who demonstrated great patience during my absences to write this book, and to the valued input of the new job seeker generation represented in part by my daughter, Sarah, my niece, Claire, and Betsy Thurman, each of whom is in the orientation phase of their overall career flow. I wish them great success. Many special thanks to my wife, Heli, for her everlasting patience and encouragement when debating several points in this book, and also for the blessing of the contentment we give each other.

As you progress through these pages, I hope you will discover a wealth of wisdom that will serve you well during each job search and throughout your entire career.

Jeffrey Garton
January 2008

Introduction

Why Career *Contentment*?

Why do most people have trouble connecting the word "contentment" to their current job or even their career path? Obviously, the world has never seemed a more confusing, daunting, and even scary place to live and work—fraught with big-picture concerns like

- terrorism and war
- global warming and looming natural disasters
- drug-resistant, civilization-ending diseases
- fraud and mismanagement in the business world
- the fear that you will *never* be able to retire.

Unfortunately, we have little control over the ultimate impact of these threats on our lives. And of course, this book could not begin to suggest how to deal with these concerns. For most of us, though, facing eight or more hours per day working in our chosen jobs or careers, worry and stress are usually driven by more mundane but no less real worries—things like

- a boss from hell
- unreasonable work demands
- career and job stalemates
- resentment from other underperforming employees.

When it comes to these kinds of issues at work—unlike terrorism, war, or unethical business leaders—*you* are in control of what happens to you. This idea that you really are in charge of your happiness, satisfaction, and contentment at work may be a surprising revelation. After all, we're all constantly assessing and measuring our careers with traditional yardsticks like salary, benefits, and convenience. Should I work harder or cut back and strive for greater balance? Do I change the direction of my career? Do I look for ways just to appreciate what I have? Do I just put my head down and power through it all and hope that everything will work out? After asking questions like these about work and career, most of us conclude that contentment with our career (what you might actually begin to think of as true job satisfaction, before you finish this book) is too illusive a goal or perhaps is reserved for only a few lucky individuals who seem to "have it all." Clearly, though, I don't believe that contentment on the job is reserved for the few, and if you choose to read this book, I hope that at some level you too will come to believe that this goal is attainable.

Job Satisfaction and Career Contentment—Apples and Oranges

The first thing people ask when I speak about career contentment is "How does this differ from job satisfaction?" My answer begins with: You have to understand that job satisfaction is controlled by employers, while career contentment is controlled by individuals independent of employers. This crucial distinction has never been sufficiently explored, and it is the focus of this book.

Everyone assumes that "intrinsic" job satisfaction is within the control of individuals. Wrong! Try experiencing any type of job satisfaction without the job provided by the employer. Jobs are here today but could be gone tomorrow, and the same applies to all those satisfactions provided by employers. They exist first and foremost at the will of the employer and are not and cannot be controlled by the employee, except through his or her choice of jobs and employers.

Once employees are on the job, their satisfaction is codependent on their performance in exchange for what the employer offers to attract, motivate, and retain them. They expect to be made satisfied, but not at the expense of wasting their time and talents in the wrong job or career. If they're not satisfied, they'll leave—and it doesn't matter how hard the employer tries to keep them satisfied. Sometimes, however, they'll stay despite the lack of satisfaction. It depends on whether their work is meaningful to the fulfillment of their calling and purpose—or what I call their "career contentment." Job satisfactions are good to have but are secondary in importance to a person's control of his or her career contentment. If you don't think so, try paying people to stay in jobs that fail to fully utilize their talents or require talents they are not motivated to use.

What employees control independent of the employer is their thoughts, emotions, reasoning, talents, and choices to fulfill their calling and purpose. An employer can only hope to influence employees' choices by trying to keep them satisfied—and now I hope you're starting to see why this doesn't always work.

Just as employers are obligated first to pay attention to the purpose of their business and only second to the commitments they make to employees, employees are obligated first to pursue their life purpose and only second to keep the commitments they make to employers. Each is in control of their destiny, and each perceives the other as instrumental to their purpose but interchangeable to suit their evolving needs. Employers change people, just as people change jobs, careers, and employers.

Because the focus of those of us in the business world has forever been on job satisfaction, without acknowledging that this satisfaction is controlled by the power of employers, we have overlooked the very real and strong power that employees have to control their reasoning and choices—regardless of employers' efforts to keep them satisfied.

By not acknowledging that employees control their reasoning and choices—and thus their career contentment—the perceived inequality of power between employer and employee in the long run contributes to employees' dissatisfaction, slovenliness, and inefficiency. As Kenneth Cloke and Joan Goldsmith (2002) put it: "Through years of experience, employees learn that it is safer to suppress their innate capacity to solve problems and wait instead for commands from above. They lose their initiative and ability to see how things can be improved. They learn not to care and to accept things as they are. They justify making mistakes and are allowed to be irresponsible and pass the blame to others for their mistakes. They become mindlessly obedient, fatalistic, intransigent, and hostile."

Also, because we've never previously distinguished career contentment from job satisfaction, there has been an ongoing confusion about the proportion of employees who are dissatisfied. Many employees could be content in their job and career but have issues with their employer-provided satisfactions. But we won't know if they are content until we make this distinction between career contentment and job satisfaction.

In any case, if an employee is dissatisfied, it's because an expectation wasn't fulfilled or he or she is in the wrong job and is wasting time complaining. By teaching employees how to recognize and pursue their career contentment, employers and career coaches could reduce complaints, improve job retention, and enhance employee contributions. Besides, we've already learned that increasing satisfaction does not result in the elimination of job dissatisfaction. What we haven't tried is recognizing the crucially important power of career contentment.

So What Is Career Contentment?

Most people think of "contentment" as freedom from worry or a state of complete satisfaction that results from either having what you want or being able to accept what you have. We have all experienced a level of contentment when everything in our lives seems to align and both our work and personal life are going so well that we feel relaxed, comfortable, and confident about the future. To use a popular phrase, we might smile and say, without cynicism, "Life is good." This feeling might be inspired by the beauty of a sunset, a rainbow, or passing clouds, by watching kids at play, while browsing through photo albums, by the touch of a loved one, or by hearing the soft sounds of a wind chime or waterfall.

When was the last time you felt this way about your job or your career? Like most people, you probably do *not* associate this state of mind with your job or career. But the goal of this book is to show how it *is* possible to feel contented about the time you spend at your job and in pursuing your career. After all, your work life takes up a majority of the hours between your birth and death, so why not spend those hours in a contented state of mind?

As a career coach, I first coined the term "career contentment" in 2002 to express how coaching helps you recognize and leverage the "feel good" elements of your work. During the early training sessions I conducted on this topic, people jokingly referred to career contentment as an oxymoron—that is, a paradox suggesting that it is impossible to work and be content at the same time. Most people perceived work as nothing but drudgery—as a series of chores, tasks, or requirements that must be finished to receive your paycheck. To most of those I have coached and trained, contentment has a negative connotation; "content" meant being laid-back, or settling for less, or simply forfeiting goals altogether. In other words, either you had a career that brought satisfaction or you didn't.

But what these individuals didn't understand—and this is one of the main points of this book—is that you can be content in your career with *or without* job satisfaction. Bear with me as I suggest how this could be true.

It isn't reasonable to expect that every day, week, month, or even year of your work life will be perfect. So by thinking of contentment as being numb to what is going on around you or as the ability to resign yourself to accept less, you are in effect creating and worsening your own job dissatisfaction. But, instead of dwelling on your thoughts and feelings of dissatisfaction, what if you were able to look at your job and career in a different way? What if you felt that you—*not* your boss, the company, your lack of windows in your office, or even your fears of living in a dangerous and confusing world—were in charge of your ability to be contented?

This book explains how you can truly create and sustain contentment no matter how these kinds of external events change by learning to be truly able to change your attitude and think of the glass as half full and not half empty. The book seeks to allow you and every reader to discover your own moments when you can make this creative mental and emotional change from dissatisfaction to contentment.

Benefits of a Contented State of Mind

If you have a contented state of mind, you feel more at ease and self-assured. You think more clearly, you have a greater tolerance for things that typically upset you, and you make better decisions. Of course, a discontented state of mind has the opposite effects; you cannot think clearly, you are less tolerant, and you cannot trust your decisions.

A contented state of mind has many benefits. First, contentment allows you to truly love what you do—no matter what your situation, ranging from a job that's going perfectly well to a job with seemingly insurmountable challenges. Second—and this is perhaps the most important element of the concept of career contentment—you will be able to endure and even thrive during times of job and career dissatisfaction. This is true because, once you really understand and apply the concept of career contentment, immediate job or career circumstances (such as a difficult boss, weekend work, and impossible schedules) become less important, and you are able to view your circumstances from a larger, more tolerable perspective. As the world becomes more and more frantic and fast-paced, this ability to rise above the moment and look at the big picture becomes absolutely essential.

Frankly, if you expect pay, benefits, perks, your employer, or any other traditional measures to provide you with contentment, your search will be long and fruitless. Career contentment must come from within you. You are in charge of assessing and viewing your life, career, or circumstances in a way that will create a contented state of mind. Your ability to step back and look at the big picture is an essential strength that you will draw upon again and again in your work life.

How This Book Is Organized

One of the great benefits of changing the way you look at your career and job choices is that the same inner resources that enable you to reason and recognize your contentment will help you attract the work that ideally suits you. In the end, this is another major goal of this book: to help you not only enjoy and be happy in the work you have chosen to do but also to use this contented state to take charge of your life and career now and in the future. The book is arranged in two parts to help you accomplish this goal.

Part I provides the foundation for recognizing and building your own sense of career contentment by recognizing and using the natural rhythm and process of employment to get the job and build the career you want by attracting meaningful work. This foundation consists of principles like

- developing a mindset that focuses on *opportunities,* which will enable you to *attract* meaningful work
- identifying, leveraging, and benefiting from *serendipity*— the unexpected positive coincidences of life
- the importance of *chemistry* and *fit* for satisfying your employer's etiquette expectations
- the key factors to consider when choosing your *ideal employer* and how to avoid the mistakes that lead to the wrong employment choices.

Part II presents all the information you'll need to keep and maintain a contented mindset throughout your career, including a detailed explanation of "career flow" and how to successfully maneuver through the three key phases of any job and career. It also includes a chapter that will help you really get comfortable with a contented state of mind even when the world around you seems to contradict everything you think you should be feeling—things like angst; a relentless search for perfection; the search for bigger, better job titles; resentment when you settle for less. Although the pull is strong to go down that path of measuring your progress by traditional measures of job satisfaction, this section will help you keep your eye on the benefits of career contentment and to use the principles of contentment throughout your career as you attract future career opportunities or just enjoy your current job or career.

An epilogue invites you to join the movement for career contentment—this book is part of a larger effort to spread the word and engage people in taking control of their career contentment. And at the end of the book, you'll find two self-assessments to help you hone in on the details of your career contentment and make a decision to stay or leave a particular job. Finally, the references and further reading section lists the works cited in the text and other pertinent research. I encourage you to consider all these sections as useful resources as you seek to achieve career contentment.

The Road to Career Contentment

My father lived his entire life in the house where he was born. He graduated from high school, got married, had seven kids, and was a farmer until the age of 40 years, when it became necessary to change careers. He sold insurance until he died at 62, and to this day I can't imagine the challenges he endured starting over with nothing and feeding a large family on commissions. He succeeded and was considered by many to be one of the happiest people in our community. His character and endurance were based not on material things he didn't have but on his ability to be content in whatever he chose to do. His advice was: "You come into this world alone and no one gets into your casket with you when you leave. What you do in between is all up to you." I've always believed that if he could do it with the circumstances he had to deal with, so could anyone else.

It's no accident that my career has specialized in various aspects of employment—from recruitment to coaching. I have an insatiable curiosity about why people choose their careers, how they are selected for opportunities, and why they change and move about. These activities amaze me, and I was fortunate that my work allowed me to stay over 20 years with the same corporation, where I could assist and observe so many people engaged in pursuing their careers. Not only was I given the opportunity to participate in the comings and goings of many people, but I could also observe many of the same employees throughout their career and work with them as they made their choices and struggled through challenges. Throughout the book, you'll find selections from what is called my Recruiter's Notebook that tell the illuminating stories of many of these fascinating people.

During my career, all the people I've met have had doubts about their ability to find work, change jobs, and survive bad employment situations—and yet they all did, and more than once. Fate had a way of working things out as if there was a position reserved for each of them. In fact, I believe things would have gone a whole lot more smoothly if they had simply allowed events to evolve the way they were meant to be. But that would have been contrary to their conditioning to take action, charge forward, and get results. For some people, it seemed that the harder they worked, the less they accomplished.

One reality I've observed is that what benefits people the most in their career isn't so much their credentials as their ability to find contentment in what they've accomplished. The people with this contentment were attractive to me as I considered them for employment, because it suggested that they had an ability to endure and get along. And the managers in my organization only wanted to hire people with these characteristics, because they knew those people would make a positive contribution to the organization. Individuals displaying this contentment always found others in the organization willing to help them succeed, and it seemed that when the time came for a change, the right job actually *found them*. Those who lacked these characteristics found that the path to career contentment (if it was ever found at all) was not so smooth and certainly more stressful—because they were expecting to be made satisfied.

Another reality I've observed is that *serendipity* plays a huge role in a person's career and ability to find meaningful work. Some job seekers with the best credentials ended up waiting two years for an interview. For others, the job seemed to be simply waiting for them—regardless of the résumé they presented, whether the position was open, or if the job even existed. These kinds of seeming coincidences and luck are the essence of the serendipitous way your career can unfold when you practice the principles of career contentment. I'm not suggesting that only the lucky succeed. But I do believe that a contented mindset clears the way for this "luck" by allowing you to relax and pay attention to the serendipity that's around you all the time by, in effect, being in the right place at the right time. Thus, in the race for the job you love, a contented mindset may be the one factor that moves you ahead of all the other applicants.

These are just some of the many themes we'll explore in the chapters to come. But far from being a philosophical discourse, this book will give you step-by-step exercises and concrete tools to enable you to find and flow with your career contentment, begin to recognize the serendipity and synchronicity all around, and always be able to see the glass as half full—even in the most tumultuous times.

Part I

Attracting Meaningful Work

The career advice you've probably heard most often is "Do what you love." Yet, as we all know, even if you are head over heels in love with your work and career choice, you can still be completely miserable due to dozens of reasons—from an unreasonable supervisor to issues of how to balance work and the rest of your life. So, in reality, this admonition is clearly not the only advice you'll ever need to be content in your chosen career and work.

Unlike other resources on the topic of employment, this book does not discuss résumé writing, cover letters, and interviewing skills in any detail. Although these basic tools, of course, are instrumental to the process of getting a job, you can find information about them in many other places. Instead, this book offers a step-by-step process to increase the effectiveness of these baseline skills so that you can get a job you love or create a career path that leads to contentment.

Part I focuses on those factors that are critical for your employment and overall potential for career contentment:

- discovering the natural rhythm to attract meaningful work
- navigating the employment process

- choosing the right employer
- enduring the challenges you'll face throughout your entire career.

But first, what does the phrase "meaningful work" actually mean? Finding meaningful work begins with building a positive impression of you with your potential employer. Negative thoughts and emotions are obvious to an interviewer, and most employers are not interested in hiring someone with the wrong "chemistry." Unfortunately, there's no formula to help you find the right chemistry, and company recruiters follow their gut instincts more than any test or assessment. The real truth in any employment decision boils down to whether you and the employer like each other. This decision may or may not have anything to do with your résumé, work experience, or interviewing prowess. The cliché "first impressions count" is never clearer than during the traditional job interview.

The bottom line is: Expectations and interviewing etiquette vary from employer to employer. It would be great if you could simply program yourself like a computer to meet these expectations. But, realistically, it is all about your personal likability. Well then, you might ask, is the job interview process a game of chance? Not really. By focusing on your goal with positive thoughts and emotions, you begin the process of attraction—of enabling these positive thoughts to propel you to success. Without this positive energy, you are just another applicant and your résumé and cover letter are nothing but pieces of paper. In fact, even the best credentials are diminished without the right attitude and impressions to back them up. But job seekers with this attitude impress interviewers as more productive, as having greater potential, and as needing less maintenance—and as a result, they get the better jobs faster.

In part I, you'll learn how to

- build and maintain the right employment mindset
- harness the beneficial realities of attraction and serendipity
- create impressions beneficial to your evolving chemistry with potential employers
- gain others' acceptance and support

- overcome inertia due to procrastination, uncertainty, or fear
- achieve higher levels of self-confidence and persuasion
- view challenges without negativity and instead as opportunities
- make employment choices that are ideally suited to you
- endure, thrive, and succeed by using your own resources.

Part I is made up of five chapters. Chapter 1—"Nine Principles for Creating an Employment Mindset"—provides the foundation for understanding the physics of attraction related to employment, the power of your thoughts and emotions to affect results, the importance of leveraging the beneficial effects of serendipity, and the importance of momentum and nonnegative "opportunity thinking" to your developing character and overall efforts.

Chapter 2—"Meet Potential Employers' Expectations"—explains the five steps to success in the employment recruitment and hiring process and the rhythm of this process, revealing the kinds of expectations that employers have when they evaluate your chemistry and the unspoken but crucial rules of etiquette that you must follow or be seen as a bad fit.

Chapter 3—"Present the Authentic 'You' to Potential Employers"—identifies the two most important factors in employment that unless you are aware of and intentionally prevent from happening will cause you and the employer to make regrettable hiring decisions.

Chapter 4—"Make Confident Career Choices"—provides detailed guidelines for deciding which employer and opportunity is ideally suited to you based on an examination of your motivations and values, or what's most important to you and about you in relation to your choices.

Chapter 5—"Keep Your Career on Track"—identifies how to recognize and leverage your inborn paradoxical qualities and resiliency strengths to stay on track, bounce back, and endure despite the inevitable challenges you'll face. It shows you how these challenges, and how you deal with them, will help you develop the characteristics that demonstrate your evolving chemistry to your employer.

1

Nine Principles for Creating an Employment Mindset

.... **In this chapter, you'll learn** ....

◆ what an employment mindset is and why it's important

◆ how to find the basis for career contentment—in nine principles

Changing jobs is easy when you're already working and the opportunity knocks on your door. It's another matter when you're on the street and you're the one doing the knocking. When you're looking for a job, you work alone and generally without an income, and your efforts are rarely appreciated by anyone but you. The process of finding work forces you outside your comfort zone, reveals your attributes and shortcomings to strangers, and exposes you to the trauma of rejection. No matter how you look at it, having to look for work is a challenge to which few people ever look forward.

But you can choose other ways to approach this task. Have you ever known people who approach a job search with enthusiasm, as if they already had the job? They're happy and excited, they have a plan and networking contacts already lined up, and it seems the very next time you talk with them they have multiple options. It's as if they have unique advantages. How do they attract what they want and breeze through challenges that frustrate others?

Creating an Employment Mindset

The real difference between the person slogging through the job search process and the truly energized job seeker is *attitude*—the sum total of your positive mental and emotional habits that enables you to have a confident stance toward possible jobs. Your attitude represents what you think and feel about something or someone. You could have a poor or indifferent attitude based on how you view your world today (the glass is half empty), or you could have a positive attitude tomorrow as your knowledge and experience evolves (the glass is half full). We do know that a positive attitude is beneficial to having a happier and healthier life and career (Peterson 2006).

Thoughts and feelings of loneliness, frustration, desperation, and rejection will not help you in a job search. These thoughts and emotions weigh you down and put a damper on your enthusiasm. More positive thoughts and emotions—like enthusiasm, excitement, joy, gratitude, and visions of success—constitute an employment mindset.

What is an *employment mindset*? If you can begin to envision yourself working in the job you're seeking, you're on the way to developing a mindset that will yield results—one based on a rational yet intuitive conviction that you can and will find a job that's a good fit and that will enable you to use and develop your skills. Although you accept that you'll have setbacks and problems during the search process, you can start dealing with the issues without allowing anything to disrupt your positive vision, thoughts, and emotions. Instead of wasting time doubting or worrying, you'll build momentum; fine-tune your optimism; and look for tipping points, serendipity, and opportunities for other people to help you succeed—in short, you'll create an employment mindset. Figure 1-1 gives an overview of the employment mindset.

Figure 1-1. Overview of the Employment Mindset

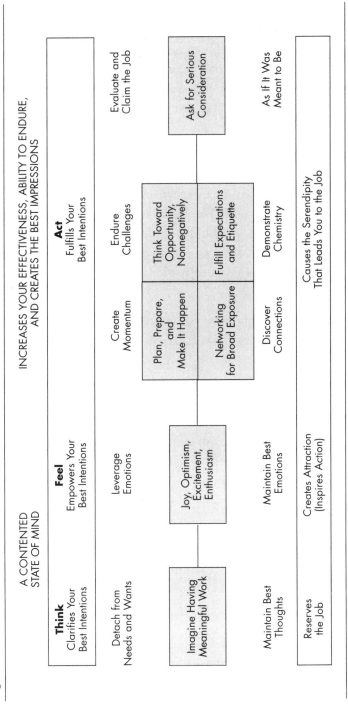

INCREASES YOUR EFFECTIVENESS, ABILITY TO ENDURE, AND CREATES THE BEST IMPRESSIONS

A CONTENTED STATE OF MIND

Think Clarifies Your Best Intentions	**Feel** Empowers Your Best Intentions	**Act** Fulfills Your Best Intentions
Detach from Needs and Wants	Leverage Emotions	Create Momentum
		Endure Challenges
		Evaluate and Claim the Job
Imagine Having Meaningful Work	Joy, Optimism, Excitement, Enthusiasm	Plan, Prepare, and Make It Happen
		Networking for Broad Exposure
		Think Toward Opportunity, Nonnegatively
		Fulfill Expectations and Etiquette
		Ask for Serious Consideration
Maintain Best Thoughts	Maintain Best Emotions	Discover Connections
		Demonstrate Chemistry
Reserves the Job	Creates Attraction (Inspires Action)	Causes the Serendipity That Leads You to the Job
		As If It Was Meant to Be

17

This employment mindset creates the energy that enables you to make positive impressions that attract potential employers who can offer you meaningful work. Without this mindset, job seekers lack distinction and chemistry in the eyes of company recruiters. And without it, even the best résumé, cover letter, and interviewing skills are not likely to produce results. And with that, we turn to the first entry in the Recruiter's Notebook, which you'll find throughout the book where the topics we're discussing can be illustrated from experience—usually, the author's.

All this information about the employment mindset might seem a bit overwhelming at this point. But because everyone likes advice dispensed in easily understood chunks, let's consider nine key principles to help you understand how an employment mindset can help you succeed in attracting meaningful work and in achieving your career goals much faster:

1. Anyone can find a job, but meaningful work finds you.
2. Recognize and obey the law of attraction and the law of cause and effect.
3. Get positive results by retraining your mind and emotions.
4. Develop the new habit of thinking nonnegatively in responding to problems.
5. Think of opportunity by converting your challenges into blessings.
6. Develop the talent of recognizing serendipity and synchronicity.
7. Maintain your momentum.
8. Remain appropriately humble and always grateful.
9. If you think it's not working, it won't, so start over and do it right.

Together, these principles help to form the basis for career contentment. Let's look at each of them in detail.

PRINCIPLE 1 Anyone Can Find a Job, but Meaningful Work Finds You

Work is meaningful when it uses your time, talents, and gifts for what you believe is a worthwhile purpose—adding value, making a

RECRUITER'S NOTEBOOK

Catch Me If You Can!

A friend of mine in the outplacement business sent me a copy of Carolyn's résumé. She knew I was recruiting for a human resources position and suggested that Carolyn was pretty good. Her résumé seemed like a fit for the job I had available, so I called her. She was happy to get my call and was excited to hear about the opportunity. I liked her enthusiasm and positive attitude right from the moment she said hello. As we continued talking, her enthusiasm seemed to rise and was infectious, and I was beginning to think we had a match. Then she said, "I've only been looking for two weeks and sent out only five copies of my résumé. Already I have three interviews scheduled, and I'm networking into three additional companies. This is the best job market I've seen in years, and by the way, how did you find me?" I suddenly realized she not only had options but had an attitude that attracted options like a magnet. Even more interesting was that I had spent the entire morning talking with several people for the same position and each of them felt the current job market was dismal. Go figure. As much as I wanted her, I knew already I wouldn't be able to work fast enough to get her.

---

contribution, providing direction, influencing destiny. When you have this kind of work, you're depended upon and feel the obligation and ability to fulfill any unfinished business related to your purpose, and this inspires you to become your honest best self and do your honest best. You strongly suspect it's why you were put on Earth, and your feelings on this matter can be so strong at times that they minimize the significance of pay, benefits, and other elements of conventional job satisfaction.

More than just for the want of tangible and transient elements of job satisfaction, you work as well for the contentment derived from using your gifts to fulfill your purpose, and that makes your work meaningful. Your contentment remains with you despite changing jobs, employers, careers, or even your purpose for working. It's why you change jobs and careers, why you'll stay in jobs that are dissatisfying, and why you'll leave jobs that are perfectly satisfying. Throughout all these changes, you are pursuing what gives you career contentment—meaningful work.

Although this might sound mysterious at this point, take it from me that meaningful work is reserved for you throughout your career. It already exists, and at certain times during your career you will experience its calling, and you will actually feel the tug when this happens. Otherwise, you'd lack the courage to look and the motivation to endure any challenges. By developing a mindset or way of thinking that envisions your new job and transcends any problems, you'll open yourself up to the beneficial effects of attraction, serendipity, and those seeming coincidences when other people want to help you—and then it happens, just as it was meant to be.

This force of attraction comes into play when you allow yourself to focus on the accomplished possibilities, when you feel the excitement of change, and when you leverage your positive emotions to help make it happen. The only thing that can prevent the attraction from working is you. By focusing instead on your needs and problems, you can inadvertently prevent this attraction from happening or even disable it. Otherwise, the attraction is there every time, and you've had the experience to prove this.

Think back to every rewarding position you've had and how you got it. You probably initiated a lot of job search activity. In the end, though, regardless of whatever problems occurred, the right work seemed to find you—and it felt like perfect timing, serendipity, or coincidence. But this did not occur until you were mentally and emotionally ready to recognize and appreciate the opportunity when it appeared.

Your readiness is apparent to employers, and the resulting attraction is what they refer to as your *chemistry* or *fit*. When they feel this chemistry, your age, appearance, attire, disability, education, résumé format, cover letter, and job experience all matter very little. Although these things are important and contribute to the attraction, if you're "the one," the employer may even create a position for you. People get hired with résumés written on paper napkins, despite missing appointments, and without even interviewing. But if you're not the one, the employer will use any excuse to reject you. This simply means you attracted the wrong position. Or the attraction may produce an opportunity you never anticipated, which explains why some careers suddenly change direction.

There is a natural rhythm to the employment process, and it's so subtle and events get so busy that you fail to recognize how things actually work or to appreciate the power of your thoughts to attract what you want. When it's over, you don't analyze what happened because your thoughts shift to celebrating—and why not?

PRINCIPLE 2   Recognize and Obey the Law of Attraction and the Law of Cause and Effect

In discussing the first principle, I alluded to the universal laws of attraction and cause and effect:

1. You attract what your attention is most focused upon.
2. Nothing happens by chance, because every cause has an effect and every effect has a cause.

These laws are "universal" because they are not subject to change. They are true, reliable, and apply to everyone anywhere in the world. They work every time whether you want them to or not, just like gravity. By not taking these laws into account, you overlook one of the primary ways to conduct your job search with productivity, ease, efficiency, and results. Three observations help to explain how these laws work in relation to employment.

The first observation is that the laws of physics at the quantum level suggest that your thinking about meaningful work causes it to exist as potential energy. Continuing to think about having it converts the energy into reality, and then you claim it as yours. So in effect, your future jobs are created and reserved as you imagine having something new or different, and these jobs seek you out. This explains why it often feels like a job finds you. This happens throughout your career, and when it does, you can actually sense the tug or calling.

According to quantum physics, this tug or calling happens because all matter has a vibratory rate of energy that when released resonates with and attracts like energy in a cause and effect manner. Your energy, released from imagining having the job you want, has a vibratory pattern based on emotions. Positive emotions release and attract more positives, while negative emotions release and attract more negatives. The bottom line: Like attracts like—you attract what your attention is focused upon the most.

Thus, if you dwell on the need of a job or problems related to not finding one, you get more problems or need more. But if you persistently imagine already having the job, you're more likely to create and attract that reality instead. It also means that if you want results that are positive, you must apply emotions that are generally more positive. Detach yourself from wanting or needing a job, and conduct your search from within the imagined position while reinforcing your thoughts with the emotions of joy, optimism, and gratitude. This is the job seeker's advantage of attraction that results from beginning with the end firmly in mind.

The second observation is that the behavioral and neurological sciences have proven that your reality is the effect caused by your thoughts and feelings. Specifically, your beliefs that were conditioned since birth produce thoughts and feelings that inspire actions that produce results that are in accordance with and reinforce your beliefs—and life goes on in accordance with your beliefs, until you change them. Bottom line: Your thoughts help to create your own positive or negative reality.

Thus, if you think you can find your job you will, and if you think you can't you won't. These are different words but mean the same thing as the first observation. This also means that your actions are insufficient to produce results. Your thoughts and intentions precede your actions, and when your actions are in alignment with and support your thoughts, they more efficiently produce the results you want. (There is more about this in chapter 6.) This is the job seeker's advantage of attraction that results from beginning with the end firmly in mind but also by acting in compliance with your positively reinforced thoughts and intentions.

The third observation is that spiritual teaching suggests that faith the size of a mustard seed can move mountains. Specifically, a belief in something that is unseen and unconditional or absent of any doubt in spite of your circumstances will achieve wondrous things. You are to ask for what you want, envision it, and confidently expect to receive it, as if you already have. The results will be in accordance with God's will and timing but also minimized or impossible when there is an absence of faith, or diluted due to uncertainty. Bottom line: You get what your faith expects.

Therefore, believe and you will receive a job, but doubt and you won't. Again, these are different words that mean the same thing as the first and second observations. This also means that your problems and circumstances are secondary to your beliefs about them, and by faith you can overcome them, whereas a preoccupation with your problems and circumstances will certainly disable your effectiveness in getting the job you want. This is the job seeker's advantage of attraction that results from beginning with the end firmly in mind, acting in compliance with positively reinforced thoughts and intentions, and also by persisting in confidence despite any problems or circumstances. This is the job seeker's mindset.

Consider that each of these three observations reflects what we accept as universal law—that either way you look at it, you have to agree that your thoughts and emotions play an important role in how you feel, what you do, and the results you achieve. Thoughts of already having the job that are fertilized with positive emotions of joy, optimism, and gratitude (cause) inspire the actions that contribute to your ability to attract the job that is looking for you (effect). However, if your thoughts are focused on the need or lack of a job, and those thoughts are fertilized by negative emotions—by fear, sadness, doubts, or anger (cause)—then your thoughts help to attract that very experience: no job or more of the same problems (effect).

Thus, like attracts like, whether you intentionally dwell on the results or unintentionally dwell on the needs, and your positive or negative emotions fertilize the thought to help ensure that it works. This will happen every time whether you want it to or not, just like gravity. It's the law, and it applies to everyone, everywhere.

What we're talking about here is really no different than what athletes or performers do when envisioning themselves crossing the finish line, making the perfect shot, or delivering a perfect performance before the actual execution, and also while simultaneously experiencing the emotions of success and the gratitude for having accomplished the desired result. Not for one millisecond do they allow themselves to dwell on the competition or need or want of the desired result, because they realize that doing so would raise the vision and possibility of failure. Instead, they apply each of their five senses to feel the excitement, see the perfect execution and result, hear the crowd roar and applaud, smell the victory roses, taste the celebratory champagne, and give thanks for the accomplishment. It's from this mindset and vantage point that they begin and play or perform accordingly until the end of the game or performance.

Of course you want and need a job, but you need to begin your search by detaching yourself from that need or want, and conduct your search with a contented state of mind, as if it was already done. Imagine yourself already there and smiling in joy and gratitude for having received your ideal position. Apply each of your senses to feel the positive emotions and excitement of starting in your new situation: see yourself driving to work and being met with smiling faces; hear the congratulations of your friends, family, and former co-workers; smell the victory roses; taste the celebratory champagne; and give thanks for the accomplishment. It's from this mindset and vantage point that you begin and continue to work accordingly. Regardless of your circumstances, and despite whatever problems develop, you can complete your search without falling into the trap of thinking about needs or wants. Everyone has needs and wants, and your ability to rise above them can distinguish you from other job seekers.

Can you create this employment mindset without knowing precisely what job you want or hope to attract? Absolutely! Note that in the previous paragraph there was no mention of any specific position, employer, industry, or location. It's great if you can incorporate these specifics, but even if you don't know them, you can still cause your desired effect by what little information you do have or can create. This is your mind at work, and there are no limitations. Right this moment, you can see yourself strapped into the space shuttle, hear the rockets roar, feel the g-forces push you backward into your seat, and enjoy the ride while the Earth rapidly shrinks beneath you through the window. Will this make you an astronaut? It could, if that's what you wanted.

You attract what you focus on the most. Your thoughts help to create your own positive or negative reality. You get what your faith expects. Keep in mind, of course, that your visioning and imagination must also be balanced by realistic and responsible thinking. You're not likely to land a position as a brain surgeon without the appropriate qualifications. Here's a story from my notebook of how one young person with vision, Jennifer, pursued her dream and found serendipity, and a job, in Los Angeles.

 RECRUITER'S NOTEBOOK

We Believed—and Did It

Jennifer tells her story: "As I was waiting for the flight that would take me to Los Angeles and the start of my new position, it occurred to me that what I had dreamed about since high school was actually coming true. In fact, three of us shared a similar dream of working in the movie industry. We naturally gravitated toward each other, and we reinforced our dreams with talk of the excitement of where we would go, and what we would do— and all our friends thought we were crazy. They said it would never happen. We thought of those people as dream stealers, and we initially avoided them until our dreams became so vivid that their opinions no longer mattered. I saw myself in the job, where I would live, and who would assist me. And as I thought of these things, like magic, I began to discover relatives and people I knew who were already there and eager to assist me. Things started falling into place for each of us, and here we are today. Is that cool? I'm the make-up and special effects artist, Shannon is the cinematographer, and Heather is the actress. We're actually doing it. Don't think I'm strange or anything, but I can also see myself one day doing the makeup for the cover models of both *Vogue* and *Cosmopolitan* in the same year. Is that like totally weird or what?"

PRINCIPLE 3   Get Positive Results by Retraining Your Mind and Emotions

Even though this chapter reveals the secret to getting not just a job but really anything you want out of life, there is a very good chance that you'll soon forget that you've read this or do nothing about it, or both. It's too easy and comfortable to focus on the lack of something or the problems, because doing so provides a convenient excuse for not taking action or not getting the results you want. Allowing this to happen is a bad habit, and by changing your thoughts, you can change your results. It's that simple—but not that easy.

Your motivation to change how you think is made difficult by the fact you don't see the danger caused by your thoughts creating the opposite of what you want. This is because of the time delay between cause and effect. For example, it doesn't take you long to pull your hand away from a flame or sharp object. Your reaction is fast because the danger is immediately apparent. But this is not true for your day-to-day thoughts. There's no danger immediately apparent when you're having coffee with friends and talking and thinking about your lack of interviews, unreturned phone calls, and needing a job. It takes too long for you to realize that these thoughts and the emotions they create are prolonging your search. If you could somehow experience more immediately the harmful effects of your thoughts, you would not spend one second thinking about your needs or problems. This is truly a situation where you must be self-motivated to change how you think.

Skepticism is normal when dealing with matters of faith or theories that are implemented inside your head, so look at it this way. You may not be 100 percent certain that a positive attitude will help to attract your next job, but there is little doubt or skepticism among hiring managers that a negative attitude repels. No one intends to attract or hire someone with a negative attitude. It happens, but these individuals rarely make it through the first cut. On the other hand, a positive attitude opens doors. Like attracts like. This is a pattern repeated thousands of times each day wherever employment decisions are being made.

This alone should provide sufficient motivation for you to improve your thoughts and emotions, and if doing so helps to attract your ideal position, what's the harm in trying, unless of course you have doubts, and then it won't work because you're focused on the impossibilities and attract that instead. Either you believe and make it work or you don't and take your chances. It all depends on how important your next job is.

In chapter 6, you'll learn more about the importance of your beliefs and thoughts and how to change them to support your intentions. But for now, develop the new habit of focusing on the results you want as if they are already accomplished. Imagine yourself saying to yourself: "I'm now doing what I want, and I love what I'm doing. I fit in, feel comfortable, competent, and valued. I have the encouragement and resources I need, the rewards and recognition I want, and there is balance between my life and career. Thank you for this job; I appreciate this, I love it, it is more than I hoped for. I knew all along that things would work out just fine."

These thoughts intentionally bring to mind the fact that your job is imminent, as if it has already happened, and all you have to do is claim it. They cause you to feel buoyant, optimistic, blessed, accomplished, and fulfilled. They energize your efforts and empower all your tactical and strategic job search tools. They create the right impressions. What you get is what you dwell on the most, and in this case, you'll have what you want and probably more. Like attracts like.

Instead of allowing yourself to dwell on the challenges, develop the habit of believing that you can, thinking that you can, and you will inspire the necessary emotions that will prompt the actions required to get things done. However, if you believe and think you can but your feelings and emotions suggest otherwise, then you're not ready or you really don't believe it's possible and you prolong attracting what you desire or attract the opposite of what you want. Before things start to happen the way you want them to, you have to develop the habit of bringing into alignment what you believe, think, and feel with the results you hope to achieve.

Thoughts and emotions that aren't in alignment with your intentions or what you hope to achieve sound like this: "Please, please, please! I need a job. I want a job. I must get a job before my money runs out or something else bad happens. When will I get a job? What's taking so long? I'll do anything. Just let me find it. Give it to me."

Thoughts such as these inadvertently bring to mind the fact you lack a job and money, need a job and money, and can't find a job or money, and that problems are expected as a result. They cause you to feel needy, desperate, uncertain, and fearful. They drain the power from your efforts and weaken the impact of all your tactical and strategic job search tools. What you get is what you dwell on the most, and in this case, you'll need more and have more problems. Instead, let's see how you can bring your thoughts and emotions into alignment with your intentions—and let's not keep just discussing this but do this quick, little, but very informative exercise from my notebook.

 RECRUITER'S NOTEBOOK

Exercise: Align Your Beliefs and Thoughts with Your Vision

Glance at each of these statements and mark each with a "+" if it gives you a positive emotion or a "−" if it gives you a negative emotion:

I am certain about what I want.

I am fully engaged to do what I must to get it.

I am capable of doing what's required to get the job I want.

I am fully capable of doing the job I want.

I am confident the job I want is looking for me right now.

My positive thoughts will help me to attract what is looking for me.

My thoughts are focused positively on getting the job I want.

Other people are ready and willing to help me.

If any of these statements produces a positive emotion, then that response is consistent with what you actually believe. But if a statement produces a negative emotion or blue feeling, then your response is probably inconsistent with what you actually believe, and you need to work on that. For example, if your reaction to the first statement was a "+" but you felt blue or uncertain as a result, then your actual belief is that you don't know what you want. Any uncertain response is the same as a "−" response. In either case, it's what you truly believe that creates the outcome—not what you think you believe. Your true beliefs about these statements provide the foundation for everything you do during your job search and how well you do it. If problems occur, return to this exercise to review whether your beliefs may be contributing to any problems.

PRINCIPLE 4   Develop the New Habit of Thinking Nonnegatively in Responding to Problems

No matter how well managed the employer's recruiting may be, or how sophisticated, it's still controlled by humans and subject to human error, including delays, rude or insensitive treatment, biases, and discrimination. Staffing is truly an imperfect process, but it's the best we have. Problems are inevitable, which is why each country has its own laws to help ensure fairness. Now that you know this, you can decide right now how to react to future problems so your thoughts and emotions will remain powerful and productive—so they'll assist and not hinder you.

Keep in mind that whatever happens is seemingly random until you assign it a meaning and react. In other words, how you react to a situation is the direct result of the meaning you assign it; so if you assign what happens a more positive meaning, your reaction and results are likely to be more positive. To illustrate, just imagine these situations, the alternative meanings you might assign to each one, and what your reaction would be to each meaning:

- Alternative meaning of unreturned phone calls: "They don't like me" or "They must be busy." What is your reaction to each?
- Alternative meaning of no feedback following an interview: "It's over" or "No news is good news." What is your reaction to each?
- Alternative meaning of being rejected after advancing to finalist: "I failed" or "That was not meant to be." What is your reaction to each?

This is not about the power of positive thinking but rather developing the new habit of thinking nonnegatively. It requires anticipating any challenges and deciding in advance to view them positively and realistically rather than negatively and irresponsibly after the fact. As you develop this habit, you begin to acknowledge problems as real, but you no longer allow them to alter the productive power of your positive thoughts and emotions.

PRINCIPLE 5   Think of Opportunity by Converting Your Challenges into Blessings

Imagine being rejected after several rounds of encouraging interviews and then going on to land what turns out to be a far better job. Later, you discover that the position for which you were rejected was eliminated due to an acquisition or some other reason. It's typically after the right job finds you that you can appreciate the blessings associated with any disappointments along the way. Rather than wait for this revelation, start looking for the blessings as they occur, right from the beginning of your search. Focus on thinking of opportunities.

Remember, you attract what is looking for you, so rejections are simply indicators of the wrong job. *Opportunity thinking* views these events as beneficial in steering you away from the wrong job and guiding you toward the right one. Like "it was fate or meant to be." If things aren't meant to be, then there is no such thing as a missed opportunity. That's fantasizing about what might have been or otherwise focusing on a lack of something, which will help create that experience. Accept the blessing that just occurred—the near miss of something that wouldn't have ultimately been for the best—and fantasize instead about having landed the right job and thus create that experience.

Opportunity thinking not only helps to preserve the thoughts you wish to maintain but also contributes to the attractiveness of your character and feeds your evolving chemistry in the eyes of the right employer. In response to adversity, you'll appear optimistic, strong, and resilient, and this is far better than suggesting that you're a pessimist or sore loser. From this optimistic point of view, every challenge is a blessing contributing to your development and in attracting the right job.

PRINCIPLE 6 Develop the Talent of Recognizing Serendipity and Synchronicity

Serendipity and synchronicity are two mysterious realities that we all experience—but may not notice—day by day, often in small events but sometimes dramatically. In a way, they are two sides of the same coin, because they both have to do with accidents and uncanny things happening. Let's look at each of them.

Serendipity

Serendipity is opportunity discovered by accident. Noteworthy examples from the business world include Velcro, Teflon, Nylon, penicillin, Post-It Notes, safety glass, X-rays, lasers, light bulbs, and Silly Putty—to name just a few. The basis for all these products was discovered when the inventor was looking for something else. For instance, Roy Plunkett, the inventor of Teflon, was trying to develop a new gas for refrigeration and instead got a slick substance, whose first application was to lubricate machine parts. And Wilhelm Roentgen accidentally discovered the X-ray while he was researching cathode ray tubes and instead noticed that fluorescent papers lit up at a distance.

The idea of putting serendipity to use in business might seem silly at first, yet every business looks for ways to convert problems into opportunities. Serendipity is a necessary ingredient to success.

In the new millennium, the employment process is driven by automation, testing, behavioral interviews, psychological profiling, and assessments. Recruiters are trained to prevent accidents by screening people out, not in, and this leaves little room for the beneficial effects of serendipity. Yet the happiest and most successful hires still occur not because of these objective tools but in spite of them—when both parties feel it was meant to be, it was the right time and right place, and the planets were aligned—because of serendipity! A recruiter hopes for this response because it confirms a good hire and suggests the possibility of success and long-term retention.

Serendipity portends the makings of an emotional connection. Watch what happens during interviews when you discover mutual acquaintances and common experiences and interests. The other person will think you have a kinship of sorts with the people, place, or position. These discoveries help to bridge gaps and create shortcuts in forming relationships by causing others to lower their defenses, listen more earnestly, and be more helpful. It creates the feeling of being in the right place at the right time, as if you were meant to be there.

Consider the example of a job seeker leaving church on a Sunday. She spots someone at a distance and senses a connection or has a premonition that the person could help. They make eye contact and contemplate speaking with each other, but they don't. The job seeker doesn't want to impose by discussing her search. The other person also felt an urge to speak, but because the job seeker didn't, the situation passed with nothing happening. A month later, they run into each other and the job seeker mentions her search. The other person says, "I wish I'd known that about a month ago, because my company has been looking for someone just like you. Do you have a résumé?"

Recall a time when you came close to making the wrong choice or were rejected, and how fortunate you were that things worked out the way they did. Maybe your job search took too long, but the delay enabled you to land a far better position. You might have felt discouraged at the time, but you later realized that the delay was a blessing in disguise. Had you known that serendipity was at work on your behalf, you could have relaxed and enjoyed your job search—something most people don't do.

Somewhere between the two extremes of looking for a job and allowing one to find you, between screening people out or in, is the serendipity that enables good things to happen—and does so whether you realize it or not. That's what makes the TV show *The Apprentice* so interesting—who gets what, why, and how in the world did it happen? Go ahead and do what you must while searching for work, but realize that some things have a way of working themselves out the way they're meant to be, though not always in keeping with your expectations. It's a combination of perseverance, luck, and other people helping you. So while you keep your nose to the job search grindstone, prepare yourself to spot the serendipitous accidents that can be converted into opportunities and seized for your benefit.

If you intend for serendipity to occur through name dropping or pointing out a coincidence, it helps when you do so in an authentic and humble manner. Otherwise—and because serendipity is supposed to be accidental—you could create the impression of manipulation or desperation. Other risks are dropping the wrong name and relying too heavily on a simple coincidence—or the wrong one. These mistakes make you to look silly and lead the other person to avoid you, if only to prevent favoritism or teach you a lesson, and you may never realize that the punishment was inflicted.

Even with the best serendipity, you still have to demonstrate the right etiquette, chemistry, or likable personality for someone to fully commit to helping you. So think of serendipity as simply getting the ball rolling—you still have to keep it moving. As you do, follow these suggestions:

- Develop an opportunity mindset—expect great things.
- Accept that everything happens for a reason and in its own time.
- Express gratitude for whatever happens and for however long it takes.
- Believe that things will work out just fine, as they always do.
- Look for the blessings and unanswered prayers as they occur, not after the fact.
- Look for the connections between you, other people, and events.
- Seek to meet more new people who are like you and appreciate what you do.
- Expose yourself to new situations and accidental opportunities.
- Listen to your hunches, and be fearless in acting on them—make it a game.
- Guide others in understanding how they can help you.

By routinely doing just a few of these things, you can't help but make accidental discoveries, and by acting on them to make the connections, you'll benefit your search and the efforts of others who want to help you. Here's an example from my notebook about my own serendipitous experience in the job market.

RECRUITER'S NOTEBOOK

Sometimes "God" (a.k.a. the Human Resources Director) May Really Be on Your Side

I was two years out of graduate school and being recruited for a new opportunity. I wanted this job so badly that I could taste it as much I could taste the free beer that came with it. At the time, I was still working as a recruiter at another company, and the job found me as result of slipping in my name at the bottom of job ads I was running for my employer: "Send your résumé to Jeff Garton, Employment."

It worked. A few weeks later, I was in Milwaukee and interviewing with Miller Brewing. I spent most of the day talking with recruiters and human resources managers. They said if they didn't call me a cab by 3 p.m., it meant I would be interviewing with "god," the human resources director. At 3 p.m., I was escorted to god's office. I was scared. He said nothing, and I didn't see his face for the two minutes he spent reading my résumé. He was sitting back in the chair with his feet on the desk.

It was the longest two minutes of my life. I sat there thinking back to the months I had spent trying to eliminate my Southern accent. I told myself I deserved to be there. I prayed that he would notice the graduate degree and would please, please, please not ask about my undergraduate degree from Glenville, a small school nobody knows in West Virginia.

Then god spoke the three words I will never forget: "Glenville State College." I died right then and there, and I know he saw me melting into the chair. Then he spoke again: "Glenville had the smallest field and toughest guys, and they beat us every year." It turned out that god had been a quarterback for West Virginia Wesleyan, only 32 miles away. He knew precisely where I'd come from and what I'd gone through to get there. I got the job, and if for any reason, it was that one coincidence. I guess it really does matter where you go to school and when god is on your side.

Synchronicity

Similar to serendipity is the notion of *synchronicity*, which is the strange coincidence of getting what you desire independent of any cause and effect, except that you had previously thought about it. It's like when you think of someone with whom you haven't talked in a while and then they call you on the telephone, or you're thinking about pizza and your friend pops in with a double cheese and pepperoni, or you think about a particular movie and turn on the TV to find it about to start on HBO. You don't plan for these things to happen, but a thought pops into your mind like a premonition, and then they do happen—giving you an uncanny but good feeling.

My awareness of synchronicity was heightened after reading *The Celestine Prophecy* (Redfield 1996), in which the author says that coincidences are significant because they lead us in the direction of personal destiny. This sounds as if there might be a relationship here to connecting with one's calling, but unfortunately it's difficult to control. I've tried but can't seem to make this happen at will, but as a precaution, anytime a less-than-favorable premonition occurs, I've developed the habit of immediately thinking of the opposite in hopes of undoing any unwanted synchronicity.

The author Carolyn North (1994) says: "If your belief system is such that intuition and synchronicity are real and significant, you will notice them. If your belief system is that they're hogwash, you won't." She says that synchronicity "gives us a sense of hope, a sense that something bigger is happening out there than what we can see, which is especially important in times like this when there're so many reasons for despair." And the authors Allan Combs and Mark Holland (1995) suggest that if you expect the unexpected, synchronicity will emerge.

From my limited knowledge of synchronicity, there's not been much conclusive research done on it, if for any reason but because researchers can't control when it will happen, except by trying to monitor intuition as it occurs. However, just having an active interest in the topic seems to make it happen more often, because you're inclined to notice it. The opposite holds true as well, in that synchronicity seems to occur less often when your thoughts are restrained by cynicism and doubt (Vaughan 1989).

The term "synchronicity" was originally coined by the Swiss psychiatrist Carl Jung (1998), who suggested that meaningful coincidences manifest when a strong need arises, and that they provide a glimpse into the underlying order of the universe. This being the case, which no one can prove or disprove, it makes sense that if any source of power unbeknownst to you wants to lend a hand, you'd be wise to take that power up on it by thinking optimistically and remaining attentive to synchronistic accidents and converting them into opportunities. In other words, get in synch with the universe and see what happens.

PRINCIPLE 7   Maintain Your Momentum

The reality that your next position will find you, and how you attract it, are not entirely the result of karma or some cosmic magic. You have to take action (cause) to get results (effect). According to the laws of physics, you are potential energy until you start working to attract, and each time you stop working, you revert back to potential energy. In other words, you fall off the radar screens of potential employers and of the people who could assist you.

For example, if you don't know what you want, how can you know where to look or when the right job finds you? Also, if you haven't communicated your aspirations clearly, how will others know how to help you? Until you decide these things and take action, you are simply potential—or a risk. Also, if there are any significant lapses in your search efforts (cause), it will prompt others to conclude that you are not diligent and they will not support you, or you may have to start over and regain their support each time you stop (effect).

The attraction works as the result of your authenticity or resolve in knowing what you want, plus consistently executing all the traditional job search efforts so that others are able to find you. Now add to this your efforts to develop and maintain your ability to think nonnegatively and think of opportunity. Once all these things are in motion, and you are maintaining your momentum, you open yourself to the beneficial effects of serendipity and coincidences associated with other people wanting to help you. When this happens, the chances of meaningful work finding you are very good. But wait just a minute...

Attraction is a two-way street, and potential employers have to do their part as well. In fact, it's often the employer's recruitment effort that gets your attention and begins the process of attraction. Employers devote months and thousands of dollars tapping into multiple sources and networks to attract people with the right fit or chemistry. When you consider the potential created by the combined effect of all employers, the odds of something matching with what you hope to attract are excellent, and if you don't believe this, then you've got some work to do on your thinking before things start happening.

Because attraction is a two-way street, the condition of momentum also applies to the employer. When you sense a possible employer's momentum lagging, possibly due to their recruiters' and interviewers' lack of interest or commitment to filling a position, it causes you to doubt their sincerity and they fall off your radar screen. Ideally, you're both ready at the same time; otherwise, it's not the right time, employer, or position.

PRINCIPLE 8 Remain Appropriately Humble and Always Grateful

As the employer narrows its list, the final selection will be influenced more by your perceived chemistry than your skills or experience. Both dimensions are important, but the tiebreaker is always whether the employer likes you and believes you fit with the other people. If you've done a good job developing your chemistry, then trust in the laws of attraction and cause and effect, and if it's meant to be, it will. In fact, if you've done a really good job, you'll continue to attract opportunities long after you've started your new position. This happens all the time.

There should be no doubt that you can leverage the eight principles given so far to attract your next job. But whether the job is meaning-ful depends considerably on your authenticity when managing your search. Like attracts like, so if you're faking it, or you don't make adjustments based on feedback from others regarding personality, ego, or performance issues, then you're not likely to get the job you want.

All you've accomplished is to fool yourself and others. Remember, we all always need to work on our lack of humility and gratitude; as the historian Arnold Toynbee said, original sin—pride—is the only religious doctrine proven by history.

For example, let's say other people have advised you to stop criticizing your previous employer because it makes you seem bitter and unattractive. But instead of heeding this advice and fixing your bad habit of speaking ill of your last employer, you stick to your script of criticizing your previous boss, harping about how your co-workers were unfriendly, and going on about how the company seemed to lack strategic direction—all things you believe are true and harmless to comment about.

However, if someone has seen fit to advise you to stop saying negative things like these, you might consider that interviewers as well are turned off by this script and prefer not to hire a complainer. Let's look at some good lessons about this process from my notebook on the next page.

PRINCIPLE 9   If You Think It's Not Working, Start Over and Do It Right

When your search seems to not be progressing, you're more than likely helping to create the delay by thinking about not finding a job. In times of need, this happens all too easily and without your even realizing it. Or you may be struggling with not knowing what you want or feel unworthy to receive it. Thoughts such as these cause unintended and unwanted effects. Rather than analyzing this, and further perpetuating the problem by dwelling on it, immediately follow four steps.

First, expand your study of the law of attraction and the law of cause and effect. These laws suggest that your next job exists as the result of your intentions to attract it and all you have to do is claim it. These laws apply to everyone, all the time, anywhere. So if you're convinced they don't work—and because they do, whether you want them to or not, just like gravity—your disbelief helps to create that experience. It is very unlikely that you're the only person in the history of the world who is exempt from what the rest of the world has determined to be

RECRUITER'S NOTEBOOK

Lessons from the Recently Employed

At networking events, the recently employed are asked to share their stories in hopes of inspiring other job seekers. As they talk, notice how they are often amazed at how their job search evolved, and you get a glimpse into the enthusiasm and personality the employer must have seen and why they were probably chosen. Their comments sound like this: "Know and humble yourself to learn and apply any lessons, persist with the expectation of positive results, and in the end, it's your attitude, genuineness, and gratitude that make others want to help you, and that's when things begin to happen. When the right job finds you, it feels like serendipity, coincidence, or being at the right place at the right time, and it can happen regardless of competition, your age, academics, résumé format, the economy, or job market."

These people achieved a point of readiness or humility before others began to help them. They listened to advice and learned what they were supposed to. They applied it to their daily efforts and, combined with thinking of opportunity, they persisted until the right position found them. Their resolve, gratitude, and expectation of positive results helped to make them irresistibly attractive and sometimes may have even led a prospective employer to create a position—as if it was meant to be.

universal laws. Start over, but think more cautiously and with unbridled optimism. You've got nothing to lose and everything to gain.

Second, reconfirm that you know what you want. If you're not sure, then you're attracting more uncertainty. Take the approach of focusing instead on your unique gifts, skills, and abilities, and seek to attract opportunities that will make the best use of your gifts to benefit others. This tactic has transformed the lives of people who ended up doing what they never realized was possible. You won't know whether this will happen to you until you do it and allow yourself to feel the excitement.

Third, never allow yourself to think you don't deserve something. Your next job is waiting and doesn't care if you deserve it. Want proof?

People get things they don't deserve all the time, so what do you suppose they were thinking? They felt deserving or their minds were open to freely receiving whatever life wanted to bestow upon them. However, if you've done something you regret (cause), you may have feelings of guilt and unworthiness (effect). When you want something, and those negative feelings are unresolved (cause), then you unintentionally help to create the experience of not receiving (effect). Forgive, forget the past, and move on. As to the present, it's always a good idea to strive for a clean conscience and to maintain a receptive, grateful mindset that allows you to receive freely.

Fourth, make certain that you associate with others who enable you to maintain only empowering thoughts and positive emotions. Every networking group seems to have one or two people who vent their frustrations as if they were in group therapy. If allowed to develop momentum, this type of thinking can be dangerous to the entire group. What each person thinks is combined with the collective thoughts of the entire group. If the group develops negative collective thinking, it can affect the results for any one individual who prefers to think more positively. When the ship sinks, everyone goes down. Positive collective thinking, in contrast, can inspire you with new ideas and solutions. It is possible that you can help to change the direction of a group by adding thoughts and beliefs of job opportunities for everyone. But if you sense this is not feasible, move to another group. If it is feasible, try passing along some of these suggestions:

- Refuse to worry about anything.
- Don't obsess about needing or wanting anything.
- Leverage each of your five senses to think and act as if you've already been hired.
- Deeply contemplate and enjoy your resulting positive emotions.
- Believe unconditionally that everything will work out the way it's supposed to.
- Create reasons to smile and laugh as frequently as possible.
- Volunteer to assist someone else in finding a job.
- And the all-time favorite: Wake each day with the belief that "this is the day." Live that day in anticipation of supernatural

results, and regardless of what does or doesn't happen, go to bed believing that you are one day closer to that which is looking for you.

Summing Up the Nine Principles

As I noted above, no one knows conclusively whether positive thoughts help to attract meaningful work. But it seems probable, based on what our universal laws, physics, psychology, and religious beliefs suggest. If this isn't enough, how about the simple fact that employers are generally more attracted to positive attitudes and put emphasis on rejecting the opposite. Like attracts like, so your best bet is to conduct each step of your search with a happy demeanor, and the joy and enthusiasm that suggest you are already there. You've got nothing to lose and everything to gain.

Achieving your own point of readiness involves far more than the preparation of your résumé and all the networking and detail work associated with a job search. Focus on doing these things expertly well, and as you do, simultaneously integrate the nine principles as if your next job depends on them. As your efforts develop momentum, you'll will begin to notice that others can sense your enthusiasm and will be inclined to assist you. When this happens, employers will start to recognize in you the chemistry they seek, and soon you'll attract the job that is looking for you as if it was meant to be. Here's an entry from my notebook explaining how this process is related to the use of résumés.

RECRUITER'S NOTEBOOK

Résumés and Reality

As a recruiter, I'm often asked, "What format should I use for my résumé, and what should my cover letter say?" Several years ago, I would have been highly critical and usually changed everything on a person's résumé, but then I discovered that by doing this I was interfering with the law of attraction. Too many times, what I thought was inappropriate was the very thing that got them the job. My advice today is this: Make sure you provide contact information, an objective, all employment listed in chronological order with accomplishments provided for each employer, education, and dates for everything. If a résumé meets these basic requirements, I don't care what else someone does with it or how long it is. Every résumé I receive is by email, and the worst ones have cover letters—which I never read. If I like the résumé, they can tell me what was in the cover letter. I get excited when there is no cover letter or at most it says, "Here it is" or "Let me know." I interpret that as a challenge that says "My résumé speaks for itself." I'll read one of these résumés every time, and I'm usually right that it is a good one.

What's Next

This chapter has explored the nine key principles of attracting meaningful work. The next chapter provides insight into what employers expect from those they hire and how to set yourself up for success. The supposedly old-fashioned concept of etiquette turns out to have a lot to do with this whole process.

2

Meet Potential Employers' Expectations: The Five Steps to Success

In this chapter, you'll learn

- how to make sure employers see the best in you—from first impressions onward
- how to follow the rules of etiquette as you interact with potential employers
- how to stay in "rhythm" with the employment process
- how to handle practical aspects—from résumés to researching employers

The employment recruitment and hiring process (we'll just call it the employment process from here on) is the persistent hurdle you face again and again as you work to get what you want throughout your entire career. You usually have to go through it each and every time you change jobs or employers. It's a dynamic process shaped by procedures, expectations, and possibilities. It's the only function in an organization where the results walk through the front door. It's about putting your best foot forward in hopes that you might be the right person to get the right job at the right time. Of course, no two employers are alike. But what you're about to read in this chapter applies to the biggest as well as to the smallest employers, because it's always a process based on making impressions, fulfilling expectations, and demonstrating proper etiquette.

The essence of the employment process is creating the best impressions—the potential employer's impressions of you, and your impressions of the employer—so that employers can attract talent and job seekers can attract opportunity. This involves fulfilling each other's expectations, plus the unspoken and unwritten rules of etiquette that set the standards for how the employer thinks you should behave and how you expect the employer to behave. If you do the wrong thing, you'll look foolish. But if you do the right thing, people will like you and begin to believe that you'll fit in. Just one small infraction of etiquette can stop the process by causing the recruiter to doubt whether a match is possible. All this can take place within a matter of seconds or several months. For this reason, the first impression is as important as the last. The process is a dance, and you both have to stay in rhythm.

The impressions you create during this process form the basis of what the employer refers to as your chemistry and fit with the organization. Everything counts, from the day your résumé is received until after the last interview. However, what matters most in the end is whether the employer genuinely likes you—from your smile to your personality, judgments, behavior, and expressed interests. Each interviewer has his or her own opinion about these things, and the majority rules unless the organization favors decisions by consensus, which means that everyone has to like you or is willing to compromise.

The greatest anxiety associated with this process is not knowing what to expect, what to do, or where you stand. You're on the outside looking in, and you want to know what desirable job the employer has open and what you have to do to get it. Meanwhile, the firm's hiring managers are on the inside looking out, and they want to know who is available and how to get him or her. Both of you are a bit nervous about meeting and eager to get it over with, and you both want the best results. No one ever intends to hire the wrong person or to work for the wrong employer. But hiring people is an imperfect process managed by humans and subject to human error and inclinations. Though mistakes happen, until something better comes along, this is the best system we have. Let's look at an entry from my Recruiter's Notebook for an example of such a mistake.

RECRUITER'S NOTEBOOK

Hard Lessons about Recruiting Flexibility

My training as a recruiter involved learning how to qualify by disqualifying, and one of the factors used was job stability. We were conditioned to follow the "2 in 5, 3 in 10" rule, which meant that good stability was demonstrated by no more than 2 jobs in 5 years or 3 jobs in 10. During the layoffs of the 1990s, we had to change our standards because more and more candidates had been through a downsizing and we were running out of stable candidates. This was a relief to the recruiters, but letting go of this standard was extremely difficult for the managers who were approving our offer packages. These human resources managers had been conditioned to rely upon the "2 in 5, 3 in 10" rule for years, and it gave them something tangible to rely on. The fact that they were slow to adapt or let go of this rule became an ongoing source of problems.

Before the interview, our managers would review the résumé and were predisposed to dislike a candidate on the basis that he or she had failed to meet the old standards. Their unchanged beliefs regarding instability were having a negative impact on their demeanor during the interview and on the flow of communication. The outcome was disastrous. The candidate was criticized, the effectiveness of the staffing department was questioned, and the candidate left upset. Several good candidates were lost for reasons that were beyond their ability to control.

This chapter explains each of the five main steps in the employment process and reveals the up-to-date expectations and etiquette that are universal to almost every employment situation. Some employers are likely to have more expectations and etiquette, but not less than what we discuss here. Realize that because this prepares you for what to expect, you must use this information to plan accordingly. By doing so, you will more than likely know more about what's going on than your competition, and in some cases, you might even know more about what's going on than the employer.

Each employer does things a little differently, and some have perfected their processes to high levels of automation and sophistication, but it really doesn't matter for your strategy. It just means they're willing to spend more to get the same results a little more efficiently. As far as you are concerned, the essence is still the same:

- The employment process does not advance without both would-be employer and employee making positive impressions at each step, and these impressions must last throughout the process.
- There will be no offer or acceptance of a job unless both parties have successfully met the expectations and etiquette of the other during each step of the process. This is a 50/50 proposition, despite what either party thinks.
- What counts most is whether the employer and job seeker like one another, believe they can work together, and can come to terms that are agreeable. Without this perceived mutual chemistry and fit, the job seeker's credentials and potential matter very little.

The employment process is accomplished in the five basic steps that we'll look at in detail in the rest of this chapter. You must stay in rhythm with the process by fulfilling the employer's expectations and etiquette at each step before the employer is willing to invite you to the next. The positive impressions you create must be consistently maintained at each and every step. In other words, your impressions build on one another and accumulate, and it's not a good idea to contradict a positive impression you created during an earlier step. Interviewers are trained to look for inconsistencies, so don't give them any.

A critical, frequently overlooked component of the process is how both your role and the employer's role change at each step. Once again, you must stay in rhythm with this evolution. You evolve from job seeker to prospect, to interviewee and interviewer, to candidate and negotiator, and finally to employee. This is especially significant because—as I've mentioned—the etiquette for each role is different, and if you're in the wrong role or miss the etiquette at any part of any step, it raises an alarm that you're either jumping the gun or losing interest by not keeping pace with the process. Falling out of the rhythm of this carefully choreographed etiquette creates the wrong impression as this example from my notebook shows.

 RECRUITER'S NOTEBOOK

How *Not* to Follow Step-by-Step Etiquette

The initial phone screens with the job seeker proved that he was a good prospect. A rapport had been developed with the recruiter and also with the hiring manager, who spoke with both the recruiter and job seeker by phone as well. Both parties were looking forward to meeting face to face, and the hiring manager had even arranged for the prospect to bring with him samples of his monthly reports to share with the division director.

When the interviewee arrived, I was pleasantly surprised that the hiring manager had already met him at the hotel and they had had breakfast. It appeared they were both eager to get things started. From my perspective, this position would be filled before the end of the day. It had been arranged that the interviewee would meet with the director immediately after lunch.

By that time, the interviewee was quite confident that he understood the position, liked the company, and was well along the way in getting to know the people—but not well enough. To our complete surprise, the director had decided that he was not a candidate. The job seeker had come across as a bit arrogant or overconfident, almost to the point of assuming that the job was his when, at this early stage of the process, the director had only just met him. He'd jumped the gun and had been perceived as lacking good judgment.

The employer's staff must also keep pace with the rhythm of the process. They must simultaneously fulfill your expectations and etiquette at each step, and if they contradict their own previously created impressions, it will cause you to doubt their viability. You can gauge their evolving interest by whether they keep pace with their role at each step. If they don't, it usually indicates they have doubts or are losing interest. But when they jump quickly to the next step, it's generally a pretty good indicator that they're interested.

So far, I've used the word "etiquette" quite a few times. Because the concept of etiquette might be sound old-fashioned or even trivial, though, before we get into the five steps of the employment process, it's best to step back and look at what "etiquette" really means. This word has an interesting history that illuminates its meaning today. Its origin is the Old French word "estiquette," meaning "label" or "ticket"—like the small cards that were printed with instructions on how to behave in the royal court or how soldiers were supposed to behave in their lodgings.

Thus, the essence of etiquette is learning the rules of correct behavior and good manners for the situation you're facing and then very carefully following them to the letter—and in the spirit, which ultimately is consideration for another person. In fact, a sage once said something to the effect that being true to your religion really means just following good manners. The etiquette of the five steps of the employment recruitment process, therefore, includes all the rules for all matters of basic good behavior as dressing and speaking with respect and—most important— *not* assuming *anything* beyond the step at hand but politely following up on each step. See the Recruiter's Notebook on the following pages for a story about the many fascinating aspects of etiquette.

STEP 1 Discover and Research Possible Employers— and Tailor Your Résumé for Each

The first step in the employment process is to discover and research possible employers—and tailor your résumé for each. Having a great résumé and being prepared for interviews may not ensure you always get the job you want, but it is hard to go further in this process without these key elements. So this first step includes doing enough research to discover each potential employer you might want to approach, and then tailoring your résumé for each employer before you send it. You might have the "inside track" on a job, or you might even get lucky, but only a small percentage of most success stories rely on luck. Instead, first concentrate on your résumé and on identifying and researching potential employers.

RECRUITER'S NOTEBOOK

Etiquette around the Globe

When I think of etiquette, I'm reminded of Emily Post, author of the book *Etiquette* published in 1922. She was our Ms. Manners, and she gave us thousands of tips on correspondence, wedding planning, hosting parties, and how to conduct yourself in the proper manner in every public or private setting. What she said was this: "Good manners can be learned. Good manner is good personality—the outward manifestation of one's character and attitude toward life."

When you put it this way, and because employers tend to hire the people they like most for their attitude and personality, etiquette is pretty darned important to getting the job you desire.

During the mid-1990s, while working for the Miller Brewing Company, I was given the job of recruiting to support our first global expansion. After a joint venture was established somewhere in the world, I was to enter that country alone and begin recruiting all the people we needed. My strategy was to hire the top people first so they could help recruit all the people beneath them. This was a several-year assignment that would take me all across Asia, Europe, the United Kingdom, and South and Central America.

To prepare me for this task, the company hired an image and etiquette expert who was familiar with the customs in all the countries where I'd be working. Her job was to prepare me for what I was about to encounter, and never having worked outside the United States before, I have to tell you this completely changed how I viewed the world. Without this training, I don't believe I'd have been as effective.

Over the next few weeks, we discussed clothing, posture, poise, approach, presentations, table manners, which countries preferred which behaviors, how and which gifts to exchange, what colors to avoid, when to avoid shaking hands, how to bow, what to say, how to say it, when to invite someone to a meal, and when not to. This evolved into my taking an entirely different approach to how I evaluated a person's fit and chemistry for our opportunities. I was accustomed to people looking me straight in the eye while talking, and I learned some cultures avoided this, and some avoided looking at your

Etiquette around the Globe (continued)

feet. I was accustomed to asking a straight question and getting a straight answer, and I learned that in some cultures it was customary to avoid asking straight questions, and it was their custom to tell you what you wanted to hear . . . and you had to probe from multiple angles to get a straight answer.

I learned that recruiting in every country was a little different, and you have to adjust for this to get the best people. After I had developed a strong listing of prospects for our positions, the next step was to fly in some of our other executives to meet and interview these candidates. Interviews were conducted in cities all around the world, and the candidates from each city were completely different from each other.

I had worked for years with our executives, but only in the United States. I knew them quite well and was familiar with their interviewing styles and approach to selecting good talent. I was curious to see how those styles might conflict with the etiquette in different countries, and what I observed completely impressed me.

Our executives adapted their style to the country where they were working. They mirrored the same etiquette as the candidates they were interviewing, so the playing field was leveled and they were able to get good information and make good decisions. Then, in debriefing sessions after the interviews, they would discuss these candidates from both the foreign and U.S. perspectives. The purpose of this discussion was to explore whether the candidate could as easily adjust to American culture and norms, because they would be working with people from the United States.

The second interview was more of a U.S. approach to employment, and you could see the tension develop in some people: straight questions seeking straight answers, rapid-fire questions probing quickly and deeply from different angles. If they couldn't adapt, it was judged too much of a stretch, and the process was repeated with another candidate. In the end, it was a matter of choosing the people who could think globally and act locally, and it worked. We ended up with a multinational staff that could work as easily in their home country as they could in the United States. It was a matter of determining whether they could demonstrate the right etiquette.

After my global assignment was completed, and there were no more countries to conquer, I was transferred to lead the staffing for Kraft Foods. All the work I did outside the United States left me with a heightened sense of awareness regarding the differences in employment etiquette between cultures. But this was just the beginning.

Although Kraft and Miller were both owned by Philip Morris, the difference in employment etiquette between a beer company and a food company was noticeable. Hiring managers from both companies expected different things, and they were basing their decisions on whether or not interviewees were doing the right things, and if they weren't, they didn't get the job. I have to tell you, we rejected some pretty highly qualified people for no apparent reason, except they didn't have the right chemistry. They didn't fit with us.

The etiquette our managers used wasn't talked about or written down anywhere. They weren't trained how to do it, and in fact, they didn't even realize they were doing it. What I observed was a sort of group think, and interviewers didn't talk about it, but they just knew whether or not a person had demonstrated the most appropriate or inappropriate manners and behaviors. The situation didn't feel right to them and they couldn't explain in words except to say that the candidate lacked the right chemistry—he or she didn't fit with the rest of our people, and, to me, this sounded a lot like etiquette.

I went back and forth to review the experiences I had in both companies and around the world. I started paying attention to what I had observed and was observing, and the etiquette became apparent. I could see it, explain it, talk about it, teach it, and it worked. There were certain things that if a person didn't do, they didn't get the job, and after becoming a global headhunter, I discovered what I call the rhythm of employment that includes fulfilling expectations and factors of etiquette, and these had applicability regardless of the company, industry, or country.

If you've ever taken a dance lesson, then you know how important it is to stay in rhythm with the music and your partner. If you don't, it becomes quite obvious that someone doesn't know what's going on. You end up tripping over yourself or the other person, and those stumbles can result in you or the other person preferring to select another partner. That's exactly what happens during the employment process, and so what I'm about to tell you helps to establish your rhythm and to enable you to monitor the employer's rhythm.

Etiquette around the Globe (continued)

Employment is the business of impression building and attraction—putting your best foot forward, and staying in rhythm. The attraction requires fulfilling each other's expectations, plus the unspoken and unwritten rules of etiquette that set the standards regarding how the employer thinks you should behave and how you expect the employer to behave. When it comes to etiquette, do the wrong thing and you look foolish, but do the right thing and people like you and believe you have chemistry and fit. Just one small infraction of etiquette can stop the process by causing the other to doubt whether a match is possible. All of this takes place within a matter of seconds or several months, and for this reason, your first impression is equally important to the last.

The greatest anxiety associated with employment is that you don't know what to expect, what to do, or where you stand. On the outside looking in you want to know what the employer has open and what you have to do to get it. On the inside looking out hiring managers want to know who's available and how to get him or her. You're both nervous about meeting the other, eager to get it over with, and want the best results.

Unfortunately, the etiquette required is not available to you beforehand, and each employer does things a little differently. Some have perfected their processes to high levels of automation and sophistication, but it really doesn't matter. That just means they're willing to spend more money to get the same results a little more efficiently. The essence remains unchanged:

- The recruiting and employment process doesn't advance without positive impressions being created at each step, and being maintained thereafter.
- There will be no offer or acceptance unless both parties have successfully met the expectations and etiquette of the other during each step of the process.
- What counts most is whether the employer and job seeker like each other, believe they can work together, and thereafter can come to terms that are agreeable. Without this perceived mutual chemistry and fit, it matters very little about the job seeker's credentials, résumé format, cover letter, or potential.

Nearly all potential employers use résumés as an initial screening tool to ensure that possible candidates are *prepared* to do the work, are *focused* on the right industry or business segment, and, overall, have an *attractive* academic record and employment history. At a minimum, your résumé should meet each potential employer's basic criteria and expectations. How any one employer judges these criteria reflects many different factors. For example, one employer may be more interested in your industry-focused experience but another may particularly value career stability. These variations in criteria from employer to employer are often hard to judge, so don't expect to get it right every time.

After reviewing your résumé, your potential employers should know that you are resourceful, goal oriented, and dedicated to achieving your job and career goals. From the employer's point of view, a résumé is impressive if it

- is delivered promptly upon request
- is to the point and grammatically correct without misspelled words
- clearly lists your name, address, telephone numbers, and email address
- includes all employment dates and explains any gaps in time
- is legible as both a printed document and an electronic document
- includes the most current information in chronological order
- communicates clearly what you have done and what they want.

As I said in chapter 1, as long as you make sure that your résumé takes care of all these basic criteria, you don't need to obsess about résumés and cover letters. They are not as crucial as some might think. And you will need to be flexible about constantly revising, updating, and tweaking your résumé as your career unfolds. You may end up keeping several different versions of your résumé on your computer. But just to help you keep your perspective, let's look at a story from my notebook about the kinds of things you should definitely *not* do in your résumé.

RECRUITER'S NOTEBOOK

How *Not* to Do a Résumé

Our staffing department looked forward each year to Christmas to see whether our favorite job seeker from Alaska would send us another updated version of his résumé. He did so four years in a row, and we looked forward to each one. We had no intention of ever hiring him for the area sales manager position he wanted, but his résumés were great to use as "don't do this" examples while training students on college campuses.

The first year, his résumé included a photo of him nearly naked harnessed to a dogsled in the snow with a bottle of Miller High Life hung from a chain around his neck. It was his version of an advertisement. The next year, his résumé picture showed him in a steaming hot tub wearing a Santa Claus hat surrounded by snow and his dogs. We recognized him immediately. He was holding a Lowenbrau, and there were beer posters pasted on the hot tub. The third year, he was wearing a cap and gown, smiling widely, and exposing a Miller T-shirt beneath his gown. It was evident that he had taken the picture himself and pasted it onto a news photo to appear as if he was in line getting his degree.

The fourth and final year, we received his résumé inside a Miller Lite bottle as if it had floated ashore as his last desperate attempt. By policy at the time, we had dutifully responded to each résumé with a rejection letter, and each time we had acknowledged his brand loyalty and creative efforts. He had become a legend, and we didn't want to lose his résumés—they were so great as examples for our training class.

STEP	Prepare for and Make the First Contact with
2	**Potential Employers**

The second step in the employment process is to prepare for and make the first contact with potential employers. If you're invited to take this step and you accept, your role changes to that of a prospect, and the employer becomes a contact. The first part of this step is typically taken via a telephone screen to answer the employer's primary question (unspoken but crucial): Are you as good on the phone as you seem on paper?

The first thing the employer's staff does is to verify their initial impressions against step one's expectations and etiquette. Once that's been satisfactorily accomplished, they want to know three basic things about you, which impose three new expectations and the associated etiquette:

- Are you genuine?
- Are you personable?
- Are you flexible?

Prepare yourself to answer these three questions when speaking on the phone and in an initial interview—though again, of course, the employer will usually "ask" these questions in a somewhat roundabout way. For example, one employer may ask you on the phone about the statements in your résumé to find out if they are genuinely supported by facts, may be observing in a first conversation how personable you are in quickly establishing a rapport, and may ask about your flexibility to accommodate the employer's schedule for an interview. Likewise, another employer may be trying to discern whether you genuinely are who you said you were in your résumé, may test you in a phone call to see if you seem personable in what might be an awkward situation, and may probe conversationally to see if you seem flexibly resilient in various life circumstances.

Etiquette at this step suggests that you must be perceived as interested and curious to learn, have personality and an ability to impress, and demonstrate a willingness to accommodate the employer's requests. If you don't seem interested and can't communicate in a lively, effective way, the employer simply will not be motivated to move forward. But remember, the impressions made at this and every step build on each other, so if any of the expectations and rules of etiquette noted above are not fulfilled, you won't be invited to the next step. Here are several more common points of etiquette that you'll need to follow as part of this step:

- Promptly return the employer's calls and emails.
- Be available when the employer needs to speak with you, or get back to him or her quickly.
- Be optimistic and positive in your comments about others.

- Be direct and answer questions honestly and straightforwardly.
- When you don't know an answer, politely say so.
- Review the company website and be well informed about the company's operations.
- Try to ask very good questions as if you have an objective in mind.
- Clearly communicate your thoughts.
- Be able to substantiate your accomplishments with ready examples.
- Volunteer information—don't make an interviewer pull it out of you.
- Relax and be engaging as a conversationalist—be someone the interviewer would like to know better.
- Demonstrate that you have a good handle on your strengths and development needs.
- Be prepared with realistic, assertive goals and expectations.
- Be willing and available for future interviews.
- Tell the interviewer that you are interested in taking the process to the next step.

To illustrate how not to get through step two, let's look at a story from my notebook on the facing page of one would-be candidate's mistake.

STEP 3   Prepare for and Get Through the First Meeting

The third step in the employment process is to prepare for and get through the first face-to-face meeting with a representative of your prospective employer. If step two has gone well, you may be invited to move on to this step. When you accept this invitation, your role changes to interviewee, and the employer becomes the interviewer. However, etiquette also suggests that your roles alternate, in the sense that you are likewise expected to interview the employer. You're likely to be asked to complete an application, and hence you may also be referred to as an applicant. Employers are cautious about this term, because it carries with it obligations of reporting to the government. You're an interviewee and/or applicant at this step, depending on the employer's definitions.

RECRUITER'S NOTEBOOK

How *Not* to Be Available

I had found the "mother lode" of résumés. In my hot little hands was a future senior vice president whose career in marketing I knew was destined to be with us. This would surely earn me a few stars. She had an advanced degree from one of our premier schools, blue chip experience, superior stability and accomplishments, was within the salary range, and was immediately available without a placement fee or relocation expense. For a low-level recruiter, it didn't get any better than this, and her cover memo even indicated that she knew one of our executives, who when I asked about her exclaimed "Get her in here—now!" All I had to do was get her in, get about 10 other people to like her, and, of course, there eventually did have to be an opening.

The telephone screen went extremely well until we tried matching calendars. Either she was out when we were available or we were out when she was available. We tried again the following week, and the same thing happened. A month later, it happened again. The initial excitement dwindled to less than a heartbeat, and we were referring to her as "the ghost" because no one had seen her and doubted that she ever existed. About four months passed, and I had forgotten her when our executive gave me a message that she had just called wanting an interview. He asked that I politely reject her with the explanation that all the openings at her level had just been filled two months ago. That's precisely what I told her.

During your interview, the conversation will first focus on confirming that you fulfill the expectations and etiquette rules given above for the first two steps. Are you as good in person as you seem on the phone? Can the interviewer put a face to the paper résumé? At the same time, the employer imposes three new expectations and the etiquette associated with them on you:

- Are you committed?
- Do you have integrity?
- Are you confident in your abilities?

You'll need to carefully prepare yourself to meet these three expectations when speaking—keeping in mind that these vary from employer to employer. For example, one employer may want to know if you can express a commitment to work, that you have the integrity to do what you have said you would do, and that you have the confidence to look beyond obstacles and challenges. But another employer may want to know if you have the commitment to advance to higher levels, if you have the integrity to be honest without exception, and if you have the confidence to say what's on your mind.

Etiquette at this step suggests that you must be perceived as serious and will do what it takes, that you are responsible and accountable, and that you are appropriately humble and have achieved closure by expressing interest in the employer and opportunity by stating something like "I would appreciate your serious consideration."

If any of the expectations and etiquette rules given above for the first three steps is not fulfilled, you will not be invited to the next step. However, this step might also include a second or third interview to reconfirm first impressions related to each expectation, as well as to observe once again that you truly demonstrate the required etiquette. The employer also may begin to check your references at this point, if he or she hasn't already, and may also impose some form of formalized testing or assessment. These are additional means of reconfirming the employer's own impressions. Here are more common points of etiquette that you will need to follow as part of this step:

- You're appropriately dressed according to the employer's instructions.
- You've taken care of travel logistics without any issues or complaints.
- You've brought a better-quality paper copy of your résumé to replace the e-résumé you had submitted.
- You've remembered to bring any other items that the employer requested in advance.
- You've come prepared to complete the application and give references.
- You've done more research on the employer.
- You can answer the employer's questions in a way consistent with what you said during the phone screening.

- You're prepared to again be honest and straightforward.
- You can ask good questions—and want to hear the employer's story.
- You have a game plan for the interview and occasionally take notes.
- You make certain to ask for and write down the names and titles of your interviewers.
- You've again been humble—despite you accomplishments and marketability.
- You're well mannered and appropriately assertive with everyone.
- You're polite enough to turn off and put away your cell phone during the interview.
- You're upbeat and positive, you smile often, and you laugh when appropriate.
- You're focused and business oriented as well.
- You know what the employer wants and have a realistic plan for your career.
- You can diplomatically address any of the employer's concerns or issues.
- You've been flexible and expressed reasonable expectations.
- You've expressed genuine interest and asked for the position.
- You've followed up after each interview with a handwritten thank-you letter to the interviewer(s).

Again, my notebook just happens to have an illuminating story about interviewing—somehow, the lessons often come through more clearly when we hear about how not to do something.

RECRUITER'S NOTEBOOK

How *Not* to Do an Interview

Because so many people were interested in working for such a fun place as Miller during the 1980s, the recruiter's job was oriented toward finding the ironclad reasons why someone should be rejected. The more deeply you dug, the better you were admired. This included reviewing the prepaid hotel bill that reflected all the meals and refreshments the interviewee

How *Not* to Do an Interview (continued)

had ordered. It was an automatic rejection if on that bill there were any competitor beer brands, wine, or hard liquor—and this occurred many times. Sometimes, we actually called the hotel to find out if anything like that had occurred before the interview, and if it did, interviewees were ordered a cab to the airport and never understood why their day had been cut so short. We thought it reflected poor judgment to imbibe anything but our brands if we were paying the bill.

One would-be interviewee's bill was a real shocker. The person had flown from Michigan to Milwaukee, and I had talked with him before his departure. He was on his way and we were looking forward to meeting and his having a great interview starting the following morning. He never arrived. The airline and hotel confirmed he was on the flight and had checked into the hotel. For an entire week, he never answered any phone calls we placed to the phone number he provided, and the hotel said they had lost track of him. I was required to send a telegram to his home asking for an explanation. He never called. Two weeks after the interview that never occurred, my boss received a bill from the hotel indicating that the interviewee had stayed for one whole week, running up charges of nearly $3,000.

People were furious. The hotel explained that they had moved the would-be interviewee's room and tried to accommodate him because he had injured his back and indicated that Miller had said to take care of him. They said the ambulance came and the interviewee explained that the medical technicians confined him to bed for one week, and he did so on room service without calling to inform us. After one week, he slipped out of town on the return portion of his original airline ticket, and we never heard from him again. Fearing the loss of my job, I fulfilled my duties by confirming that his bratwurst had been washed down with Miller High Life.

STEP 4   The Employer Makes a Decision—and Possibly an Offer

The fourth step in the employment process is that the employer makes a decision—and possibly an offer. An invitation from an employer to take this step is essentially the same as an invitation to consider an offer. If you accept an offer from the employer at this step, it means you are willing to consider the offer, but of course there is still the option that you and the employer may reject each other rather than advance to the fifth and last step. At this fourth step, your role changes to that of a candidate, and the employer becomes the negotiator. However, etiquette also suggests that your roles alternate, so you are likewise expected to negotiate if and when you discuss an offer with the employer.

The initial conversation at this step focuses on the fact that a decision has been made to move forward. The employer's representatives try to envision you as an employee and determine whether you've done your job in evaluating them and are just as serious. This means exposing any recent contradictions or doubts you may have about the expectations and etiquette rules given above for the first three steps. For example, if you are not prepared or not serious, it may not make sense to move to the next step. But if there are no outstanding issues from the earlier steps, the employer imposes three new expectations and the etiquette associated with them:

- Are you selective?
- Are you decisive?
- And are you grateful?

Prepare yourself to meet variations in these three expectations as you speak with different potential employers. For example, one employer may inquire whether, rather than being selective, you're not just settling for this job; may ask when you will make your decision to see if you are decisive enough to not cause any delays; and may see whether you spontaneously express gratitude for the offer. Another employer may find out if you're being selective by determining whether you've done your homework, whether you are decisive in stating that you know what you want, and whether you express your gratefulness by seeming truly happy with the offer.

Etiquette at this step suggests that you have explored your options but are being selective in favor of this employer; that your decision will be timely, consistent with how you've acted in the past; that you thoroughly review all the finer points; and that you are genuinely appreciative of having received the offer. The etiquette for this role also suggests that if an offer is extended and you don't like it, you are expected to negotiate and not flatly turn it down. If you fail to demonstrate the etiquette at this step, you may not be given an offer, or sometimes the employer may give you an offer and later rescind it. Some employers may also ask or require that you to complete a drug screen and health examination before they can consider moving on to step five. Here are more common points of etiquette that you will need to follow as part of this step:

- You're excited and appreciative of the offer.
- You've diplomatically negotiated any issues with the thought of accepting.
- You've promptly given the employer your answer.
- You've been flexible and accommodating on the starting date for the job.
- You've followed up with a nice thank-you letter to your prospective boss.

Once again, see a story from my notebook on the facing page about what not to do at this step—please don't accuse me of negative thinking; it's just that we can often learn so vividly from our mistakes.

STEP 5   Start the Job

The fifth and final step in the employment process is to start the job. This step is reached only by accepting a job offer and then successfully completing any medical testing. When you actually start a job, your role, of course, shifts from candidate to employee. After you become an employee of a new organization, you can really impress your new employer if you remember to follow these common points of etiquette:

- Make it clear that your old employer has been notified of your intent to leave and appropriate transition time has been given.
- Confirm the start date.
- Promptly return any new-hire paperwork requested.

RECRUITER'S NOTEBOOK

From Job Offer to No-Show

Finally, we were done, and I had to admit that no one worked harder on getting this offer done than the candidate. He had all the details from his salary history and was able to justify the cost of our providing an interim housing allowance in addition to a one-time hiring incentive. We moved mountains to get him what he wanted just so we could get him on board. The hiring manager had stuck his neck out as well because the base salary was in the top quartile of the range and exceeded the average paid to his existing staff. This was truly an exception, if not also a precedent. We also agreed to pull strings in town and help his wife get an interview with another company nearby.

We worked collaboratively with the candidate to get this done, and you can imagine our surprise when, after giving him what he wanted, he couldn't make a decision. He asked for two weeks to consider the offer, and during that time he was slow in returning our phone calls. His actions at this point were contradicting our initial impressions, and this caused us to doubt whether we should have extended the offer. At the very least, he should have been gushing with thanks at our accommodating his compensation expectations. The hiring manager was beginning to suspect that he was leveraging the offer to get a counteroffer or that he might be bargaining with another employer. I was asked to start looking among the résumés we had put on hold in the event he didn't accept. We had also considered whether it was appropriate to rescind the offer because he hadn't been so accommodating in returning our phone calls, even though the two weeks had not yet expired.

After we gave him a one-week extension, he called to explain that he would not be accepting the offer. He explained that his original willingness to consider the offer was based on his wife's company agreeing to transfer her to Milwaukee, and during the now three-week review period they had changed their mind. He didn't want to ask her to resign without having another job immediately available. He had failed to disclose this fact during the interview. Everyone agreed that we had been duped and that it was a blessing that he hadn't accepted. Had he accepted, I'm quite confident, based on his mishandling of the situation, that he would have been starting with one mark already against him.

Figure 2-1. Making and Maintaining the Right Impressions

| Five-Step Process | Evolving Roles | | Expectation: "What must I do to appear...?" | Etiquette: "How can I demonstrate that I have or I am...?" |
	You Are	Employer Is		
Research and Discovery	Job Seeker	Reputation	Prepared	Ready, and Resourceful
			Focused	Goal and Plan to Accomplish
			Attractive	Eager with Intent, and Purpose
First Contact	Prospect	Contact	Genuine	Interested and Curious to Learn
			Personable	Personality and Ability to Impress
			Flexible	Willingness to Accommodate
First Meeting	Interviewee	Interviewer	Committed	Serious, and Does What It Takes
	Interviewer (Applicant)	Interviewee	Integrity	Responsible, and Accountable
			Confident	Humble, But Achieved Closure
Decision and Offer	Candidate	Negotiator	Selective	Options and Is Selective
	Negotiator	Negotiator	Decisive	Timely, Consistent, Thorough
			Grateful	Genuinely Appreciative
Job Start	Employee	Employer		

So the completion of step five has brought you to the brink of an exciting new phase of your career. You can look back on this and the first four steps with thankfulness—until it's time to go back to step one again!

Summing Up the Five Steps

As mentioned above, although processes may differ among employers, they generally boil down to the five basic steps to success given here. By consistently fulfilling the employer's expectations and the rules of etiquette for each step, you'll enhance your evolving chemistry and the employer will perceive you as a good fit. For your review, and for a handy summary of the five steps, see figure 2-1.

The greatest frustration you or the employer can experience in the employment process is to make it to step five but then have the candidate decline the position or be rejected by the employer. It's always better to find this out sooner rather than later—but this is difficult to admit if you need the income or need employees.

The decision to hire is frequently made by the end of step two but not communicated at that point. The balance of the process continues with the hope that impressions will change or improve, but that doesn't always happen. Expectations are allowed to build unfairly. The moment when either you or the employer fails to fulfill an expectation or does not demonstrate the proper etiquette, an alarm should go off for both parties that it probably was not meant to be and should go no further. At the very least, failed expectations and a lack of etiquette expose a tendency or weakness of the offending party, and that's a strong clue what to expect from them in the future. This is referred to as "a peek under the tent," and you want as many of these as possible to help verify the authenticity of your final decision. On the following pages are two final cautionary tales from my notebook—which I hope really drive home how crucial it is to follow each and every aspect of the five steps with great attention to the details of what you say and do and how you act at every moment of contact with a potential employer.

RECRUITER'S NOTEBOOK

Close, but No Offer

It took several weeks of searching, but we finally discovered our next director of marketing, and the interest was mutual. The only question that arose during the phone screen and initial interview was about her level of empathy in dealing with subordinates. It didn't seem that serious at the time, so we agreed to take a second look.

The second interview occurred two weeks later and involved the chief operating and chief executive officers. We also held a reception at which senior members of the marketing team had an opportunity to visit with the candidate and her spouse. From all accounts, it was a go. But nagging doubts persisted regarding a lack of empathy in dealing with people.

Before being extended an offer, the candidate requested an opportunity to speak with a couple of the people who might eventually be reporting to her. We took this as a sign that our initial concerns had been unfounded. The results of our reference checking were good as usual. The profiling assessment did suggest that the candidate had some developmental needs related to leadership, but nothing we couldn't handle—plus, she had the endorsement of one of our executive coaches, who happened to know her. The Compensation Department had developed an offer, and we were now ready to conduct the final debriefing involving the principal decision makers—but one of them had a surprise for us after speaking with the candidate's potential future subordinates.

Information from these potential future subordinates led us to reject the candidate for making two fatal errors. First, when meeting with the two members of her future staff, she had failed to inquire regarding either of their backgrounds. Second, when ushered between interviews, she had asked her escort, "So what's broke that I have to fix around here?" Our consensus was that she lacked empathy with subordinates and was insensitive to imply that there were problems. She gave the impression that she was being brought in to fix things that we didn't think were broken—so back to the drawing board.

RECRUITER'S NOTEBOOK

Always Be Prepared for Eccentricity

I was one of the rare exceptions in our division to be hired without interviewing with our division head. I don't know how it happened, but because I hadn't met him, I was concerned that it might affect my advancement. My colleagues knew I had slipped through that crack, so I thought their stories about the division head being an eccentric were meant as a joke and part of my initiation as a new recruiter. They forewarned me that he might unexpectedly let himself into my office, even while I was conducting a closed-door interview. To emphasize this point, they explained that this was the reason each office had been assigned two visitor chairs, and I was to make sure of this just so he would have a place to sit. They said that if he came in and said hello, just return the hello, say nothing, and keep working. But if he came in and said nothing, I was to ignore him and continue working as if he wasn't there. That he did this unexpectedly was to ensure that things were running the way he wanted them to, and if they weren't, I could be fired— or become what they referred to as a "Friday casualty" because that's when they usually fired you. They had my attention, and even though I was green, I wasn't that dumb, and besides I wanted to meet him.

I did meet our division head the day I was asked to interview a candidate for one of our human resources positions, and I soon realized that my initiation was not that I had been told about this but that I had only been given a fraction of the true picture. We had already ended the interview, and I was explaining the benefits of working with our organization, when my door opened and in walked what looked to be a frail 80-year-old man with thinning purple hair who was wearing Coke bottle glasses and an orange suit. I assumed it was the division head, and because he closed the door and sat down without saying a word, I knew to say nothing and keep working. I guess that's why I felt compelled to restart the interview. The chief had a lit cigarette hanging from his lips, and as I began asking many of the same interview questions, all I could think about was why his eyes weren't watering as the smoke went up and under his glasses.

The candidate was completely perplexed, and I could hear rustling outside my door and knew my colleagues were listening. I tried giving eye signals to the candidate that I hoped he would interpret as "Ignore him" and "Play

Always Be Prepared for Eccentricity (continued)

along." He didn't get it. I held my breath as the candidate suddenly introduced himself and stated that he was interviewing for a human resources position. The division head shook his hand limply and said just one thing: "Why should we hire you?" The candidate gave a nice answer and then waited, but there was no response. Then the candidate spoke again, and again there was no response. As the candidate began telling his life story, he looked like a cracker you might crumble in your hands and watch as the pieces dropped one at a time to the floor. In the meantime, I was watching a cigarette ash grow to about an inch long, and when it fell onto the division head's white shirt, it glowed red and left a small brown spot that I assumed was a burn.

I was mesmerized by this while the candidate was literally squirming in his seat, and when the division head had had enough, he quietly got up and left the room, leaving me to try and explain to the candidate what had just happened. By the time I heard back that the division head had said "Get that guy a cab," the candidate had already told me that he didn't want anything to do with our company. Good choice. My initiation was complete, and from then on, I started each interview by explaining what to do if we were interrupted.

What's Next

People who have experienced a bad employment situation will often admit that they had strong feelings of doubt during the first three steps of the employment process but did nothing about it. It was a hunch they chose to ignore and later regretted. Whenever people have these hunches, there is a more than 50 percent chance that the employer has had the same hunch and likewise chose to ignore it. Thus, by commission or omission, both parties contribute to bad decisions that could have been avoided. In the next chapter, you'll find out how to avoid these bad decisions.

Present the Authentic "You" to Potential Employers— and Avoid Job Inflation

---

In this chapter, you'll learn

- how to keep from overpromising and underdelivering on the job
- how to avoid job inflation
- how to avoid projection, or the me-too syndrome

The worst nightmare for either a job seeker or employer is to discover that the employment process has failed after a person starts a new position. In a week, a month, or perhaps even a shorter amount of time, it may become absolutely clear that things are not working out as planned. In this unfortunate situation, usually no one wins. If you're the job seeker, leaving a new job will mean having to explain why this job lasted such a short time whenever you interview for other jobs. And no matter how well you explain it, your potential new employer will still wonder about your judgment or perhaps even secretly question the truth of your story. Clearly, you should do everything you can to avoid living this irrevocable scenario. This chapter helps you find your authentic self and thus avoid the most common reasons for being the lead character in the employment nightmare of a failed employment process caused by job inflation and projection.

Avoiding Job Inflation

Job inflation is exactly what you might imagine: dishonesty of any kind in the interview process. Whether you call it fudging the truth, stretching the truth, spinning the truth, padding, embellishing, exaggerating, misrepresenting, distorting, bluffing, or telling a white lie, it can still be called employment fraud.

Court cases involving employment fraud have referred to job inflation as "counterfactual imaginings"; as "characterological dysfunctions"; and my favorite, a condition referred to as "pseudologia fantastica." When you inflate your employment history and related credentials, you might be mentally ill or not able to tell the truth, but probably you're like most people and simply want things to appear a little better than they actually are. It happens all the time, but it's becoming increasingly more difficult to get away with, thanks to the Internet and the rapid availability of information. Just Google any person's name.

Why Job Inflation Happens

From your perspective as an employee, job inflation may happen under the stress of a phone screen or interview, when you might imagine the past as being different from what it really was or you might spontaneously imagine the way you wanted it to be. Or maybe you just want to make things sound better or you left things off your résumé that if known might make a difference in the outcome you wanted. Likewise, an employer can also be tempted to inflate the content of a job to enhance its appeal when attempting to recruit you. Either way, this kind of inflation, by stretching the truth to the point where it misrepresents the facts, ends up being the opposite of telling the truth.

For you as the job seeker, job inflation most often occurs with respect to

- your reasons for leaving a job
- your job titles
- your dates of employment
- the omission of some of your former employers
- whether your education was not completed
- your earlier experiences and accomplishments
- your scope of involvement in projects
- your memberships in professional organizations and the like
- your extracurricular activities, acquaintances, and friendships.

In sum, job seeker inflation can affect just about anything about you, including where you live.

For the employer, job inflation occurs most often with respect to

- job duties
- performance expectations
- difficult personalities (they don't make it possible for you to meet the bad ones during interviews)
- required travel
- work culture
- career path and promotions
- pay increases and incentive payouts.

This inflation of a job's content by an employer can also occur if there is a lack of full disclosure on planned reorganizations, acquisitions, divestitures, and changes in leadership—or of trade secrets that couldn't be talked about during the interview because that information hadn't yet been released to employees or the press. Because the focus of this book is on your career, from here on we look mainly at job inflation as it pertains to the employee's record.

How often job inflation occurs is difficult to say, because the majority of incidents are never discovered, especially today when past employers are often reluctant to provide references and instead give little more than dates of employment. For instance, each year, a career columnist will publish an article saying something like this hypothetical statement: "As many as one-third of all job seekers 'embellish' their accomplishments, while up to 10 percent 'seriously misrepresent' their work history and academics." But such estimates are well below what actually happens, as shown by these reported instances of inflation:

- ◆ The Society of Human Resource Managers estimates that 53 percent of all job applications contain false information (www.hrmreport.com/pastissue/article.asp-268485&issue-172).
- ◆ According to the FBI, approximately a half million people in the United States falsely claim to have college degrees (www.das.state.ne.us/personnel/nkn/IIF/2006-04 /newsletter_2006_04.pdf).
- ◆ Online "diploma mills" sell fraudulent diplomas to willing buyers for as little as $425 for a bachelor's degree, $550 for a master's degree, and just a little more for a PhD (for example, see www.inquestscreening.com).
- ◆ The Association of Certified Fraud Examiners estimates that occupational fraud and abuse cost organizations about $600 billion annually, or roughly 6 percent of gross revenues (www.cfenet.com).

This job seeker inflation is a serious problem, and believe it or not, some employers are willing to tolerate a little inflation because they inflate their available jobs as well. But what employers won't tolerate are boldfaced lies about academic degrees you don't really have; gaps in employment that are hidden due to terminations; or any inflation that you handwrite on an employment application, which is termed "falsification of company documents"—a cause for immediate termination if discovered. This danger of falsifying documents is why employers insist that you not leave any blanks on an employment application. A lie documented on an application is the ideal defense in an equal employment or wrongful discharge case—provided by the employee himself or herself.

Getting Caught
The inflation of a potential employee's record is rarely discovered during initial screenings. It usually emerges further into the process, when

the focus is primarily on you versus multiple interviewees, and most often when your references are being checked or you're a candidate and a job offer is about to be made. Or it may be discovered after you start the job and are unable to prove yourself or deliver on your promises.

Recruiters are trained to discern whether the inflation is only puffery or actual intentional fraud. They start by looking for gaps in chronology, the absence of any dates, overlapping work experience, and/or unrealistic and vague qualifications and explanations; they refer to these as "red flags," "stupid stuff," "word magic," and "clever positioning." They watch and listen for the lack or misuse of industry-specific terminology, and "extreme descriptors" and what they really mean, like "top performer," "key contributor," and "functional lead." If they misjudge an instance of employment fraud, they not only fail in their duties but also expose the employer to lawsuits if unqualified employees are put into situations that may jeopardize the health and safety of the public or other employees. So they have a strong incentive to catch anyone engaging in job inflation before he or she is hired. Let's look at an example from my notebook.

RECRUITER'S NOTEBOOK

Caught in a Lie

The telephone screen I had with the job seeker probed all the basics, including goals, academic degrees, stability, accomplishments, strengths, developmental needs, issues of relocation, preferences about supervisory styles, pay and benefits, work cultures, and examples that demonstrated fit with the competencies for which I was recruiting. After 45 minutes, I had collected sufficient information, and then it was the job seeker's turn.

The job seeker probed the details related to the position, employer, team, job description, and structure, and he tried to get a sense of what the immediate supervisor was like and the initial goals and objectives for the position. He seemed organized, his questions suggested that he knew what he was doing, and I was sufficiently impressed. I suggested that he take the evening and browse the employer's website to see if any further questions came to the surface. We agreed that he would call me the next morning and that if there were no problems we would meet that afternoon. We met, and I went through his résumé again to confirm everything. He had just a couple of questions. I probed and helped him to resolve his doubts or hesitations. Once they were resolved, we discussed his availability for interviews. He was good to go, and I wrote a summary of my interview notes and sent that along with his résumé to my client.

The client asked that I arrange a phone screen for the next day. It was set for 3 p.m., and I prepared the candidate for what to expect. He was to call me afterward with his impressions. He did, and he was clearly excited. He said the opportunity was everything I said it would be and that he was ready to move forward. I asked whether the employer had discussed any next steps with him. He said they would get back to me and were just getting started and planned to interview others. Red flag!

I called my client, who said they had no interest because they thought it was important that the person in this job have a completed degree. It turned out that the job seeker began the conversation by stating that he wanted to clarify a mistake in the wording of his résumé and that he was actually one semester short of finishing his bachelor's degree but would have that done very soon. I apologized as best I could and then called the job seeker. He said it wasn't that big of a deal and that he thought the employer would understand because his experience was more important. He said he didn't tell me because he thought it might prevent him from getting the interview.

The Perils of Job Inflation

Every adult knows the implications of being caught in a lie, so we won't dwell on that. Suffice it to say that it creates the wrong impression and also long-term consequences that you really don't want to deal with for the remainder of your life. Take, for example, these excerpts from the Internet available worldwide until the end of time (the names have been omitted here but do appear online; the pertinent sources and URLs are not given here, but you can easily search for them):

- Bausch & Lomb's CEO falsely claimed an MBA from New York University's Stern School of Business. He attended the program but never graduated.
- Veritas Software's CFO said he earned an accounting degree from Arizona State University and an MBA from Stanford.

All he really had was an undergraduate degree from Idaho State University. Merrill Lynch downgraded Veritas after the disclosure.

- The research director at Institutional Shareholder Services, the influential firm that advises shareholders on whether takeovers are good deals, was terminated when it was discovered that he didn't have a law degree from the University of Southern California, as he had claimed (he was a few credits short).

- A now-disgraced Salomon Smith Barney analyst said he attended the Massachusetts Institute of Technology, when he in fact studied at nearby, less prestigious Boston University.

- An investigation by *Washington Technology* and *Government Computer News* turned up more than 60 government and contractor information technology workers *claiming* degrees from unaccredited schools. One of those employees was a senior director in the Department of Homeland Security. She was placed on administrative leave while the department investigated her bachelor's, master's, and doctoral degrees from an unaccredited school in Wyoming.

- A presidential appointment to head the Federal Emergency Management Agency was replaced in 2003. An investigation by *Time* found discrepancies in his online legal profile and official biography, including a description released by the White House at the time of his nomination. He lacked emergency management experience as proclaimed, and also the academic institution he graduated from could not confirm that he was on the Dean's List, a professor, or outstanding award winner as his bio also proclaimed.

- A Notre Dame football coach was forced to resign five days after starting his position when it was revealed that he had falsified information. He did not have a graduate degree as proclaimed, and he had exaggerated his own playing experience. He lost the millions of dollars he was due under his new contract and the several million dollars he would have received had he stayed with his former employer.

- A writer with the *Washington Post* was hired with fake educational credentials. She won a Pulitzer Prize in 1981 for a story that was untrue. She resigned and the *Washington Post* returned the prize.
- The dean of admissions for the Massachusetts Institute of Technology resigned in 2007 after it was discovered that she did not have a college degree, as her résumé claimed. The fraud had gone undetected for nearly 28 years.

The stories of how recruiters discover these kinds of falsifications are of course fascinating. Let's look at one from my notebook.

RECRUITER'S NOTEBOOK

Disaster Averted

A recruiter I know well discovered that a finalist candidate he was representing for a senior vice president of administration position did not have an academic degree as claimed on the employer's application form. The candidate had had a very successful career within the financial services industry, most recently as a senior vice president of human resources. He had navigated two interview visits and been favorably evaluated by an independent assessment service, and the results of his reference checks had all been extremely positive. While the employer was in the process of preparing the offer, the college could not verify his completion of the degree he had listed. I asked him to contact the school to help resolve this discrepancy. He claimed that the issue had come up only once before a year earlier and had been successfully resolved. However, the college's records indicated that only two semesters had been completed, and there had been no efforts by anyone during the previous year to investigate or resolve this matter. Throughout this awkward process, the candidate insisted that the degree had been completed but that his copy of the transcript had been lost in a flood at his parent's home. When he was advised that the employer would be unable to proceed, he volunteered to further explore this matter with the college. Fortunately, this job inflation disaster in the making was averted before an offer could be extended.

The employment process is imperfect because it is managed by humans and subject to human errors and inclinations. Decisions have to be based on impressions, and attempts to verify them are not always successful. As was mentioned above, it's human nature to engage in a little inflation, but a lot of inflation or inflating crucial facts like degrees completed is cheating. Although it may be easy to cheat, the consequences will haunt you the rest of your life. At the time, it may seem hard to not cheat—but you will be forever glad you did not.

Projection, or the Me-Too Syndrome

Everyone has heroes who inspire and motivate him or her. Sometimes you might even make changes in your life or attitude to be more like your hero. Job seekers sometimes play this game of psychological projection and assume they have the same qualities as those they admire. But if you don't truly have the experience and credentials to back up these projected imaginings, you are courting disaster in the form of what psychologists call "projection"—or the "me-too syndrome."

Bruce Learns Contentment

The movie *Bruce Almighty* provides an excellent example of the effects of this projection and the resulting career discontent. Bruce is a news reporter who appears to be doing what he loves but doesn't really love what he's doing. He feels something is missing, that there should be more. He wants to become a TV anchorman before he gets too old and misses his opportunity. The only problem is that he lacks the skills for the job and is more ideally suited to his reporter position. He projects the qualities he lacks and wants onto the anchor job and pursues it with the intent of finding his contentment there.

When an anchor opening occurs, Bruce competes against a better-qualified co-worker, who is given the position. Bruce is devastated, and in his state of discontent he stops thinking clearly and makes some very bad decisions that result in his being fired. He then meets God, who explains to Bruce that he was endowed with free will and can choose to believe whatever he wants, but that he was created with a gift for reporting the news and entertaining people. Despite the career coaching directly from God, Bruce chooses to persist in his faulty, grandiose, projected belief of his destiny as anchor and tells God that his way of doing things is better. So God decides to take a vacation and leaves Bruce in charge of the universe.

The now–"Bruce Almighty" discovers that genuine contentment is from within and not dependent upon another position or employer, or even material things made possible by his "Almighty" powers. He returns to his old reporter position and his authentic self, and he is successful, content, and lives happily ever after.

Bruce's story demonstrates that your life and career go a lot more smoothly when you choose to think responsibly and when your beliefs are realistic and not based on faulty projections. Bruce also demonstrates that your beliefs about work are more difficult to keep realistic, change, or let go of because they are linked with your pride, aspirations, respectability, and income. You are conditioned to pursue what satisfies these things, but the measures of success do not always enable genuine career contentment. It wasn't easy for Bruce to defy his conditioning and find contentment in just being himself and to accept that he was doing what he was created to do.

The Perils of Projection

When applied to employment, projection involves your bestowing upon the position or employer certain characteristics you want them to have but they don't actually possess. It's otherwise referred to as infatuation, wishful thinking, or being out of touch with reality. You're so focused on believing what you want that you overlook the truth, or choose to ignore it. Actually, this is far more dangerous than job inflation because you don't always know you're doing it, and the employer does it as well, as evidenced by the way they describe you as a water walker, self-starter, superstar, person with fire in the belly, entrepreneurial, high potential, promotable, upwardly mobile, and so on. You only wish you could live up to some of their projections—but what if you can't and they've already hired you?

Projection works like this: Let's say that in spite of any problems or issues, you choose to view the employer as ideal and possessing all the attributes you're looking for, and the employer chooses to view you as a person with high potential. Later, when the facts are finally acknowledged, you each start to perceive the other as a fake, scam, con artist, or something less than what you bargained for, even though it was your false impression of the other that created the problem, not the other's intention to deceive you. You projected onto the other all the characteristics you wanted them to have, even though they didn't actually possess them. You were infatuated and not thinking clearly. You wanted it that badly, and it happens all the time. Let's look at an example from my notebook.

RECRUITER'S NOTEBOOK

Infatuated at the Employment Agency

While attending graduate school, I decided to explore part-time opportunities through a local employment agency. I made an appointment to visit its offices, and its owner indicated that they didn't have anything suitable for me at the moment. But he was thrilled by the fact that I was a graduate student and was pursuing a career in human resources and employment, so he offered to let me work for him on a commission basis to learn the ropes.

The employment agency owner immediately arranged for me to meet with one of his recruiters to get an idea of the work. I did, and I soon realized this wasn't what I needed at the moment. I needed a steady part-time income to help me get through the remainder of school. I was about to disclose this fact when I spotted a woman out of the corner of my eye. She was absolutely gorgeous, and I had to get to know her. I pretended to think I knew her from somewhere and asked the recruiter who she was. It turned out that Suzie was single and dating the owner's son. I eagerly accepted the position and started work the next day.

Over the next two weeks, I became absolutely convinced that Suzie and I were meant for each other and that she would be the ideal mother for our children. Then I worked up the courage to ask her out on a date. We dated for two months, and it turned out that Suzie wasn't exactly what I wanted. I also discovered that my heart wasn't really in the work either, so I started looking elsewhere.

This example is true and may be silly, but it helps make several points. The employer projected high hopes onto the candidate, while the candidate was projecting high hopes onto Suzie. Projection is more dangerous than inflation, because you don't always know if or when you're doing it, and you may not know if or when the other is doing it. It just happens, and it may sometimes be referred to as an honest mistake, though the only intentional dishonesty is by you to you, which makes them stupid mistakes due to your lack of due diligence or irresponsibility and wishful thinking. But because you now know that this can happen, you must be on guard to prevent it from happening to you. Instead, you can and must do everything in your power to find the true you and present your true self to would-be employers. Now that we've covered all the bad news in this chapter, let's move on to this much more pleasant topic: authenticity.

Summing Up: Try Authenticity

Job inflation and projection have the effect of prolonging your search as you waste time researching, pursuing the wrong trail, and presenting and selling yourself as the right person for the wrong positions or employers. (See table 3-1 for a handy summary of job inflation and projection.) You're chasing suspects when you should be chasing genuine prospects, and the net result is to cause yourself a lot of unnecessary grief and disappointment due to rejections or false starts—if you make it that far.

The direct opposite of inflation and projection is *authenticity*, which involves viewing others, and yourself, as they truly are, not what you want them to be or what you think they should be. It allows you to present yourself as you truly are, despite what anyone else thinks you are or wants you to be. Authenticity is an aspect of integrity, and both these basic human qualities contribute to your contentment.

Job seekers don't often think about the term "authenticity" because they're preoccupied instead with their persistence, hope, and optimism. This is a good thing, but only to a point. Each individual and organization have their own DNA, and you're not likely to change it from the

Table 3-1. Job Inflation and Projection from the Employee's and Employer's Perspectives

Inflation or Projection	Employee's Perspective	Employer's Perspective
Inflation Exaggeration or puffery to get what you want	False or misleading information on résumés, applications	False or misleading information on job descriptions, offers
Pride that prevents you from being who you truly are	Comments made or withheld during interviews	Partial truths regarding viability, reorganizations, staff changes, etc.
Projection Attaching the qualities we lack and desire onto others and things	Overlooking a mismatch to the people, place, and particulars	Overlooking a mismatch to the qualifications, personality, and potential
Endowing them with the power to make us happy	Misreading personalities and conditions	Unrealistic performance expectations

outside looking in by thinking wishfully. It's possible, but why waste your time trying? It is what it is, and that's a good thing because it enables you to form an opinion and make your decision. Otherwise, you'd drive yourself nuts dealing with the inconsistencies and trying to hit a moving target. Here's a story from my notebook about finding authenticity.

RECRUITER'S NOTEBOOK

Authenticity: The Sweet Spot in the Middle

Jobs find people, and my job as recruiter involves facilitating introductions that were meant to be. To help ensure that they are the right introductions, my approach involves deciding whether I like you and then trying to place you with people I like. I have to believe that you're representing yourself as you truly are, you know what you want and don't want, and you're content about these facts. If during the initial conversation you radiate an attitude that says "convince me," I'll appreciate your objectivity, but I'll also question whether this is the job that's calling you. I'm looking for

Authenticity: The Sweet Spot in the Middle (continued)

some sense of enthusiasm that suggests I shouldn't have to sell or convince you that this is meant to be.

However, if you radiate the opposite extreme during that first conversation—"This job was made for me"—I'll value that reaction as a positive clue, but I'll also consider the possibility of whether you're inflating or projecting. I'm looking for that sweet spot in the middle referred to as authenticity, and when I find it, I'll be more likely to move you from suspect to prospect and to facilitate the introduction.

During our initial conversation, your authenticity is recognizable as a doubt-free and honest inclination to one extreme versus the other (a simple yes or no), or as a balanced inclination to both extremes (maybe), and I'll try to sense whether you're realistically evaluating your inclinations against the resolved certainty of knowing what you want, or whether serendipity has opened your mind to this being the possibility that you have an inkling that it's meant to be. When your authenticity is there, my job becomes helping you evaluate your options, and you'll know instinctively whether my motives are to benefit you or me. Only you can sell yourself—and when you sell yourself with authenticity, that's when I decide I like you.

What's Next

The next chapter is devoted to helping you make the right decisions—those decisions most in tune with the noninflating, authentic self we've learned about in this chapter. But don't feel overwhelmed if this sounds grandiose—there are handy guidelines for making these decisions. By following these guidelines—factors that can be summed up as the "four Ps," people, place, the particulars involved, and what's personal to you—you'll develop the ability to make confident career decisions rooted in your authentic self that feel deeply right to you both mentally and emotionally.

4

Make Confident Career Choices: Follow the Four Ps

In this chapter, you'll learn

- ◆ how to recognize the kinds of people you'd prefer to work with
- ◆ how to analyze a potential employer as a place to work
- ◆ how the particular aspects of the actual job mesh with your career goals
- ◆ how your personal character fits the job

Determining which opportunity you're ideally suited for can be challenging, particularly if it involves a geographic move, a change in lifestyle, or a compromise in some dimension of your life and career. Of course, you don't want to make the wrong decision. But your ability to make the right decision depends on what you consider most important for your potential contentment—and that can involve more than you realize.

First, remember how you reached this fork in the road. Whether you were looking or forced to look for a new job, you were somehow "called" to something new, and you managed to have it find you. There will be other new callings again in the future, so keep in mind that this decision determines what you do next, not necessarily what you'll do for the rest of your life. In fact, don't burn your networking bridges, because your job search never really ends. It will continue throughout your career. Having said this, what was so important about your last job that made you decide to accept it? And what did you learn from that decision that can help you make even better job decisions in the future?

You already know what you don't want, and you know that accepting anything that compromises your authenticity is not a good idea. To prepare yourself to reject what doesn't feel right mentally and emotionally, you'll need guidelines to help you determine what's most important. Providing them is the purpose of this chapter.

Everyone is different, but what's most important to any job seeker is a combination of factors that you can easily remember as the four Ps:

- the people
- the place
- the particulars involved
- what's personal to you.

Within each of these four factors is a host of considerations that should not be overlooked.

As you review the material given here, keep in mind the subtle dangers of making decisions that ultimately are opposed to your authentic motivations and inspirations. For instance, let's say that the people with whom you work are ultimately most important to you but that during the course of interviews for a job you discover they are not so great. Nevertheless, you accept the job because the money is extraordinary, the employer is located within two miles of your home, and you're confident that the career path will catapult you to the next level within 18 months.

In accepting the job, you've made a compromise with what you thought was most important, which means the people were not really that important. If they really were the most important factor, you just blew it by choosing to spend the majority of your waking hours with the wrong people, and the situation will worsen if all the other alluring attractions don't pan out as you imagined. This can all begin to get confusing—what's ultimately most important to you? That's why it's so important to examine the four Ps before you accept a job, rather than after.

P1 The People

People make the organization. We depend on each other to get things done, and when things don't get done, the problem is usually the result of an issue between people—your leaders, supervisors, co-workers, subordinates, role models, and mentors.

Recall from previous chapters that employment decisions really boil down to whether you and the employer like each other. That's because your normal tendency is to associate with the people you like the most or who are most like you. This is important, because 60 percent of your waking hours will be spent with the people you work with. That's more time than you spend with your family. So if you don't like them, why would you consider working with them? Ideally, the people you work with should be encouraging and compatible with you, and you'll avoid the people who you dislike, don't respect, or don't trust.

However, there's another important reality to keep in mind. Because the employment process involves people when they are trying to make good impressions rather than give the full picture of their behavior, it's highly probable that the people you meet when job hunting are on their best behavior. So you'll need to look toward the future and try to imagine dealing with them at both their best and worst. This is almost impossible, because you don't really know them. But you can ask about the most important relatively identifiable aspects of on-the-job behavior that will help you get to know them:

- leadership
- supervision
- role models and mentors
- teams, colleagues, and subordinates.

Let's briefly look at each.

Leadership: Looking for Openness in Downward Communication

The people leading an organization are always important. You may not get the opportunity to meet them, and the people you do meet will be cautious in what they tell you about them. They don't want to give you a bad impression, and they might be concerned that what they say could come back to haunt them. However, because you're already there, it means they like you, so you'll probably be given just enough positive and negative information on which to base a decision. What you look for, and what's truly most important about leadership, is openness in downward communication.

The best leaders are open and truthful with their employees regarding strategies, business plans, decisions, and course corrections. Everyone is informed and rowing in the same direction, and surprises are kept to a minimum. Because communication is free flowing and straightforward, you'll know where you stand and what you can do about it. When these conditions exist, people seem to be confident in knowing where they're headed, in taking pride in their contributions, and in being supportive of their leadership. Contrast this with people who seem to be uninformed or working in the dark. They spend their time dealing with assumptions, second-guessing decisions, and competing with each other for limited attention from above. Look for signs of openness in downward communication. What do the people you speak with know about what's going on?

Supervision: Looking for Trust in Upward Communication

Middle managers and supervisors are likewise important due to their immediate impact on your day-to-day affairs and peace of mind. They help to create a comfortable, productive work environment. They sign your performance appraisal, determine your contributions, and moderate your pace and flow. But what's really most important is whether they demonstrate trust in their upward communication.

Good managers and supervisors demonstrate their willingness and ability to intercede on your behalf and make it possible for you to do your job. They strive to keep you informed about information from above and around you. You should expect this from the people you meet, but when their communications upward are selective or the information is being filtered or scrubbed to control what is known at the top, this indicates that things are probably not as they seem. Either a problem exists at the top and they are powerless to fix it, or they are creating problems. Neither situation is good.

Weak managers tend to attract problems. They want to know if you can help *them* and don't necessarily keep in mind the overall good of the organization. Stealthy, controlling managers tend to build fiefdoms and use information as their greatest weapon. They want to know if you're a team player for their fiefdom, not the overall organization. Look for signs of trust in upward communication. Among the people you're speaking with, what effort is made to keep the senior management team informed?

Role Models and Mentors: Looking for Morals, Ethics, and Values That Match Your Own

Organizations tend to showcase their assets, and when it comes to employment, they make sure you meet the right people—or at least they should. Expect to meet at least one person to whom the organization thinks you might relate, who understands the organization, and who seems willing to enlighten and assist you. What's really most important is that you observe solid morals, ethics, and values, and that you believe they match your own.

If you were not introduced to one of these people, they may not exist, or the organization may not be sufficiently evolved. Otherwise, you may be dealing with the wrong people. Look for people you can affiliate with, aspire to be like, or trust will support you later. What do they stand for, and are you willing to stand beside them? If you find that one person, but the organization doesn't make the connection possible, there's a problem with that person or there's something the organization doesn't want you to know. In either case, it should send up a red flag that you should probe, particularly if that's the one person you identify with. Look for morals, ethics, and values that you respect and that tend to mirror your own. Take note of any opportunities the organization gives you to speak with special people.

Teams, Colleagues, and Subordinates: Looking for Competence and Evidence of Appreciation and Gratitude

Teams, colleagues, and subordinates are the people who will be sharing your foxhole day by day. To put it mildly, it's a good thing if these people are competent and pulling their own weight; otherwise, you can expect to be doing most of the work. As they talk, try to get a sense of whether they feel recognized, valued, and appreciated for their contributions or are seeking to build or regain credibility—and you're their path to it. Also, do they willingly express their gratitude for what's occurring in their environment and for the opportunity to influence outcomes? Are they engaged and contributing, or are they looking for direction and new sparks of hope? Do they talk positively about each other, or do they give you tips on how to deal with the other? What's most important is that you see evidence of competence, appreciation, and gratitude—and you might as well throw in loyalty while you're at it. Take note of what the people at your level are saying.

P2   Place

You can tell a lot about an employer simply by the people who work there, but there's a lot more you should be looking for. Specifically, is the place where you work genuinely stable, safe, and attractive within the community and overall? Do your research and ask about what's most important:

- viability as a place to work
- products and services
- location; image and identity
- size, pace, and aesthetics.

Let's look briefly at each.

Viability as a Place to Work: Looking for Stability, Vision, and Direction

That your target employer has existed for many years is a fairly decent indicator of its viability but doesn't eliminate the possibility that the firm might be acquired, divested, downsized, or right sized just weeks after you join it. You have to investigate the firm's performance and what's going on, including whether its employees have a clear vision for the future and are taking purposeful, decisive steps to get there before the competition.

Do the people with whom you speak seem to share the same vision regarding the company's future direction? Are they on the same page and fully disclosing what they know, or are they just as much in the dark as you? But don't stop there. The company may be doing well, but plans could be under development that will have an impact on one or more people, departments, or divisions that will in turn directly or indirectly affect where you'll be working. Look for signs as to whether the existing scenery and environment are evolving, and get a sense of what they will look like within the period of time that is most important to you—like when you're working there.

Chances are, it might be better when you get there or into the future, but you have to make sure you know what you're walking into. What's most important here is that you find evidence of stability, clear vision of worthwhile goals, and purposeful movement toward them.

Products and Services: Looking for Acceptance and Affiliation

What the staff members of your target employer do or make to generate revenues is something they're proud of and intend to further perfect to increase revenues. This is true whether they're doing one thing or are diversified to do several things. What you see is what you get, and what's important is you accept this as fact, and ideally feel an affinity for the firm's main product or service. You need to be able to believe in it and, thus, play a willing role in its promotion, selling, and usage.

This, of course, brings up the basic reality that not everyone wants to work in the alcohol, tobacco, defense, nuclear, meatpacking, or other industries that people find fault with on a daily basis. If you're one of those people, don't work in one of those controversial industries. Many do and try to rationalize it, and in their hearts they doubt or have suspicions—but this is the same as opposing the will of the employer, and sometimes the will of your family and friends. It wears on you until you finally admit it—generally when you're walking out the door and not intending to return. What keeps you there is usually an alternative motivation or something you consider more important, like salary and benefits. That's OK, as long as you can rationalize it without it having a negative impact on your performance and potential for contentment. But what's really important is that you look for authentic acceptance of and affinity for the product or service.

Location: Looking for a Reasonably Accessible Employer

On the surface, it seems obvious that you would want to look for an employer that is reasonably accessible, so you can work close to home or otherwise in locations with favorable traffic patterns and public transportation. However, the lure of an attractive job—caused by another motivation or something else that seems more important than location—may tempt you to make compromises and justify commutes that are unreasonable because the money is go good, you think you can endure the commute, the family will eventually move, or the situation is not likely to stay as is. Don't count on it. What's most important is that you choose an employer that is now reasonably accessible. If you really want the job, move near the employer if you're not now accessible, unless you can move the work closer to you.

Image and Identity: Looking for a Reputable, Desirable Employer

The factor of image and identity focuses on the reputation your target employer has as a place to work, regardless of its product or service. This is important because by joining a particular employer, you immediately take on its existing image and reputation in the eyes of your friends, neighbors, and colleagues who work elsewhere. You become one of "them." What's important is that you find out what a firm's reputation is and whether you consider it desirable for you.

This is not a significant point if your target employer is too small for community recognition, but the fact that it doesn't have a reputation may be a factor if you want the benefit of its identity. When applying for a mortgage or car loan, it's definitely an advantage to work for a prestigious, well-known organization, and it can just as easily hurt you if your target employer has a less-than-positive reputation—guilt by association. What's most important is that your target employer has a desirable reputation, or one that is in keeping with your standards and that you can be proud of.

Size, Pace, and Aesthetics: Looking for a Positive Climate and Work Culture

When observing the people who work with your target employer, try to imagine keeping pace with them amid whatever their working conditions may be. They've probably become acclimated to whatever's going on and may not even recognize the things you see as unusual or cause for concern. What's important is that you try to recognize what they think about the place where they work—or otherwise judge for yourself whether you could make the same adjustments, because you may have to.

Each time you enter a prospective employer's environment, try to purposefully experiment with each of your five senses. What does the place look like, smell like, sound like, and feel like? Even try the food and coffee. If you don't like the factory floor, stick to an office. If you can't stand working in an office, find what turns you on and stick with that. If you need time to contemplate, avoid fast-paced, multitasking environments. If the firm thrives on meetings, PowerPoint presentations, and many memos to cover rear ends and you don't, find something else. What's most important is that you find what matches your ideal climate and work culture. Be yourself and see what happens. Let's look at an illustrative story from my notebook.

RECRUITER'S NOTEBOOK

Performance: Excellent; Product Affinity: Nil

No one had any doubts that Paul would be a great addition to the regional corporate affairs team, and he felt the same way or he certainly wouldn't have accepted our offer. For most of his first year, he had excelled at everything, and we were questioning whether he had been brought in at too low a job level. It was obvious that he had potential beyond his job, and in some areas he was stronger than his boss. And he also had humility, so it wasn't an issue that he had to wait a while for that opportunity. His job involved governmental affairs and required him to work closely with industry lobbyists and multiple state legislatures to promote bills that benefited the brewing industry and to kill bills that didn't. He was a whiz at this and had several successes under his belt when all of a sudden it seemed as if things were starting to slip and were getting worse rather than better.

Because of Paul's earlier successes and the good relations he'd established with many of our executives, he was brought to the corporate office to discuss whether anything could be done to help him. We had no idea what the problem was, but he had been on the job for one year and we assumed he might be dealing with pressures related to his need to constantly battle the forces that were intent on further controlling our industry—alcohol. But the problem wasn't our industry but that of our parent company—tobacco.

In his meeting with the corporate honchos, Paul admitted that from the very beginning he had had ethical doubts about whether to take the job because our parent company sold tobacco. One of his family members had been diagnosed with lung cancer and had been getting progressively worse during the past three months. At the same time, because Paul was so effective, he'd been increasingly relied upon to leverage his contacts to help the parent tobacco company. This situation was wearing on him, and he could no longer take it. We couldn't change the fact that we made cigarettes as well as beer, so if Paul couldn't adjust, he would have to make the decision to resign.

Paul did resign, with the sympathy of all but one senior staff executive, who asked one question: "Who hired this guy?" At that time, we were maintaining "job files" for each position that had been filled, and the search was on to find the original interview notes, reference checks, and which recruiter had signed the offer package. The only reason this didn't result in a "Friday casualty" for this unfortunate recruiter was that the he was already gone—but it certainly got the attention of the rest of us. From then on, I made a point of ensuring that all our candidates fully accepted the products made by the overall corporation.

P3   The Particulars

The "particulars" mean the actual job and everything associated with your getting, starting, and enjoying it. There's a lot more to the particulars than most people realize until they're reminded of them, and then it's usually too late. So take the time now. Let's look at the gamut, from job competencies and expectations to the budget and resources.

Job Competencies and Expectations: Are They Realistic and Challenging?

You're usually not going to look for or take a job that doesn't interest you or for which you're inadequately trained. The real issue, and what's most important, is whether the competencies and expectations associated with that job are realistic or sufficiently challenging in relation to your abilities and interests.

Employers have become increasingly cost conscious, resulting in fewer employees doing the work that was previously done by many more. Competencies and expectations have been elevated accordingly—but not necessarily the pay. Watch for hybrid positions that blend job functions that seem like unusual combinations but are presented as providing rounding for career development. What's most important is not to get too far in over your head at the start. Alternatively, this could be a good thing if the job has an element that enables you to find a refreshing new challenge, rather than more of the same old thing. In either case, what's most important is that the competencies required for and expectations imposed on the position are realistic, are compatible with your interests and abilities, and offer fresh challenges.

Recruitment and Selection: Looking for Swift, Fair, and Engaging Processes

Because the business of employment involves creating good impressions, and recruiting presents your first, most lasting impression with the employer, how do you think they're likely to treat you in the future if they fail to impress and involve you during your recruitment? Probably not very well!

In most human resource departments, the recruiting function is occupied by entry-level staffing specialists who are doing their time before advancing. The function may also be outsourced. Their mind may not always be in the game. However, there's no excuse for an employer that is disrespectful and causes you to feel processed rather than finessed. Don't justify your decision by making excuses for the employer's bad efforts, particularly if you're also their customer or consumer. What's most important at this delicate phase of your relationship is that your recruitment is handled in a swift, fair, and engaging manner. If not, consider whatever happens as providing a glimpse into your probable future with that employer.

Career Paths and Opportunities: Looking for Progress Toward Your Goals, Not the Employer's

Not everyone wants to be company president, but if you want to advance, it would be nice to have that option. However, if you want to remain stationary and not be pressured to move, that would also be nice. What's most important is that both options are available and that the choice is yours and in keeping with your career goals, not the employer's.

Before you accept a job, it's important to get a sense from the prospective employer of what the future might hold for you. That's because after you start the job, you'll be working at the will of your employer and placed where you're needed. If they don't have a plan, you may not have any place to go; and if they do, you might be limited to where they want you to go—and neither alternative is particularly good. What's important is that your plan counts, whether the employer has one or not. Let's look at a story from my notebook on the following page about how this can unfold.

Pay and Benefits: Looking for a Fair, Competitive Package

It's diplomatic to comment during interviews that the work is more important than the pay. Nobody really buys this comment—or if they do, they leverage it to buy you for less. People aren't always willing to work if they don't have to, so of course the money is important. It's one of the most important reasons you're working, and it should be fair and competitive.

RECRUITER'S NOTEBOOK

Kevin Excels—Right Off His Career Path

Kevin's experience illustrates what happens when someone follows the employer's plan rather than his or her own: "My academics and experience were specialized in marketing research. I knew this stuff like the back of my hand, and I enjoyed the work. My clients appreciated my contributions and one day suggested that I should move into the brand management function.

"Although this suggestion was a compliment, it was something I hadn't given any thought. I was on the succession plan to become marketing research director within two years, and that was exciting enough. My boss was very encouraging and helped arrange a series of exploratory interviews. Everyone made certain that I was given all the information I needed, and though no one ever said anything, it felt as if I was being asked to move.

"After a couple of weeks, I had a good idea of what the brand management job entailed. I knew I could do it, but my heart was still in research. By this time, things were too far along to back out. They made an offer, and I accepted it as any good soldier would. Within two months, I was regretting my decision. My old job had been filled, and I was stuck doing what I didn't particularly like. I became the proverbial fish out of water. I did what I could, but that was never enough.

"Two years later, I negotiated with my boss and the Human Resources Department to be put back into my old job. But by now I could have been the director of marketing research. The only way I could get that job soon would be to go elsewhere, but I've been out of research now for over two years. Who would want me?"

Employers work within salary ranges, and problems arise when your current compensation is far below or above what the employer is willing to pay. It forces them to find a solution, and they don't like doing things that are out of whack with how their existing employees are paid. If this situation arises, it should alert you to a potential problem with either the industry you've chosen or your target employer. The latter is the bigger problem.

If you're coming in below range, are you taking on more than you should, and where will that put you in relation to other people doing the same job? It's understandable now; but a year from now, others will wonder if you're the weaker performer simply because your pay is lower. Conversely, if you're coming in at the high end of the range or above, are you overqualified for the position, and why would they want to do that to their existing employees? Also, could this high pay limit your ability to increase your income when your performance deserves it? Finally, how does the compensation they're talking about compare with what you're finding elsewhere? What's important is that you're paid fairly and competitively.

Induction and Orientation: Looking for Efforts to Integrate You

Every employer has an induction process, sometimes called onboarding, but not all make an effort to orient you properly. Not that you need any hand-holding, but it certainly helps to be given the resources you'll need or information on how to get them so you can thrive in your new environment, not just survive.

The absence of a new-hire orientation program is not a bad thing, because even when employers have such programs, employees don't make full use of them because they're so busy getting started, and supervisors would rather have them on the job. However, as they learn about things they wish they'd known earlier, they unanimously regret not having gone through a formal orientation process. What's most important is that you find out in advance how your target employer plans to integrate you after you've started working. If there are no plans, you'll essentially be on your own, and probably for more than just the orientation. What's most important is that the employer has plans to fully integrate you rather than allow you to stumble on your own.

Training and Development: Looking for Timely, Purposeful Programs

Training for the sake of training is not good, but no training is even worse. Employers want to be on record as valuing training. But what exactly does that entail?

It's important to find out what training will be offered, if it will be available when you can take it, and whether it will suit your needs—and if not, what can be done about it and when. The same thing applies to memberships in professional and trade associations. Does the employer pay for one membership that others are expected to share for information, or does each employee get his or her own membership? What about attendance at professional networking and development events? What's most important is that training applies to your needs and is available when you can take it.

Budget and Resources: Looking for Adequate Funding

It's wonderful to be recruited for specific projects, when the employer is extremely excited and expects great things. However, before you accept a job offer, it's a good idea to make certain that the employer is willing to fund any achievements they expect. Nothing is free, and they shouldn't expect miracles or put the burden on you to become resourceful without a budget.

It's important in any job that you have all the resources you need to fulfill your basic requirements, and particularly any special projects discussed during your recruitment. Employers get upset when the results fail to materialize or cost too much. It doesn't matter after the fact whether or not enough funding was allocated; what matters is that you failed to meet expectations. Beware of resource sharing, outdated equipment, inadequate staff levels, published budget restrictions, and so forth. Fiscal responsibility is good, but not when it inhibits good performance or when the employer is obviously doing well but not willing to make an investment in doing the right things. That's greed, and it signals other problems that will occur into the future. What's most important is having adequate funding and resources to meet all the requirements of your job.

P4   What's Personal to You

You might be asking "What's in it for me?" Actually, everything up to this point has already addressed that question. You might also ask "Why not me?"—and that question should be avoided at all cost. It assumes the negative and discounts the employer's right to half the decision. The more important question is "What's most important about me that makes this the right choice?" This does not refer to your credentials but rather to whether you're truly passionate, willing, and able—for all the reasons that are most important to you. Those reasons boil down to whether you're pursuing authenticity, passion, emotional maturity, competence, professional image, and rounding and balance. Consider whether you are meeting the following criteria for each of these qualities as you consider whether to accept a position.

Pursuing Authenticity

When pursuing authenticity, you're in effect saying to yourself: I'm not fooling myself or denying myself anything. You're on the right track if you're

+ making this job decision on your own accord rather than to please someone.
+ resolved in knowing what you want and what you'll accept.
+ certain you've honestly considered all the pros and cons.
+ confident what you've attracted satisfies all of your most important needs.
+ using fewer terms like "but," "what if," "maybe," "what about," and so on.
+ feeling increasingly upbeat, positive, confident, lighter, and self-assured.
+ sensing that it was coincidental, the right time or place, or meant to be.
+ hearing more encouragement than discouragement from yourself.

Pursuing Passion

When pursuing your passion, you're in effect saying to yourself: I'm focused on the right thing and it feels good. You're on the right track if you're

+ envisioning yourself already in the job.
+ so excited and eager to start that you can't wait.

- absolutely certain there's nothing else you'd rather be doing.
- confident you're not overlooking a missed opportunity.
- thinking this feels so right that you're not as concerned about money.
- feeling proud, happy, and inclined to tell the world about it.

Pursuing Emotional Maturity

When pursuing emotional maturity, you're in effect saying to yourself: I'm adaptable and energetic. You're on the right track if you're

- thinking realistically versus irresponsibly or wishfully.
- able to flex to accommodate challenges without complaining.
- capable of adjusting to any new or surprising demands.
- prepared not to make any excuses.
- feeling compatible with the people you've met.
- not regretting anything about what you're getting or not getting.
- feeling the risk is worth taking, almost as if there is no risk.
- increasingly unconcerned with what others might think.

Pursuing Competence

When pursuing competence, you're in effect saying to yourself: I'm enabled to use my motivated and inspired skills and abilities. You're on the right track if you're

- feeling up to the task and already know what you're planning to do.
- matched positively with the organization's pace and demands.
- not feeling underqualified or overqualified.
- willing to do whatever it takes or otherwise to give it your best.
- expected to use the skills you are motivated or inspired to use the most.
- not forfeiting or underutilizing any special or desirable abilities.
- not giving anything up by taking the opportunity.

Pursuing Professional Image

When pursuing your professional image, you're in effect saying to yourself: I'm accepted for who I am, my fit for this, and my readiness. You're on the right track if you're

- going in at the right level.
- confident you look and feel the part, and the employer also thinks that.
- associating comfortably with the right people.
- not compromising or making concessions—and neither is the employer.
- fit and attired to meet all expectations for the position.
- not worried about fitting in or being accepted.
- setting or increasing the standards for the position.

Pursuing Rounding and Balance

When pursuing rounding and balance, you're in effect saying to yourself: I'm growing from this and will still have a life. You're on the right track if you're

- leveraging existing talents.
- developing new talents.
- learning new things.
- broadening your horizons.
- increasing your marketability for the future.
- still able to balance family and career.

Summing Up the Four Ps

To sum up, the four Ps highlight what's universally most important about meaningful work: the people, place, particulars, and what's personal to you about all these things. An important aspect to keep in mind while evaluating these factors is realizing that no person, employer, or job is absolutely perfect. What you need to determine is the acceptable middle ground for each. In other words—and considering both the positive and negative aspects of each—what do you find most acceptable about each that can still fulfill your purpose?

Finally, if the job offer opportunity matches what you believe is the acceptable middle ground, you might consider using affirmations something like these to get the best perspective on the situation: "What I'm looking for is right now looking for me. We are drawn together like powerful magnets, or sewn together, and I'm drawing the thread so tight that my excitement has grown to where I feel I've already started working there. I feel a strong affiliation with my employer and compatibility with all the smiling faces. My work is meaningful and engaging, and I feel valued. My authenticity is at its peak, and I feel completely confident about this, blessed and extremely grateful. I believe this and so it is." We'll revisit these kinds of affirmations in chapter 6, after we explore how you can actually change the way you think and feel—the realities that underlie the four Ps.

What's Next

The next chapter presents ways to keep both your job search and career on track—the keys to resiliency. It moves beyond what has been explained in these first four chapters to the stage where you're in a new job and need to stay on course, whatever the challenges. We'll particularly examine moving from negative to positive feelings and the role of contentment in the whole process.

5

Keep Your
Career on Track:
Use Your Paradoxical Qualities
and Seven Keys to Resilience

In this chapter, you'll learn

- how to move from negative to positive feelings—using your paradoxical qualities
- how to recognize, strengthen, and use the seven key traits of a resilient person
- how it's all undergirded by and infused with contentment

In the first four chapters, you learned how to attract meaningful work, navigate the employment process, develop the right impressions, view your situation and others' as they truly are, and make the right choices. What you haven't learned thus far is how to stay on track, bounce back, and turn around a bad situation that seems headed in the wrong direction—in other words, how to endure despite the challenges and frustrations along the way.

Endurance is portrayed in movies and books as physical strength and stamina—a person's hardiness, thick skin, fighting spirit, strength of character, and will to survive. In the real world, we see endurance demonstrated time and again by the meekest people who might seem incapable of climbing even a flight of stairs. In fact, our greatest examples of endurance come from everyday people who started from backgrounds of poverty, abuse, or dependence, who were beaten down repeatedly by misfortune, and yet who managed to climb back up to become an example to us all. How did they do it?

You only have to open up a newspaper or a magazine to find an amazing story of someone who has survived some unbelievable catastrophe, trauma, hardship, or misfortune. Sometimes these stories center on an individual's astounding success despite growing up in difficult circumstances. Other times, the stories demonstrate that humans can survive seemingly impossible physical trauma or abuse and live to report the details. So what's the point? It's simple: These stories demonstrate that human beings have a nearly inexhaustible capacity to endure and even thrive through adversity.

The good news is that this wellspring of strength exists in us all. We just have to find a way to access it and use it. A large part of this innate capacity to survive is simply your attitude (the glass is always half full) and your ability to draw from this well of strength and human pluck. And some of it comes from sheer physical force summoned by this attitude—we've all heard of the petite woman whose adrenaline enabled her to lift the car off her child. And here's more good news: You already have the tools to access this never-ending source of strength and will. Moreover, you have probably been using this capacity your whole life without even acknowledging it. The trick is to find a way to access this force of will directly and purposefully and use it to your advantage to develop the career and the life you want.

The first step to accessing your inner strength is to acknowledge that you'll never be absolutely consistent in your thinking or resulting actions. For our purposes, we'll call this human tendency our "paradoxical qualities"; we'll look at these just below. And the second step is that you must acknowledge that you're just as resilient as the person in line with you at the movie theater, next to you on the subway, in the adjacent car stuck in traffic—or the company executive or grocery store clerk who happens to live in the house across the street.

Your Paradoxical Qualities

Any job or career search tests your ability to maintain a positive mindset, even if you believe a positive attitude is your natural tendency. If things are not going well, even the most positive people will find themselves becoming pessimistic. Although you might see this as a negative direction, it can actually be used to help you build your natural tendency for resiliency—I'm referring to your ability to be both one way and its opposite. Here's a list of these paradoxical qualities that exist in all of us:

- pride versus humility
- happy versus sad
- aggressive versus relaxed
- serious versus playful
- formal versus casual
- logical versus intuitive
- self-appreciating versus self-critical
- optimistic versus pessimistic
- angry versus forgiving
- task oriented versus people oriented
- trusting versus cautious
- selfish versus giving
- positive versus negative
- critical versus accepting.

Once you recognize that you won't always be able to maintain either a completely positive or a completely negative attitude, that you can be critical of people sometimes and highly accepting at other times—in short, that you're human—you'll discover more resiliencies to move toward an attitude that attracts the work and career you desire. Try this exercise from my Recruiter's Notebook to build resiliency. And then look at another notebook entry about two of the most important paradoxical qualities: pride and humility.

RECRUITER'S NOTEBOOK

Exercise: Trying on Positive Feelings

Although this exercise in trying on positive feelings might seem too simplistic, it does work. You'll need to try it several times, when you're feeling each of the ways it identifies:

- If you're feeling *pessimistic*, recognize that feeling and imagine how you would feel if you were *optimistic*.
- If you're feeling *beaten down* and stressed by circumstances—and even notice your shoulders slumping—try *standing up straight* and walking taller.
- If you're feeling *tired*, imagine what you'd feel like with more *energy*.
- If you're feeling *sad* or even depressed, imagine a *smile* on your face.

Try out each of these new feelings for 20 seconds. Then repeat the exercise a few times. You might think that this cannot possibly help, but most people are surprised to find how quickly this helps them begin to find their inner strength to endure. (For more on this approach, see the discussion of "flip switching" in chapter 6, and see Anthony 2005.)

RECRUITER'S NOTEBOOK

Lessons from Marge in Humility versus Pride, Endurance, and Triumph

Being a highly consumer-oriented company, it was in our DNA to be extremely image conscious, and this carried over into our employment decisions. Because Marge didn't look the part, we overlooked the one person who—if she'd been given the opportunity when she asked for it—would've enabled us to avoid a four-year quest to fill one position. During that four-year period, we placed three different people in the same vice president position, and the final and most enduring was Marge.

The initial opening occurred as result of a resignation, and Marge asked for consideration. She was told she lacked the necessary depth of related experience, but in the meantime she would be given some of the vice president's duties on an interim basis. From the perspective of her management, it was not that she was incompetent but that she was just plain ordinary. Her image was such that it was difficult for anyone to imagine her doing the job.

Although Marge's pride was hurt by this decision, she chose instead to humble herself by admitting her lack of executive experience, and she threw herself into the interim duties. The person we hired proved within 15 months that he was not the gregarious type he had portrayed himself to be but was a mentally unstable tyrant who was feared by his entire division. We waited and took advantage of the first opportunity to terminate him, and we didn't have to wait long. Marge once again asked for the position but was told that even though she had done well over the last 15 months, she required a little more seasoning to be effective in such an important job.

Marge privately admitted that she was angered by the situation, but she chose instead to forgive and forget. Then, to make matters worse, she was not asked to take on any special assignments because we already had a candidate from within who we thought was much better. It was her peer, and he had less seasoning compared with her, but he was well polished and had an impeccable image and presence. Marge first reacted fairly negatively, but she eventually chose instead to act positively and devoted herself to helping her new boss succeed.

As it turned out, we had projected some pretty hefty capabilities onto the new boss that he didn't actually possess. Within a year, he realized he was in over his head and left voluntarily to accept another job elsewhere. Marge once again asked for the position but was declined because we didn't need another internal mistake. The company instead chose to invest in the services of a prominent executive search firm. In the meantime, Marge was asked to fill in as vice president while the search was being conducted.

At this point, Marge had become more openly critical and intolerant of the fact that she had not been given serious consideration for the vice president job—if not exploited for her expertise. Yet rather than remain critical, she once again chose to stick things out and try to be more accepting of the situation, and she performed the duties as if they were officially hers. Her mature handling of the situation resulted in our asking the search firm to interview Marge along with whomever they surfaced from the outside. They interviewed Marge and thought she was worthy of consideration but that stronger candidates were available from outside the company. However, after paying a search fee of over $70,000, it was one year later and we still had no viable candidates who were as good as Marge. This was not so much due to the search firm's inability to do their job as it was to the fact that Marge had done an exceptional job in hers.

The decision was made to officially put Marge into the vice president position, where she remained until she decided to retire. She was the real deal, and despite her challenging circumstances over an extended period, she managed to endure in a positive manner that caused others to eventually change their beliefs about her.

The Seven Keys to Resiliency

I was first drawn to the topic of resiliency during the early 1990s when exploring how to find endurance to combat the challenges associated with my own job dissatisfaction. The book I focused on at that time was *The Resilient Self: How Survivors of Troubled Families Rise Above Adversity* by Steven Wolin and Sybil Wolin (1993). Although this book focuses on the adult children of dysfunctional families, its message enabled me to find relief and see a relationship with my career. Since then, we've seen emerge *The Survivor Personality* (Seibert 1996) and the new positive psychology, which offers greater insight and resources (Peterson 2006). But I still enjoy my earlier resources simply because the seven resiliency strengths the Wolins propose make sense and are practical for everyone. For a more updated perspective on resiliency, you may wish to investigate *The Resilience Factor: Seven Keys to Finding Your Inner Strength and Overcoming Life's Hurdles* (Reivich and Shatte 2003).

Your *resiliency* is your ability to quickly bounce back from misfortune. As a paradoxical trait, the opposing side is burnout or a lack of energy to resist or bounce back. This happens quite often in response to seeming setbacks—things like a series of unreturned phone calls, a lack of response to résumés, delayed interview decisions, and outright rejections. When these things happen often enough without a home run in between, they tend to deplete your resiliency reserves of any bounce-back energy. You can tell when this is happening when in response to frustrations you begin to experience a victim or blaming reaction. But remember: True endurance comes from within, so it does no good to find fault elsewhere.

When your resiliency or bounce-back energy gets to this low point, it's a matter of refilling your tank, recharging your batteries, and putting the spring back in your step. The classic solution for most people is to take a vacation, but that's not always feasible or advisable when you're unemployed or in job search mode. Short of flying to Tahiti, what can you do?

You may not realize it, but several times each day, you make use of one or more of your seven natural resiliency strengths. These strengths come forth automatically when you need them, and they're always available when you want to use them. You depend on them. They feel good to draw upon, and they enable you to cope when bad things happen. You also replenish your resiliency strengths daily, without expensive vacations, by doing things you don't realize are accomplishing the same result. The solution to developing your ability to more consciously draw on your power to endure is to move your resiliency strengths beyond automatic pilot—to intentionally leverage them to your benefit and keep them recharged. The sidebar highlights the seven keys to resiliency. Let's look at how to recognize and build each of these seven keys.

Seven Keys to Resiliency

1. insight
2. independence
3. relationships
4. initiative
5. creativity
6. humor
7. morality

Key 1   Insight

The first of your seven natural resiliency strengths is *insight—your ability to ask and answer the tough questions*. This is the ability to get to the heart of the matter and figure things out for what they are versus what you'd like them to be. It might also be referred to as second sight or a level of understanding that's not usually present—for example, how you sense things are going and what the outcome might be during an interview.

To maximize your insight, pay close attention to your hunches and intuition about employers and interviewers. This inner wisdom is your insight strength. It's free, it'll keep you out of trouble, and you'll get to learn how smart you really are. Recharge this strength by making time to admire when and how well it works—and be sure to smile when you do this.

Key 2   Independence

The second resiliency strength is *independence—distancing yourself from the source*. This involves the ability to get away from it all, to take a break or breather until you can regain strength. This strength enables you to instinctively know to move away from and not waste time with employers that seem incapable of giving you straight answers or making a decision.

To gain the most independence, don't turn your back on problems you have to deal with, but do walk away from situations and people you feel are sapping your strength, or when it doesn't seem that you're getting what you want. The break gives you strength, and you can go back when you're ready. Take frequent breaks—take a nice relaxing walk and go out to lunch where the employed people eat. You're probably working harder than they are. Recharge this strength by intentionally getting away from it all and thinking about anything but finding work.

Key 3   Fulfilling Relationships

The third resiliency strength is *fulfilling relationships with others*. These include developing and relying on a support network; the people you play with, trust for support, seek out for a diversion, and with whom you replenish yourself. They also include mentors, networking groups, and others in transition.

To build stronger relationships, schedule a weekly appointment with one or two people who know you, give you straight answers, provide new perspectives, and cheer you through and beyond any challenges. At least talk on the phone, and see them and do something recreational—even if it's only walking around the block and stopping for a cup of coffee. These trusted people appreciate you just as you are; you enjoy each other's company and they give you strength. Recharge this strength by getting out with them—and also by mentoring someone else through a job change. You'll be amazed at the strength this produces.

Key 4 Initiative

The fourth resiliency strength is *initiative—taking charge*. This includes your ability to organize a response and implement it, to deal with things and move forward—that rush of adrenaline and how you become transformed in response to any emergencies, as well as how you charge back with another wave of résumés and networking contacts.

To strengthen your initiative, make it a daily priority to move faster than employers. Waiting kills enthusiasm and hope because it allows disappointments to accumulate. Move to the next thing without relying on the outcome of the last. Taking action feels good because it gives you the sense of forward progress. It's a source of strength. Be cautious not to create tasks that simply occupy or waste time. Keep your activities purposeful and moving toward your goals. If you're down to one preferred employer, and you're confident waiting will not cause you a problem, then devote time to writing your first 100-day business plan exclusive to that opportunity. Recharge this strength by doing things around the house that you can complete relatively quickly and from which you'll derive a sense of accomplishment—even, when you're really down, if it's only taking out the trash.

Key 5   Creativity

The fifth resiliency strength is *creativity—your imagination and expression*. This includes your ability to express yourself through other channels, such as your inclination to write a book, paint a picture, engage in hobbies, start a creative project, or engage in some other diversion that takes your mind off things.

To enhance your creativity, restart or start a diversionary off-hours hobby that allows you the opportunity to express yourself and take your mind off other things—and where you can do exactly what you want, be in control, and really create something you can admire. Do something with your hands like keeping a journal, taking pictures, painting, gardening, playing an instrument, pursuing a sport, or even singing like a contented bird. This allows the release of any pressure caused by suppressed emotions—which are suppressed because you're limiting yourself to creating only positive impressions, acting diplomatically, and dealing continuously with things beyond your control. Get it out. Recharge this strength by developing your curiosity about new things, how they work, how they might be used or designed differently.

Key 6   Humor

The sixth resiliency strength is *humor—finding the comic in tragedy*. This is your ability to not take things too seriously, to laugh as relief, and to vent any emotions. It happens automatically without disrespect, when you laugh at what the employer does or doesn't do and your response to how others describe their situation.

To strengthen your sense of humor, laugh and smile intentionally and frequently during the day. Your body does this automatically, even in the midst of when bad things are happening, so you should be able to do it intentionally whenever you like. There should at least be one thing you can think about right now that will produce a smile, regardless of your circumstances. Try it. This is a source of strength, because it feels good and it's good for you. In fact, when you smile or laugh you can't simultaneously hold a disappointing or sad thought in mind. Try that, too. So there's no better way to initiate a phone call or project than with a big broad smile. Recharge this strength by simply smiling and laughing more frequently and by doing more fun things that make you smile and laugh.

Key 7 Morality

The seventh resiliency strength is *morality—acting on an informed conscience.* This includes your inclination and ability to seek out and do the right thing when appropriate, such as resisting the temptation to embellish your résumé or not taking credit for accomplishments during interviews. You do it because it feels good to do the right thing.

Thus, morality means doing the right thing despite the opportunities to do less. Doing so feels good and becomes a source of strength. The more you do the right thing, the more the wrong things start to look like the traps they are. Job change offers the potential for a new beginning. Shed yourself of any questionable ethics, norms, or customs you might have inherited from previous employers. Stick to your own principles regardless of the ethics of others. Recharge this strength by appreciatively recalling your roots and the values that have made you what you are today. From that point, you'll know what to do in any situation.

Using the Seven Keys

Resilient job seekers draw upon these seven keys with the belief that things will work out. They try to find value and benefits even in the worst situations, and they draw from their paradoxical nature to turn things around. They don't waste time dwelling on the "why" questions (Why me?) but ask the "what" questions (What can I do about it?), with the intent of learning from their struggle and applying the benefits to their efforts to find meaningful work. They think in an opportunity-oriented way by viewing setbacks as temporary. They develop a talent for serendipity and learn to rely on their intuition and hunches rather than be stymied like a deer in the headlights by potential consequences. They also make time to recharge their resiliency strengths. Let's look at an entry from my notebook that tells the story of how Josie learned to use her resiliency strengths.

RECRUITER'S NOTEBOOK

From Vacation to Resiliency and "Singing Like a Contented Bird"

When we first met, Josie had been laid off as part of a corporate downsizing. She was already into her 14th month of unemployment. She was afraid and uncertain, and she was looking for positions in sales, human resources, or logistics, and also considering whether to pursue a law degree. I suggested that she give herself a one-week mini-vacation and just have fun. One week later, she was back on the job looking for work, but there was a noticeable difference in her attitude. She was more upbeat and positive.

During her break, Josie had joined a church choir and was now spending considerable time rehearsing, and she was being recognized by her group as having a fantastic singing voice. She was beaming and quite proud of this. Each week she was becoming more inspired, optimistic, and confident, despite the fact that the job market had worsened rather than improved. With greater confidence and clarity than before, she began to focus her search into pharmaceutical sales. And within six weeks after our meeting, she had the pleasure of choosing between two offers and got the sales job she wanted.

What was Josie's secret? She suggested that you try "singing like a contented bird." She was able to inspire her own contentment through the initiative of independence, the creativity of singing, and her relationships with other choir members. As she got more deeply into her singing, the fog that had been clouding her thoughts finally cleared and she was able to decide what she wanted to do. She got more than she had hoped for by simply leveraging her resiliency strengths after first finding contentment in another area of her life—like a singing bird.

As with most natural things, recharging your resiliency strengths is accomplished in a very straightforward manner, by simply using them—particularly humor, relationships, creativity, initiative, and independence. (Figure 5-1 shows how these strengths are related to contentment.) Although it's not a bad idea, you don't have to take a vacation to recharge these strengths. Simply start by not taking anything that happens so seriously. Sure, it's important to find your next job, but isn't it supposed to find you? It will happen a lot more quickly when you develop a mindset that enables you to attract a job versus dwelling on the lack of it, which is exactly what a lack of resiliency does.

Recharging Your Resiliency

You can actually have fun recharging your overall resiliency by focusing daily on expecting good outcomes. Be curious about the things around you, ask more questions, and learn how to make yourself laugh so you don't have to rely on outside sources. Counterbalance a tendency toward seriousness with a spirit of playfulness. Get out with the people you enjoy and have some fun experimenting with your paradoxical qualities. That ought to drive them nuts and give you a few laughs. Make it your objective to learn how to find the positives in what happens and to gain strength from any unpleasant experiences. Ask yourself: "How can I deal with this in a manner I can benefit from?" Practice how to give and accept compliments, and to show empathy for all the difficult people you meet. And of course, forgive and forget with the intention of meaning it. You'll know you're recharging when you start

Figure 5-1. Resiliency Strengths to Maintain Contentment

THINK To maintain best emotions	FEEL To inspire best actions	ACT To fulfill best intentions
Insight	C	Increased
Relationships	O	effectiveness,
Creativity	N	resolve, and
Humor	T	endurance—
Independence	E	despite
Initiative	N	inevitable job
Morality	T	dissatisfactions
	M	
	E	
	N	
	T	

to hear yourself reflect on the benefits of whatever happens or you sense that things will work out fine as they always do. That's your resiliency at work.

Your resiliency strengths and your enjoyable efforts to recharge them have the effect of prolonging your life and enabling your success. They are based on medical research involving people who have endured the most unfortunate situations like holocaust, natural disasters, plane crashes, terrorism, and other crises (see Seibert 1996; Reivich and Shatte 2003; Sapolsky 2004; Wolin and Wolin 1993). They offer the potential to relieve the stress you experience in dealing with employment challenges, and they enable you to move beyond any adversity to get the job you want—and much faster than if you didn't do these things. So is resiliency important—even a little smile that grows and warms your heart as you think of your cat on the windowsill at home? Absolutely!

Summing Up: How Resiliency Helps Your Job Search and Career

Any lack of resiliency in your ability to deal with challenges that arise during the employment process creates the impression of weakness and immaturity. Increased resiliency, however, enhances your ability to thrive despite adversity and to create a more favorable impression with an employer. Resilient job seekers are presumed to be more productive, have greater potential, require less maintenance; and as a result, they get the better jobs faster. This is no different than natural selection, whereby the strongest survive. And so you don't forget your resiliency strengths, it's a good idea to develop the habit of intentionally using them. It feels good when you do, and they'll serve you well—and the fun of recharging them is a bonus.

Your resiliency strengths enable you to rebound faster and roll with the punches. People who use them naturally tend to avoid blaming others and to believe that there's a higher plan guiding them to something better. Said another way, they're *already* content in their ability to endure. Despite whatever happens, they're predisposed to believe they will win and that things will work out. They're mentally prepared, optimistic, and confident in their ability to endure, and their beliefs are realistic and self-empowered, and this enables them to leverage their contentment as a source of strength to pull them through their challenges.

Being already content in your ability to endure implies having some degree of insight or anticipation about potential challenges. Some people achieve this by paying close attention to their instincts and to the serendipity that occurs around them. They keep their eyes and ears open for any clues, consider their possibilities, and have a plan and a few contingencies in mind. They're ready to adapt whether or not something happens.

More than you realize, you rely on one or more of your seven resiliency strengths each hour of every day. Just think of the potential that you could muster if you used them intentionally whenever you wanted to. Your resiliency would be limited only by your lack of imagination. As a paradoxical quality, the opposite of lacking imagination would be imagination, and that is limitless—which explains why you can accomplish anything you put your mind to. What you do in between is all up to you. Let's look at a selection from my notebook that shows how resiliency can enable you to transform the worst circumstances into an opportunity to find contentment.

RECRUITER'S NOTEBOOK

From Exile to Resiliency and Contentment

Not long after our new marketing vice president started, it became clear that a wholesale reinvigoration of the division's creativity was on the horizon. The vice president hired a creativity consultant to conduct a day-long off-site meeting involving the entire division. The morning was spent listening to the hype of a professional motivation guru who had the confidence—if not temerity—to try to inspire the marketers who'd already transformed their industry with some of the most entertaining TV advertisements ever seen.

This motivation guru accomplished far more than he realized. What started with a bang at our meeting ended up as a crisis that shook the entire company and tested the resiliency of several individuals, including me. The guru's

From Exile to Resiliency and Contentment

challenge at the meeting was to "think outside the box," and the challenge for our division was to meet that challenge by breaking into teams and producing competing make-believe commercials for our brands. In the spirit of fun and unlimited thinking that the consultant had aggressively drilled into those of us at the meeting, each group produced a five-minute commercial that captured what it believed was its highest level of fun and free-thinking creativity.

The afternoon was spent critiquing our live stagings of these commercials and enjoying the camaraderie and laughter that came from seeing peers and managers act out their various roles. Unfortunately, not everyone reacted to one of the commercials in a positive manner—and this commercial that provoked a negative reaction happened to be the one made by the group that included the division's most senior members. Within a few hours, news of the offending event managed to reach the highest levels of the organization. The top managers wanted to be on record for doing the right thing, and that meant someone was in deep trouble.

The next day, the new divisional vice president volunteered to resign, but instead a reluctant decision was made to suspend without pay the highest-ranking members of the group that had filmed the offending make-believe commercial. What had been intended as a fun, creative team-building event had split the team—some were offended, some were dazed and couldn't believe their peers were reacting this way, others didn't care and just wanted it over, and some thought management had overreacted as usual.

But no matter what people thought, or whether what happened was deserved, one small group of people had to endure the humiliation, pain, anger, fear, uncertainty, and embarrassment that resulted from being dismissed from the building; suffering the duration, loneliness, and uncertainty of suspension; and reexperiencing many of these same emotions again upon their return, without knowing whether or not they would be welcomed.

I was a member of this exiled group but can only speak for myself. That morning, I reported to my boss everything that had happened the previous day. That same afternoon, as if we hadn't had that conversation, he read a prepared statement to me like a perfunctory bureaucrat who enjoyed the task. His boss sensed the same thing and interrupted to say, "We have no choice, just take the bullet and come back in two weeks and it will be like nothing ever happened."

Although I was to derive a lot of hope from those words over the next two weeks, I nearly vomited as I walked to my car. We had been instructed to talk with no one, including each other. We were on our own. I first tried to find the positives in what had occurred, but I couldn't think of any. I then took stock of all the good things I'd accomplished during my career and decided to dwell only on those things. That lasted about a half an hour. I then forgave anyone I was angry with, and I began to paint my living room. When I was done, I advanced to the family room, and then I did the dining room. I also painted the kitchen and I put in crown molding where there hadn't been any, and I painted that, too. Then I painted the ceilings and stenciled the stairways and doorways with patterns I discovered and thought were unique. I then called a designer and we upgraded all the window treatments.

When I was done, the house looked spectacular and the suspension was over. It was time to go back to my real job, and regardless of what had happened, I felt accomplished and refreshed, and I'd been too busy to think about anyone at work or what had happened. I returned almost glad for the opportunity to get a few things done around the house, and my boss remarked: "I honestly believe that if I had to go through a job-threatening problem like this, I don't think I could come out of it as well as you have." I honestly swear that as he finished speaking those fateful words, I had the insight or psychic certainty that what he believed and spoke aloud would one day become his reality. (To be continued in chapter 7.)

What's Next

This concludes part I of the book. Part II will show you how to recognize and experience career contentment, so you'll be able to find greener pastures in whatever positions you choose and whatever happens to you in them and not long for some imagined job satisfaction. We'll look at how your contentment will enable you to decide when to change jobs. And we'll explore how your career callings will continue throughout your lifetime and consider a model to help you decide the timing and direction of your next and future moves in keeping with your career flow and contentment.

Part II

Choosing to Be Contented with Your Life and Career

Contentment is something you may not often think about in relation to your career. Normally, what you think about is job satisfaction, and you're always measuring it in your head against your time and talents. For example, job satisfaction is derived partly from your income, benefits, working conditions, career path opportunities, quality of supervision, training and development, and other things that come with a price tag. Because you're working for these things, you can point to them. And if you lack just one of them, you can legitimately claim a lack of job satisfaction, even though you may have an abundance of other things.

Contentment can't be measured. It comes from within you and thus doesn't depend on other people or material things that are transient and unreliable. Instead, it connotes the willingness to accept and make the best of your current situation—whether or not some need has been met. You can choose in your mind and heart to be contented because you are using your gifts to fulfill your purpose and to make a contribution—whatever the reaction or feedback from others, who ultimately cannot control what's in your head and heart. You can recognize contentment as you use your ability to reason and find the acceptable middle ground in any situation, even during times of job dissatisfaction. And because your contentment comes from within, you can stay contented despite changing jobs, employers, careers, and even your purpose for working. It's the one constant as everything else about your career changes.

In part II, you'll learn how to

- evaluate, change, and control your beliefs
- leverage your beliefs to support your career intentions
- recognize your career contentment in any situation
- distinguish among the three career flow phases
- understand and use a three-phase career flow model
- anticipate and sense when it's time to progress or recycle among phases
- purposefully control your career flow
- leverage your career assets and sovereign power to manage your career flow.

Part II is made up of six chapters. Chapter 6—"Learn to Master and Change Your Beliefs and Thoughts"—discusses the importance of your beliefs and thoughts, and how you can learn to control them to help you pursue and enjoy the career you desire.

Chapter 7—"Forget Job Satisfaction and Look for Contentment"—explains contentment as a relaxed, centered state of mind that enhances your effectiveness and ability to endure. It shows how, although it's important to do what you love, it's just as important to look for ways to love what you're already doing. As you learn to do this, you'll find the contentment you need to guide your career.

Chapter 8—"Manage Your Career Contentment with the Career Flow Model"—presents a model of career flow that moves through three phases defined by time, your developing expertise, and your pursuit of contentment. It explains how to use this model to anticipate, plan, and decide on the timing and direction of your job and career changes.

Chapter 9—"Maximize Your Career Contentment by Controlling Your Career Flow"—explains how you can control your career flow so you'll work toward the career you want rather than one others want you to have. It delineates how you can use your assets and sovereign powers to recognize your career contentment.

Chapter 10—"Becoming Comfortable with Career Contentment"—reviews all the aspects of how to recognize career contentment—from maintaining the right mindset to attracting meaningful work to proactively managing your flow and maximizing your remaining career time.

Finally, in an epilogue—"Toward a New Paradigm of Career Contentment"—you'll be invited to join an effort to carry the lessons from this book out into the world of work.

6

Learn to Master and Change Your Beliefs and Thoughts

In this chapter, you'll learn

- how your beliefs and attitudes are at the heart of contentment
- how to think differently as you seek contentment
- how your thoughts can, in turn, create positive instead of negative emotions

---

Without a fundamental awareness of how you think, your life, career, and contentment will be limited to only what your brain decides is best for you, even though you may want to do something differently. To gain the career you want, and the contentment that goes along with it, you'll have to learn how to think differently—and thus become the master of your beliefs and thoughts, not let them automatically control you.

You may not realize it, but this is a very exciting time for scientists working to better understand how the human brain functions.

Advancements since 1997 in imaging technologies used to diagnose disease and to study anatomy and chemical processes are enabling physicians and researchers to observe the living brain in real time like never before. Magnetic resonance scanning equipment is revealing things that were previously unknown about the brain and also reconfirming that your beliefs and thoughts play a significant role in determining how you feel, what you do, and what you can achieve.

Several books about these recent discoveries have been published during the past 10 years (for example, Seligman 1998, 2002; Peterson and Seligman 2004; Peterson 2006), but learning about your brain and how you think probably isn't at the top of your list of things to do. That's because most of your thinking occurs naturally or you take it for granted—although that's the last thing you should want to allow. Why is this so?

Research on brain scanning confirms that, as you think, your brain functions in six areas simultaneously. But only one of those areas represents your conscious thoughts—that is, what you intend to think. The remaining five-sixths of those functioning areas represent your subconscious or unconscious (or "nonconscious," in the newer terminology) thoughts, or the thinking that occurs without your awareness and while you sleep. Though all six areas are influential to your effectiveness, your nonconscious thoughts have the potential to overpower your conscious intentions, which helps to explain why your willpower is sometimes insufficient to overcome bad thinking that yields no results, the wrong results, negative feelings and emotions, procrastination, or a lack of motivation (see Doug Bench's "Mind Your Brain: Greater Achievements by the Numbers Video Series," available at http://scienceforsuccess.com). You must be constantly attentive to how you think to prevent this imbalance from creating regrets—or the life, career, and contentment you don't want.

My understanding of contentment has benefited significantly from the works of Martin Seligman (1998, 2002), Christopher Peterson (2006; also see Peterson and Seligman 2004), Al Seibert (1996), and William James (1950, 1975, 2005), and also from the research of nonscientists or "brain hobbyists" like Doug Bench. Since retiring as an attorney,

Bench has been devoting himself to summarizing the results of new brain scanning research—and I believe he's doing an amazing job (see his website, http://scienceforsuccess.com). He began his career as a science teacher, so he has an empirical foundation, inspired by amazing curiosity.

For those of you, like me, who are interested in the brain and psychology but are neither a brain surgeon nor a psychologist, I suggest, to gain a deeper insight on these topics, starting online at the University of Pennsylvania's Positive Psychology Center (http://www.ppc.sas .upenn.edu/index.html). There you'll find a summary of current research, a listing of books and articles, and links to research databases on topics such as happiness, learned optimism, learned helplessness, resiliency, and well-being, to name just a few. My favorites are Chris Peterson's book *A Primer in Positive Psychology* (2006) and all the works of Martin Seligman (1998, 2002; also see Peterson and Seligman 2004).

Your Brain's Job

The purpose of your brain is to keep you alive and safe. It does this so well that your instincts to survive can overpower your will to do almost anything else, including routine tasks required to locate your next job or even to enjoy it. This is due to the conditioning you received while growing up. The moment you were born, your caregivers began to structure your reality by teaching you what to believe and how to think and act in certain ways. Your mind naturally created meanings from these experiences, and this enabled you to make sense of your evolving world. You listened, you learned to respond, and you were corrected by the "can-do" encouragement that empowered your beliefs and by the "can't-and-shouldn't-do" discouragement that suppressed your beliefs (James 1950).

Over time, your beliefs were formed and reinforced, and they were sometimes changed when you made new discoveries as you advanced to adulthood. The thoughts your beliefs produced eventually became automatic, and you lost the awareness of even having them (James 1950; Hassin, Uleman, and Bargh 2006). Now they just pop into your head, and you respond without always considering their validity or impact. Although this automatic thinking may help to save your life in an emergency situation, it can also prevent you from stopping to think freshly and without preconceptions about how you can discern and seize opportunities for networking, sending out résumés, taking a certain job, recognizing your contentment, or living your life to its fullest.

Before the end of each day, your brain processes tens of thousands of thoughts—and sadly, it's estimated that over 80 percent of them will be self-limiting or life suppressing, thanks to your conditioning that, in effect, establishes the boundaries of your comfort zone (James 1950; Hassin, Uleman, and Bargh 2006). These are automatically negative thoughts, like "I can't," "I shouldn't," "I won't." And the consequences of all these thoughts can be even sadder. Because your intentions to change jobs or careers sometimes stretch the boundaries of your comfort zone, you'll understandably feel alternately positive and negative, skeptical and optimistic, dependent and self-reliant, vulnerable to doubts and disappointment—but those automatic thoughts always orient you toward staying within your comfort zone.

Your five-sixths, or nonconscious, thoughts provide a sort of failsafe guarantee that if your one-sixth, or conscious, thoughts don't protect you, or if your conscious thoughts intend to move you beyond your comfort zone, your nonconscious thoughts will kick in to prevent you from doing things they think aren't good for you (see Bench's "Mind Your Brain" videos). For example, say you want to attend a career-networking event, but for whatever reason you've been conditioned to believe that these events are impersonal and uncomfortable. One-sixth of your brain thinks you should go to the event to see about locating a job, but the other five-sixths thinks this is contrary to your beliefs—and so you hear, "Don't go; it's a waste of time, you won't know anyone, you won't know what to do or say, and you'll probably look and feel uncomfortable."

Thus, to ensure its effectiveness in holding you back, your nonconscious mental "guardian" perceives these beliefs and thoughts as real and true. It has a built-in inability to distinguish between what's real or fake, true or false. So rather than take the risk, it simply perceives everything as real to keep you in your comfort zone. It doesn't care if you get a job or not; its only concern is to keep you safe and comfortable. Thus, you're constantly faced with the primal mental challenge of determining what to do or who to believe—your conscious intentions or your nonconscious guardian!

When it comes to your career, it's essential to realize that you're always facing this mental challenge, because finding meaningful work and being able to enjoy it are dependent upon your thoughts and the actions they inspire. Your beliefs allow you to filter and interpret what you see and to reason and decide what jobs are good or bad for you, what tasks are possible for you to achieve, how you should feel and react to your circumstances and other people, and whether or not you can recognize your contentment. In turn, how you react influences how others respond to you.

Therefore, in effect—and this is crucial—your beliefs and thoughts define your circumstances, determine how you respond to them, and influence how others respond to you, even though it may seem to you that you're living in response to your circumstances and other people. So instead of really responding to the outside world, your mental guardian is controlling your responses to all your career possibilities, thinking those automatic thoughts that keep you safely in your comfort zone—not exactly what you want as a basis for making the best choices to fulfill your greatest potential.

Now let's get back to how your brain does its job. Your ability to reason and identify the satisfactory middle ground in any employment situation is situated in the left portion of your brain. That you have the power to reason in this manner makes your circumstances unimportant, random, or meaningless until you assign them a meaning and react. Think of it like this. The words you're reading right now are merely a conglomeration of symbols. Your conditioning enables you to interpret them as letters and to combine them to form words, and neither the letters nor words make any sense until you assign them a meaning and react. For example, your conditioning might cause you to interpret the letters A and O as simply vowels and C and F as consonants. But to others, A means excellent, C means average, F means failing, and O is for Oprah's magazine. When you put them all together, they form the word FOCA—meaning nothing to some but to others a beautiful resort city in the Aegean region of Turkey. Or if you travel to Asia or happen to wander inside a shop where artifacts are sold, you might be shocked to see prominently displayed the swastika symbol that Western people associate with Nazism. But in Hinduism, this is a holy symbol used during festivals and special ceremonies like weddings. It's not the symbol or word that causes a shock, but the meaning you assign to it that makes it shocking. You create the reality.

An example closer to home involves the effects caused by the meanings you assign to your circumstances. The term "biological stress" was invented in 1934 by Hans Selye, who once commented that he regretted using the word "stress" because "strain" better describes the effect caused by the actual force, circumstance, or stressor (Selye 1977). He made the point that what most affects your health is not the stress, but your reaction to it—the strain. Even with the knowledge gained from reports regarding the harmful effects of stress, you still empower your circumstances with meanings that "stress you out." The meanings you assign and how you respond are far more critical to your health than the stressor could ever hope to be. But it's easier to place blame on the stressor than take responsibility for the effect of your beliefs.

How many people have you ever heard make a comment something like "My job sucks because of how I react to the horrible meanings I've assigned to the people I work with"? Probably none! But you must have heard something like this: "If they would've just done this I might've reacted differently and things would be a whole lot better." Notice the similarity? You can acknowledge responsibility for your reaction, but not to having caused it by the meaning you assigned. Your co-workers created the circumstance, but you assigned a meaning that was bad and created the reaction, and that's a function of how you think. It's always easier to blame someone else, and here you thought you'd grew out of that bad habit. Here's a story from my Recruiter's Notebook about how you can control the meanings you give events much more than you might imagine.

RECRUITER'S NOTEBOOK

Enduring Horror by Minimizing Meaning

We knew our co-worker was a Vietnam veteran, but he really didn't talk much about it. In fact, not until Hollywood made the movie *Hamburger Hill* did we realize that he was a true war hero whose commentary would be used in making the movie. A movie crew came to our offices to interview him, and in response to his sudden notoriety among us, he made the comment "No big thing." If you've seen the movie, you know this was the typical response by soldiers to the sudden and ongoing deaths of their comrades during that conflict. To endure their circumstances, they chose to empower themselves by assigning a meaning that minimized or helped to make what was happening more tolerable. They chose to make a horrifying experience "no big thing." They found contentment through self-empowerment, and it helped give them the ability to endure a life-threatening situation and on more than one occasion. After what we learned about our co-worker, we assigned him a new meaning: "real big thing."

Why What You Believe Matters

As an adult, you certainly must acknowledge your circumstances for what they are, but you should also realize your contributions to them. Give them the attention they deserve, but don't empower them with beliefs that may dominate you by impairing your bodily functions. Again, this leads us back to the brain's work: as thoughts occur, your brain releases a chemical that fuels an electrical transmission or neuron and you respond. Angry thoughts fuel increased muscle tension and heart rate, and may even cause dizziness. Happy and contented thoughts fuel increased muscle relaxation, slower heart rates, and breathing. Telling a lie triggers a strain or stress response that increases muscle tension, heart rate, blood pressure, and sweating (Seligman 2002). You can realize your contribution to the situation, but you can also be aware of the power you possess to alter your thoughts and to help shape your reality—and even your health.

Now let's look at the big picture of how your brain's work affects your emotions and actions. The father of American psychology, William James (1842–1910), points out that what you believe influences your thoughts, and what you think inspires the emotions that prompt you to take action (James 1950; also see Bandura 1997). Your results reinforce your original beliefs, and life goes on in keeping with them. This process is illustrated by figures 6-1, 6-2, and 6-3.

As you study these three figures, you can see that positive or empowering thoughts inspire confident feelings and resolved actions, but negative or conflicting thoughts inspire doubtful feelings and halfhearted actions. In both situations, the results speak for themselves and reinforce the original beliefs. This think–feel–act sequencing is critical, because your beliefs and thoughts provide direction and purpose; otherwise, if you feel before thinking, you risk being criticized for reacting emotionally. Similarly, if you take action without thinking, you risk being criticized for being impulsive or impetuous. As figure 6-3 shows, mixing up the sequencing of thinking, feeling, and acting leads to no results, mixed results, untimely results, or the wrong results.

What are the consequences of this? Well, life goes on in keeping with your thoughts until you decide to change them. But when you do decide to change your thoughts, you can also change your life, career, and potential

Figure 6-1. All We Do and Achieve Begins with Our Beliefs

Can Do	Able to	Confident	Resolved
1. Beliefs	**2. Thoughts**	**3. Feelings**	**4. Actions**
Don't, Can't, Shouldn't	Unable to, Don't Try	Fear, Anxiety, Discomfort	Nothing Halfhearted

Will Do		
6. Expectations		**5. Results**
Can't/Won't Happen		Always Speak For Themselves

Beliefs Are Conditioned from Birth, and We Rely On This
Mix of Good and Bad to Make All Our Decisions

Figure 6-2. Problems Occur When Our Thinking Gets Out of Alignment

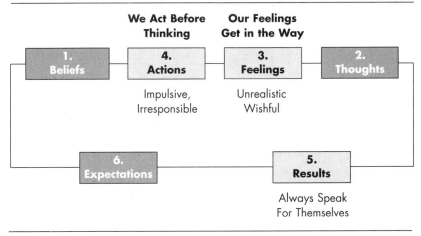

Figure 6-3. Problems Compound and Ruts Develop When We Fail to Control How We Think

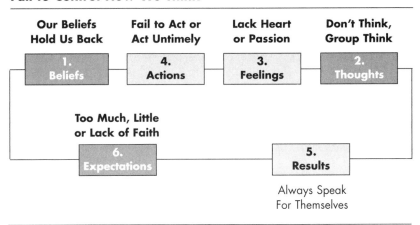

for finding contentment. The point here is that what you believe and think can be so powerful that it has the effect of creating your reality. You can't work, navigate your career, or even live your life by truly responding to possibilities because they're all controlled by your beliefs about them. This occurs whether you want it to or not, because unless you've assigned something a meaning, you won't know how to react to it. Once again, a negative lesson can illustrate this—here's another selection from my notebook about the effects of assigning meanings.

RECRUITER'S NOTEBOOK

Unlearning Contentment

Leslie had already started her career and was learning how to adjust to her new circumstances. She was a first-generation Chinese American who had come to the United States to complete a graduate degree in engineering, and her U.S. work experience had been limited to student project teams. Her noncitizen work permit allowed her to begin her career within the United States, but she was completely unfamiliar with the norms associated with office work and unaware of how people attempted to deal with them.

At the start of her new job, Leslie was her authentic self—content with her accomplishments, happy for the opportunity, and intent on succeeding despite the challenges that immigrants normally endure. Her family back home in China was as much delighted with her accomplishments as she was. She genuinely looked forward to the start of every work day.

Life was good until a few months later, when Leslie began to notice that she had become just as unhappy as the people she worked with. It began when she recognized that the people she knew as happy were sometimes unexpectedly unhappy, and for no apparent reason. A pattern emerged: They were typically unhappy on Mondays. She began to probe this but was told nothing and so life went on, even though she seemed happier than others.

When the situation persisted week after week, Leslie probed again and was finally given an explanation by her co-workers: People normally felt down on Mondays after returning to work from the weekend, a phenomenon referred to as "blue Mondays." At first she thought this was ridiculous and was amazed that her co-workers didn't appreciate that they had it so good. She persisted in being her happy self until, one Sunday evening, the thought occurred to her that she wasn't looking forward to going to work the following day.

The same thing happened the next Sunday and the next—even though Leslie was genuinely excited about working on several projects. She believed that if she was going to live and work in the United States, she had to learn to adapt just like everyone else. Therefore, it was her "right" to be just as unhappy as everyone else. She now dreaded Mondays just as much as anyone else!

Avoiding the Career Rut

"Getting into a rut" is the expression commonly used to describe what happens when you can't or don't want to change your thinking. You do the same old things and get the same old results. Scientists refer to this as establishing a neural or thought pattern due to thinking repetitively, and you then resist new ways of thinking so you can maintain those patterns. This is why the older you get, the harder it becomes to change your mind about certain things. Your neural patterns are "set in their ways," and you resist thinking differently. However, research also indicates that you can climb out of these ruts and improve your thinking—provided, of course, that you believe in this unseen possibility (Amen 1999). Stated another way, what you believe determines your potential, and what you think determines the outcome. Let's consider how one person took advantage of believing in himself in this page from my notebook.

RECRUITER'S NOTEBOOK

The Payoff from Persistently Believing in Yourself

Dana came from Detroit and was truly gifted in his abilities to establish a rapport and relationships with many kinds of people. We referred to him as a "mover/shaker" because he had the knack for getting into the heart of the action, isolating the decision makers, and getting things done on short order. He was hired into our department as a recruiter, and within a year he was already bored. Despite our hiring volume, he was not sufficiently challenged, and his supervisors perceived him as a potential misfit. They believed he was impatient because they had paid their dues and felt that he should pay his dues as well. But Dana felt differently.

At the time, Dana had an eight-year career already established in human resources and recruiting, and he believed he was as good as the people he reported to. As his time in the job slowly passed by, he grew more impatient each day. As a relief from dealing with his issues, he began to spend more time with the people outside our division, and eventually he was encouraged by his new friends to make the transition to a marketing role. He contemplated this; then one day he realized that he had the basic skills to succeed at whatever he attempted. He believed he was as good as anyone he had met, he realized that his transition would involve picking up a few new skills, and he believed he was up to the challenge.

By this point, Dana's frustrations had become so great that he felt his only options were to make the transition or leave the company. He made an appointment to pitch his proposal to transfer, and although his managers were willing to accommodate his proposal, marketing had already requested his immediate transfer. Dana was on his way. Not only did he excel in marketing, he later again moved to sales and eventually to leading one of our largest geographic regions as director. Dana believed in himself when others didn't.

Changing Your Patterns of Believing and Thinking

If you can suspend your set-in-ways skepticism and really begin to believe something different is possible, you really do have the ability to create as many new neural patterns as you like (Dispenza 2007). But you still have to contend with the old or existing ones by reconditioning, updating, modifying, or releasing the self-limiting and negative beliefs that cause you problems, hold you back, or suppress you. If you can do these challenging things, you can create a better reality, improve upon your results and contentment, and even change how people respond to you. Your reality, relationships, and potential related to career and contentment depend on your beliefs and whether they empower you to think and act in accordance with your intentions. Even though others may control whether you get a job or a promotion, you can control your patterns of beliefs and thoughts—and change them so you can change your life, all the while resting on a mental and emotional cushion of contentment, not the same old doubts, anxieties, and lassitude.

So now the big question: How do you undo years of conditioning and reinforcement to change your beliefs, empower them, stop the resistance, and create new kinds of thinking?

Self-help audios and books such as the one you're reading right now can help to inspire changes in your thinking, but the results can rarely be sustained. That's because the changes you make using these materials occur at your one-sixth conscious level of thinking and depend on your willpower to sustain them. However, your willpower may not work if your five-sixths nonconscious thoughts have remained unchanged and—more important—if your nonconscious senses you're holding onto a belief that contradicts what you're consciously intending to do. In other words, although you might want to do something, your nonconscious says "No way, José."

This disconnect between your conscious and nonconscious thinking explains why you're unable to keep your New Year's resolutions or to make changes you know you should. For example, say you want to send out an extra 20 networking emails and résumés each week and you know that's a good thing. You start to identify the people you want to contact, but you settle for sending out only five extra emails and five extra résumés. The next week, you send out only three extra emails, and so on. You feel guilty for not hitting your goal, and you start thinking that the problem is due to a lack of networking contacts or leads. But no matter what you do, you don't seem to get the effect you want. The unknown cause of this barrier is more than likely a subconscious belief that is contradicting your intentions; your good old mental guardian is thinking for you: "Networking doesn't work, and besides, if I send out those extra emails and résumés, I'll have to spend time following up on all of them and end up having to explain my situation to strangers who really aren't willing to help me."

Negative nonconscious thoughts and beliefs such as these that contradict your conscious intentions produce negative emotions that attract negative results. Like attracts like, so you don't follow through in doing the things you intend. As I explained above, it's the job of your mental guardian—your five-sixths nonconscious thinking—to keep you in alignment with your conditioned beliefs and to prevent you from doing things that take you out of your comfort zone. This puts severe limitations on even the strongest willpower. Although hypnotherapy deals directly with the nonconscious to affect changes— like how to quit smoking and help resolve fears and phobias—the results are not always consistent because your earlier conditioning is so ingrained and, thus, not easily undone. Your nonconscious is a design feature that works very efficiently for self-preservation—but not necessarily self-actualization!

Changing Your Beliefs: A Gradual Process of Using Seven Levers

The trick to changing and improving your thinking is: There is no quick fix. The psychologist and writer Howard Gardner suggests that changing your beliefs doesn't always occur as the result of a sudden epiphany or "aha" moment but as a gradual process that can be actively influenced. You recondition your thinking by creating new habits that your nonconscious will cautiously accept in time as the redefined boundaries of a new and improved comfort zone. But you have to want to change to begin with, and that includes changing your underlying beliefs and thoughts. Gardner (2004) identifies seven levers that—when the first six are aligned and the seventh is minimized—can bring about significant changes in your perspective and ultimately your behavior. These levers include

- reason
- research
- resonance
- representation
- resources and rewards
- real-world events
- resistances.

Lever 1: Reason—the influence of a logical argument or explanation. You can be persuaded to think differently by someone who makes sense to you. Try seeking out the credible people who hold the beliefs that you admire and aspire to hold—especially if they care enough for you not to just tell you what you want to hear but are even willing to play devil's advocate and throw a wet blanket on your projections and unfulfilled resolutions!

Lever 2: Research—the influence of data that convinces you otherwise. You can be persuaded to think differently by what you learn. Try seeking out data that do not confirm what you currently believe and confirm what you aspire to believe. For instance, spend some time browsing in a news store that carries a wide variety of magazines and journals, and look for ones that pique your interest and offer practical analyses and information on a subject you're passionate about but frightened to actually pursue—such as the excellent magazines for professional writers, if you've always imagined yourself writing the great American novel or travel stories now that you've survived to middle age mellowness and can recollect your wild youthful experiences in tranquillity.

Lever 3: Resonance—the influence of your thoughts and feelings being in alignment. In other words, it not only makes sense to change but also feels right. Try to simultaneously open both your mind and heart to new thoughts and to what you aspire to believe. One idea: To get a taste of this, give yourself a day off when you can afford to, and just wander on foot around some favorite place, allowing your mind to also wander. Be open to what's in front of you, and I almost guarantee the serendipity will point you toward a new awareness of how some half-forgotten dream all of a sudden begins to seem like it might be practical, and you even begin to envision particular steps to fulfilling it. Some books on creativity call this making a date with yourself, as if you're actually meeting afresh that childlike intuitive creative person you used to be—who is still inside you somewhere, waiting patiently behind the nonconscious guardian.

Lever 4: Representation—the influence of multiple media that present the same message. You hear about it on the radio, and see it in words, pictures, and graphs on TV and on the Internet. Don't allow yourself to stop at just one source. Keep working at it. The more you immerse yourself in these interesting messages, the more you'll stimulate your heart's desire—and realize, say, that more people no smarter than you are actually pursuing the kind of job you've always imagined having, and so why can't you, too?

Lever 5: Resources and Rewards—the influence of rewarding or reinforcing a specific belief that benefits you and advances the fulfillment of your intentions. Material rewards are likely to change behavior, but not necessarily your beliefs. Focus on recognizing the beliefs that contribute to your genuine contentment. For instance, if you always get depressed imagining redoing your résumé to show that you really could do that challenging job that your mentor clued you in on, reward yourself with a DVD of that movie you've really wanted to see—once you've done and sent the résumé.

Lever 6: Real-World Events—the influence of events that have the potential to affect the beliefs of multiple observers simultaneously. Be mindful of the news and events that pertain to the beliefs you aspire to change, and acknowledge that they make sense to you—and could also be persuasive for others. If you're pursuing a project that might seem quixotic to your superiors, find out about events that validate its ultimate practicality—like that fact, if you're in retail, that despite the prevalence of large chains, shoppers are desperately longing for unique stores and that, through imaginative and attentive market differentiation, your retail firm can capitalize on some of its mothballed brands to create those unique stores once again, while still benefiting from the chain's economies of scale.

Lever 7: Resistance—the influence of your unwillingness to change how you think or to think differently. This, as noted above, is the one level that you want to minimize and not maximize. If you're attempting to change your beliefs by using the first six levers, do so while at the same time you're lessening the effect of your resistance to new ideas, beliefs, and thoughts. But how? One way would be through negative reinforcement—say, using the reward lever to give yourself a treat once you do make a change that you've been resisting, like making all those cold calls to potential new clients for the service your firm offers.

Your Efficacy Beliefs and Their Four Underlying Factors

Your beliefs in your ability to get the results you want by exercising control over your thoughts, feelings, and actions are called your *efficacy beliefs*. According to the psychologist Albert Bandura (1997), your efficacy beliefs are formed based on four factors related to what you think you can achieve: experience, modeling, social persuasions, and physiology.

Factor 1: Experience. You're more likely to take action and do what's required if you believe you'll succeed, or if you've succeeded before and think you can do it again. For instance, try keeping your résumé updated as a reminder of your accomplishments and what you believe you can do in the future.

Factor 2: Modeling. You observe that others can do something and think that you can do it, too. Try reading inspiring biographies, watching Oprah, and getting out and taking notice of other people and what they're doing to inspire your confidence to think differently. And if one of these inspiring people is making a personal appearance nearby, by all means make the effort to attend—there's nothing like being in the presence of a charismatic person to imprint his or her confidence and spur you to imitate that person's efforts!

Factor 3: Social Persuasion. You feel encouraged to do it. Associate with the people who help to encourage you or otherwise help you to recondition your self-limiting beliefs. Again, this personal contact is irreplaceable—don't just talk on the phone; make an appointment to spend some time with your mentor and capture his or her, and your, full attention to talk through your career issues with him or her, together come up with some really different ideas to pursue, and hear your mentor say to your face "You can do it!"

Factor 4: Physiology. You feel resilient and emotionally strong enough and capable of doing it. As you are working on changing your beliefs, don't forget to also take care of yourself physically and emotionally, including paying attention to the meanings you assign to your circumstances. For example, when you encounter rejection in pursuing the kind of more challenging job you are newly convinced you can do, take a little break but don't start telling yourself "I told you so." Instead, practice strengthening your resiliency—see the pointers in chapter 5—and then get back on the horse—pursue another similar job.

If your efficacy beliefs are high—that is, up to the "can-do" levels— you're likely to think things through, find the most efficient course of action, and then go ahead and just do what's required. You simply believe it will happen. And if for some reason it doesn't work out, you'll find some balanced explanation, won't beat yourself up or wallow in rejection, and move on to the next solution that does work. Higher efficacy beliefs yield greater resiliency and emotional strength.

But if your efficacy beliefs are low—down at the "can't or shouldn't do" levels—you're likely to view what's required as being more difficult than it actually is. You'll procrastinate, feel the gnawing discontent of performing unsuccessfully outside your comfort zone, function erratically, and have unpredictable results. If for some reason what you're trying to do doesn't work out, you'll attribute the results to your inabilities, thus reinforcing the "can't or shouldn't do" low beliefs, and life will go on inside the rut created by your same old neural patterns.

Five Tips for Learning to Think Differently

Your reality, relationships, and potential related to career and contentment depend on your beliefs and on whether these beliefs and the thoughts they engender empower you to act in keeping with your intentions. However, your career and contentment also depend on having a high level of belief in your ability to get what you want by altering how you feel, think, and act.

According to the psychologist and writer Robert Anthony, another solution to changing how you think is to act in the moment, before you lose the thought or forget you had the emotion. He refers to this as "flip switching" (Anthony 2005). As a negative thought or emotion occurs, and intends to hold you back, you "flip a switch" by looking for ways to feel better in any one moment, no matter what's happening around you. He suggests holding the new thought for 17 seconds so that it can have a chance to positively influence your emotions. For example:

- "Don't even think about it or try it."/flip switch/"Do it."
- "This situation is hopeless."/flip switch/"This is doable."
- "I'm worthless and can't do anything right."/flip switch/ "I can."
- "That's been tried before and I know it won't work."/flip switch/"Give it a go."
- "Someone else will get that job before me."/flip switch/ "That's reserved for me."

- "They won't like me."/flip switch/"This will go well."
- "Nothing will ever go well for me."/flip switch/"Things will work out fine."
- "Networking doesn't work."/flip switch/"This is going to work."

Without flip switching or something like it, one automatic thought fuels another, and before you realize it, you're immobilized. According to Anthony, the more you practice and develop flip switching, the easier it gets. It becomes automatic. The net result is greater control over your thoughts and emotions so that you can achieve the results you want. So get to work on changing each thought one at a time as it occurs. To help you do this, here are five tips.

TIP 1 Pay Attention to Your Automatic Thoughts and Feelings

The first tip is to start paying attention to your automatic thoughts and the feelings they inspire. It's impossible to catch all the thousands of thoughts that pass through your mind each day, so at first focus on the automatic ones that seem to pop into your head as if they had a life of their own. They may be experienced as a very few words or as a brief image or memory. They pass through your mind with lightning speed, and you may not even be aware they're racing by, but they usually predict the worst and incorporate a "can't do" or "shouldn't do" message. And regardless of how irrational they might seem, you almost always want to believe them, and as a result, they tend to hold you back, limit, or suppress you.

TIP 2 Focus on Moments When You Suddenly Feel Negative

The second tip is to focus on moments when you suddenly feel blue, sad, guilty, or uncertain. These and other negative feelings are the result of not complying with your automatic thoughts. They're penalties imposed by your five-sixths nonconscious mental guardian for attempting something that may cause you to move beyond your comfort zone. For example, a job search involves telephoning leads, attending networking events, and asking others for help. You know you have to do these things, but when you begin to prepare to do them, you suddenly feel dread, fear, or sadness. These are warnings issued by your nonconscious mind to not act upon your intentions or risk destruction by the hard, cold world—it will be much better to huddle under the covers.

TIP 3   When You Have Negative Feelings, Pinpoint the Culprit Thought

The third tip: At the moment you have negative feelings, pinpoint the culprit thought that caused them. The culprit thought that creates a negative feeling will be something like

- This won't work.
- They won't like me.
- I'll be wasting their time.
- This will make me look stupid.
- I hate doing this.
- I'm going to screw this up.
- They don't want to talk to me.

Challenge these defeatist thoughts rather than accepting them as viable or true. Ask yourself: "Is this real or just my nonconscious believing it's real with the intent of holding me back? How does this thought help me to get or keep a job or to recognize my contentment?" Try to imagine how you would react if these culprit thoughts had been spoken to you by a stranger. You'd probably ignore them. Do the same for yourself—but be prepared, because your nonconscious guardian is ready and waiting for you to do this. What you'll hear is: "No, that's not the thought, and besides, it doesn't matter because the threat is real, not just a feeling—you'll be sorry."

These culprit thoughts may seem overpoweringly strong. But remember, your nonconscious is too strong for your willpower to control it every time, so just *don't listen* to these thoughts that it is issuing. Your nonconscious doesn't care about your new job or contentment. All it cares about is keeping you safe and comfortable. But you have to do what you have to do to live your life and not just slink back to your old negative mental and emotional habits, in spite of how comforting they are. Yet if your thoughts still seem suspect or suppressing, ask yourself these questions:

- What is my belief underlying this thought?
- What is the direct opposite of this thought? Have I considered this?
- How else can I look at this situation, and does this prompt any different thoughts?
- How does maintaining or eliminating this thought help or enable me?
- What has to happen for me to change this thought to a better one?

TIP 4   Think Again to Produce a More Positive Emotion

The fourth tip is to think again, or change the thought, to produce a more positive emotion. To do this, substitute or "flip switch" the culprit thought with something more in keeping with your intentions:

- This is going to work.
- I can do this.
- I can make this work.
- It's worked before so it will work again.
- This can't stop me.
- I think the best thing to do is this.

Again, you have to decide whether you're going to control your thoughts or let them control you. Don't compromise your dreams by doing and accepting less. Decide what you're willing to do, what you're willing to give up to get it, and then commit yourself to doing it. Thank your nonconscious guardian for intending to help you, but let it take a vacation.

TIP 5   Fully Leverage the New Positive Emotion to Do What You Want

The fifth and final tip is to fully leverage the new positive emotion to do what you want. Take the new emotion that you've helped to create with the new thought (joy, excitement, enthusiasm, confidence, and the like) and spend no less than 17 seconds savoring the pleasant feeling. Imagine this will be the same positive feeling you'll have when you've done what you need to do. Seek to feel the excitement of change. Leverage the power created by the new feeling. Just do it, be glad you did, and start enjoying the results now.

Summing Up and Techniques to Try

As you really begin to change your thinking patterns, you'll realize that when you start to think with fewer self-limitations, you're likely to discover some of the faulty underlying feelings and beliefs that were causing your problems or holding you back to begin with. For example, if you once believed that networking doesn't work, and your results suggest otherwise, you'll probably notice that belief and want to change it. This is something your willpower could have never hoped to accomplish on its own. But now that you're starting to see the evidence, it will become easier and easier to maintain the new belief if you keep doing the same positive things and getting the same positive results—what psychologists call positive reinforcement. Do it right the first time and—eventually—for good, by changing your thinking one thought at a time, as each thought enters your mind.

Making Affirmations to Help Change Your Attitudes

If you're having difficulties attempting to change your thoughts, you may want to introduce some new thoughts by incorporating the use of affirmations. Affirmations have been shown by psychologists and others to be effective in helping you to see your life in a holistically new way (Peterson 2006; Anthony 2005). The sidebar gives several sample affirmations; rewrite them to your specific needs, or write your own. Speak them aloud with conviction several times during the course of your day, when you're struggling with a particular thought, before you fall asleep each night, and just before you get out of bed.

Attitude-Changing Affirmations

- I am feeling stronger and better every day. I know that what I'm looking for is already looking for me. We're sewn together with the thread pulling tight. I believe this, and so it is.
- I am blessed with other people who are willing to help me, even without my knowing this is happening. I see all their smiling faces. I believe this and so it is.
- I am receptive to unexpected blessings, and I'm grateful and excited because this happens each and every day. I believe this and so it is.
- I am worry free, and any challenges I'll encounter will only help to improve my readiness. I believe this and so it is.
- I am full of joy and vitality. I'm confident and capable of doing whatever is required, and I do so gleefully and with unbridled enthusiasm. I believe this and so it is.
- I am in charge of my own life and my own thoughts. I'm fully able to change my thinking whenever I like. I believe this and so it is.
- I am content, and I want to smile right now. As I do, I feel the energy swelling inside me, filling my resiliency reserves so that I can use this happy energy anytime I like. I believe this and so it is.
- As I hold my arms out wide, I can slowly enclose them around the energy being radiated somewhere out there by my new job. Like a powerful magnet, we're pulling close together, faster and stronger each time. I see and feel this happening. I believe this and so it is.
- I am proud of and thankful for all my talents. They've served me well, and great things are happening to me right now. I believe this and so it is.
- I am completely relaxed and at peace with all my past experiences. I now feel propelled forward as if shot from a cannon toward my target, and I'm so excited, because where I'll land will be where I'm supposed to be. I know this will be great. I believe this and so it is.

Envision Being and Having—Not Wanting or Needing

If you decide to write your own affirmations, keep in mind the advice from chapter 1 regarding beliefs. The two sets of weakest words to avoid are "I want" and "I need." Instead, use the two strongest two words: "I am."

Your dreams, visions, and aspirations are thoughts with potential. You're told that to make them real, "You have to want it." Unfortunately, wanting and wishing inspire emotions associated with needing, lacking, and not having—or, in other words, dreaming with a deficit mindset. The better approach is to dream of being and having, not wanting, because having inspires the more positive emotions of joy, optimism, and excitement. Leverage your desires rather than your needs, and believe.

Children use their imaginations to do this all the time. But as you grow older, your desires fade and diminish to idle wishes or you doubt the power of your jaded imagination. Without the desire to have, all you get is what you're given or settle for, and that's not good. Instead, renew and use your imagination to dream of having, and detach yourself from wanting or needing. Then use the levers, tips, and guidelines given above to begin to create the new mental and emotional you—a person who practices contentment, who pursues efficacious ways of thinking and feeling, and who has given your old mental guardian a very long vacation. Here's an illuminating notebook story from my own childhood on making your dreams come true.

 RECRUITER'S NOTEBOOK

Five Steps to Making Your Dreams Come True: From the Sears Catalogue to Your Career

Growing up in rural America during the early 1960s, we had no malls and megastores were too far away. Computers, email, text messaging, and faxes had not yet been invented. To reach a wide customer base, major retailers would distribute mail order catalogues to homes. These colorful publications were usually two inches thick and were packed with product descriptions and photos of clothing, household goods, tools, and toys. They were our principal resource for easy shopping. You could see the current styles and new product innovations, make your selections, and then send your order form along with a check for payment—or "Green Stamps," depending on the catalogue. People held onto their catalogues for long periods of time, and neighbors even borrowed them back and forth. You always wanted or needed something, and catalogues allowed you to dream of having.

Each November, our grandparents allowed us to choose one item for less than $15 from the catalogues supplied by either Sears Roebuck, J.C. Penney, or Montgomery Ward, and if you were good that year you might get what you asked for on Christmas. Each child was required to identify the product, the catalogue it came from, and the page and product ordering number. In our little minds, this was big business, and wishing had nothing to do with it. Once you supplied the correct ordering information, it was the same as owning the item, and you could begin to imagine having it. Then all you had to do was wait and to demonstrate your worthiness with good behavior and by expressing your gratitude as if your desire had already been fulfilled.

However, the wait seemed like an eternity, and if you weren't careful, your thoughts would dwell on the frightful possibility of order errors and out-of-stock inventories. By the time you could make this discovery, it might be too late to order anything else, and the replacement might be out of stock because it was closer to Christmas and a zillion kids had probably ordered the same toy. There was no end to these worrisome thoughts, so the best way to keep yourself from wishing or wanting was to strengthen your desire of having by revisiting the catalogue photo, but you had to wait your turn because other kids and even adults were in line to do the same. Contemplating the picture made it easier to imagine having the item and holding it in your hands, and how you would care for it. As you did this, thoughts of any problems seemed to melt away, and your desire became so strong that you couldn't imagine not having it. Eventually the time would pass, and your dream would come true.

It was the duty of the oldest children to mentor us younger ones on how to make our dreams come true. They gave us simple instructions that were easy to remember and were promised to work if we followed them precisely:

1. *Know what you want.* Do your research, and be specific in what you ask for or no one will know what you want.
2. *Do what's required.* Do what you're asked and supply what's required, or you might get the wrong thing or they'll just give you clothes.
3. *Be real but think positive.* Problems are possible and worrying won't fix them, and neither will being a pest by asking "Where is it" or "When will I get it?"
4. *Don't stop believing.* If you think you made a mistake, or you forgot what you ordered, don't ask because it's too late. Go back to the picture, stay excited, and say a prayer, but don't tear out the pages.
5. *Be grateful and act like you deserve it.* Behave, be excited, and be grateful as if you've already received it. That way they won't change their mind.

Five Steps to Making Your Dreams Come True: From the Sears Catalogue to Your Career (continued)

The grandchildren are now grandparents, and those heavy catalogues no longer exist because the expense became too great and people didn't want to pay for something they had once received for free. Now you go online to see the picture, and you can order using a credit card or just go to the mall. If you want, eBay will even sell you one of the original free catalogues. Of course the products have changed and you'll have a hard time ordering, but they're still good for dreaming.

After all these years, the only thing that has remained unchanged is our ability to dream, and the five steps for making your dreams come true. And now I promise you, whatever your dreams may be, these steps will work for you as you pursue your career dreams if you follow them precisely, and leverage the desire of having by thinking like a kid before Christmas.

What's Next

As this chapter has pointed out, your circumstances or other people do not create your reality. Instead, what you believe and how you think about things shape your reality by influencing how you respond and how others respond to you. Your career, life, health, and relationships all depend on what you believe, how you think, and your ability to change your negative, limited thinking and actions—and so too does your potential to recognize your contentment in any employment situation. The next chapter shows in detail how to accomplish this.

Forget Job Satisfaction and Look for Contentment

In this chapter, you'll learn

- ◆ why job satisfaction is a myth
- ◆ the nature of true career contentment
- ◆ how relationships at work can be good—or bad

Most of us expect our employers to reward us with a reasonable amount of money in exchange for our time and talents. True, we might also expect other intangibles, such as a generous amount of paid vacation or an office with a view. But money is usually the first item we check off on our employment decision list. Depending on the circumstances (for example, you decide to take the job because the office is two blocks from your house, but the pay is lower than you want), you'll either be satisfied or unsatisfied by the deal you made. Your satisfaction may decrease or increase after you begin working at your new job, but you'll essentially have only two ways to relate to your job: positively or negatively.

But what if you could look at your job and career choice from a middle ground that would allow you to take charge of your *own* satisfaction on the job? What if you could go to work, and no matter what happened to you during the day, the inner strength and resiliency you bring to your job and career choice could be sustained and bring you contentment?

The Myth of Job Satisfaction

Job satisfaction is usually gauged by specific employer-provided metrics, such as pay, benefits, supervision, training, job opportunities, working conditions, work relationships, life balance—things and more things. Because you're working in exchange for things, you can point to them and claim that because you don't have one of them, you don't have job satisfaction.

In contrast, contentment has no metrics per se, because being contented means that you've learned to balance your expectations from your job and employer. You don't expect the traditional rewards given to you by your employer to give you job satisfaction. As an employee who understands career contentment, you know that not every day will be perfect, but your salary will be enough to compensate for the work you have to do, the boss you have to endure, the petty politics you have to play, and the endless meetings you might have to attend. You can find career contentment when you are able to use your inner strength and resiliency to keep a positive attitude no matter what happens, and thus you can truly feel that *you* are ultimately in control— and not passive in the face of the usual ups and downs of a job controlled by higher-ups.

Unfortunately, the career advice you received from parents, teachers, and other supporters gave you the idea that you would succeed in finding job satisfaction when you somehow achieved your highest potential while doing what you love. But in between starting your career and achieving that imagined success, if it ever happens, there's an awful lot of time when you're not reaching your highest potential. The bleak message you get is that you will not have job satisfaction during all those weeks and months and years when you're waiting for this success.

In contrast, career contentment allows you to appreciate the reality that, ultimately, the highs and lows of your career—even the less-than-satisfying experiences—play an important role in your evolution as both an employee and a person. Employees who understand the principles of career contentment continue to love what they do even when aspects of their work provide little satisfaction by traditional measures. Once you learn this contented approach to work, the good news is that even if you're working without the employer satisfactions you want, the time you spend getting a new job or changing jobs will be a lot less stressful and happier. And the contented attitude that you've shown in dealing with whatever your current employer may throw at you will probably help you as you move toward the job or career you really want!

Getting Our Terms Straight: The Illuminating Origins of Key Words

As we launch into a detailed look at how you can recognize and sustain your career contentment, it's illuminating to first consider the origins of words like "satisfaction" and "contentment." The place to start is the dictionary, and what you're about to read is one of the most critical parts of this book for your understanding of career contentment.

Webster's defines *satisfaction* as "fulfillment of conditions or desires, being made satisfied, pleased, and contented," and *contentment* as "ease of mind, being pleased and satisfied." Thus, it would appear that these words mean the same thing. In fact, pay attention to people's comments and you'll hear them use these terms interchangeably. Even more interesting, as you read a report about job dissatisfaction, you'll see that it states workers are dissatisfied with one thing but have contentment about another. What are these people and papers trying to say?

These tangled meanings and undisciplined uses of the terms "satisfaction" and "contentment" dilute the significance of each. This is unfortunate, because the actual origins of these words suggest that they ultimately have quite different meanings—and that we need both. For example, in situations where you're not happy or entirely satisfied, how can you still be content? Do you see the difference, and why we might need both meanings?

Let's resolve this right now. Turn on your computer and visit the Online Etymology Dictionary (www.etymonline.com). There you'll find the origins and root meanings of most words, and sometimes what you'll find is not what you'd expect.

Take, for instance, the word "satisfy." The Latin roots of this word mean "sad" and "factitious" and have the sense of "comply, make amends, doing enough or sufficient, sorrowful and artificial." In other words, something has to be done for you to be made satisfied, and potentially you may never be completely satisfied. This is not unlike what my parents tried to tell me years ago when with seven kids on a farmer's income we weren't always satisfied: "Give me, give me, give me."

Now let's look at the word "content." The Latin roots of this word mean "contain" and have the sense of "hold together" and "enclose," suggesting that a "person's desires are bound by what he or she already has." It's easy to imagine a contented person as self-contained and to see logically that when you're feeling contented, you are indeed holding yourself together with a calmness protected by self-sufficiency. Once again, this is like something my parents tried to explain: "Be thankful and content with what you already have—we can't afford more." We learned to be content, even if we weren't satisfied.

Both terms represent a state of mind, but with major differences when you consider their origins. You need to simply think with the right perspective to begin to feel content, but you have to wait on something or someone else to do something to make you feel satisfied—while your thoughts spiral down into enervating worrying. Thus:

- Your satisfaction depends on a need, want, obligation, effort, result, or expectation being fulfilled. You either have it or you don't, and getting it depends on other people and material things that are not always within your control. As such, there's no guarantee that you'll ever feel completely satisfied, and by your reasoning alone you cannot bring this state of mind into existence.

- Your contentment depends on how you reason to recognize the acceptable middle ground in any situation. It depends on how you think about your situation, which enables you to feel a certain way, rather than waiting for material things or other people to make you feel a certain way. When you think in a self-sufficient way, you recognize your contentment even if external circumstances have not made you happy or entirely satisfied.

Note that, from this point of view, contentment does not really involve settling for less but rather finding your resiliency strength. By reasoning your way to recognize the silver lining, rainbow, and light at the end of the tunnel, you can empower yourself to endure, persevere, make due, get by, and eventually make things happen even if you're not completely satisfied. Contentment proves that you can live without satisfaction but not without your ability to reason. Without it, your only option would be dissatisfaction.

We're fortunate that our ancestors saw fit to create and evolve the two words "satisfaction" and "contentment" with their logically useful different meanings, and if we could remember to distinguish between them, it might help make our beautiful but imperfect world more tolerable when things don't go our way.

So what does all this mean for you and your career? Your job satisfaction is codependent on your hard work, time, and talents, which you give in exchange for the goodies that your employer provides to attract, motivate, and keep you from leaving. Either you have satisfaction or you don't, and unfortunately you can't control the will of your employer. But what you *can* control are your thoughts, emotions, reasoning, talents, and choices—all of which enable you to create your own contentment and to maintain it in the face of almost anything.

Your career contentment is not related to any one job, employer, or satisfaction but rather is recognized when you guide your career despite these things toward fulfilling your calling and purpose. You can be content with or without job satisfaction, but not without your ability to reason and pursue meaningful work. And considering that nothing is perfect or always goes your way, if you're dissatisfied it's because you haven't learned how to be content. You're either expecting too much or you're in the wrong job. For more on the deeper meaning of contentment in the face of trying circumstances, let's look at this selection from my Recruiter's Notebook.

RECRUITER'S NOTEBOOK

*Survivor—***Corporate Snake Pit Edition**

During the early 1990s, the morale in our department had plummeted to an all-time low, and it was so bad on one occasion that we thought one of our co-workers had committed suicide when she was home sick but hadn't called to report her absence. Even our client groups were openly referring to our department as the "snake pit." Our department manager was the primary source of our problems, but he was able to keep his job because he obsequiously kept his bosses happy and in the dark. If you wanted to keep your job, you were expected to keep quiet, follow the chain of command, and help maintain the impression that everything was just fine—even though this was far from the truth. Our manager rewarded loyalty with favoritism, and this encouraged spying among us just to maintain his favor. When you weren't in the room, he talked about you, and we knew this because we told each other when it happened. This was the only time during my corporate career when I felt I had to watch my back.

To make matters worse, the business was still performing poorly; there was no place to move, and only a few people were lucky enough to do so. They made a point of calling to remind us how wonderful it was to have escaped from the snake pit. The only other place to go was outside the company. But rather than jump ship, we began to participate in our own little game of *Survivor*—but instead of an exotic island, like the TV show, all we had was our island of sanity as we stuck it out by pursuing real accomplishments and not office politics. We hunkered down by taking the initiative to perfect our policies, develop and implement new programs for our client groups, revitalize our jobs to be more interesting, get closer to our client groups, and eliminate unnecessary reports and paperwork. We put our problems aside, and in the course of doing our jobs to the best of our abilities, we excelled in recognizing our contentment without job satisfaction.

As a result of this surge in self-sufficiency, and the fact we were still looking to downsize, it became apparent that our manager's job might no longer be required. We had also matured in our jobs, and the senior management team was starting to break the chain of command to learn directly from us what was happening in our client groups. This is how the problems in the snake pit finally came to light.

The person assigned to investigate the problems in our department was our manager. We knew this would go nowhere, but it was his turn in the barrel, and his predicament became a source of entertainment for us, giving us something to think about instead of our lack of promotional opportunities. The first thing he did was delay the investigation for two months, no doubt thinking we would forget about it. Not a chance. We couldn't wait for the fun to begin, and we delighted ourselves in timing our visits to ask him when the results would be available. Because our department had more than 20 employees at the time, we could make it quite obvious that the problem wasn't going away, so he finally began his interviews. We each had the opportunity to express our concerns, including our displeasure with our immediate supervision and his lack of concern for employees.

When the interviews were completed, our manager held a departmental meeting and announced that our department's morale problems were due to the flattening of our industry and the resulting lack of career opportunity. This explanation was, of course, only partially true, and an insult to our intelligence—it left out the key cause: our manager. It was also the final straw that prompted people to begin calling the division vice president with their own impressions of the problems. Events had finally evolved in accord with the manager's spoken beliefs less than two years earlier (see the Recruiter's Notebook entry titled "From Exile to Resiliency and Contentment" in chapter 5): "I honestly believe that if I had to go through a job-threatening problem like this, I don't think I could come out of it as well as you have." Fertilized by the emotions of fear, the manager's own thoughts had finally become his reality, starting with his demotion and soon followed by his termination. In the meantime, and despite our less-than-satisfying circumstances, we had developed the ability to recognize our contentment, and it enabled us to endure.

The Path to Career Contentment

Pure contentment is a relaxed state of mind that suffuses you automatically or even intentionally when you pause, take a second look, and appreciate the things around you. When you have a contented state of mind, you feel calm and collected, and this allows you to think about and see things more clearly, to experience a greater tolerance for things that are upsetting, and to make better decisions.

This contented state of mind is what the psychologist and writer Christopher Peterson refers to as "savoring" (Peterson 2006). Rather than expecting everything to be perfect or go your way, you delve into what you already have and savor it for all it's worth—provided, of course, that you've put yourself in a position that is meaningful to your calling and purpose. Thus, contentment is both a resiliency strength and a paradoxical quality, as discussed in chapter 5. In a discontented state of mind, on the other hand, you're less tolerant, making it difficult to think straight or reach good decisions. But a contented mind makes you more emotionally strong, effective, and able to endure and surmount your challenges—including job dissatisfactions. Here's another story from my notebook illustrating these benefits of contentment.

 ### RECRUITER'S NOTEBOOK

Her Career Contentment Was Always There—but Hidden

Joanne's job as a customer marketing manager was to function as a go-between. She made certain that corporate marketing was sensitive to the needs of retailers and that retailers understood and implemented the strategies and plans prepared by marketing. She helped to improve communications, worked with retailers to develop their marketing plans, and monitored the trends that allowed both entities to recalibrate to meet the demands of consumers. Her career had originated in sales, so her knowledge of the customer exceeded her knowledge of marketing and branding. Thus, her good works were frequently scrutinized by marketing to ensure that the branding was maintained in accordance with their strategies, and this continued long after she had proved that she had the abilities to do this brand work quite well.

Although Joanne's region consistently outperformed other regions, she dreaded the calls from marketing because she believed they were too critical, and the deficits they highlighted were due to her lack of earlier marketing experience. Despite her favorable results, it seemed that she couldn't do anything right, and the harder she worked, the more difficult those conversations became. She was stressed and self-conscious of failure, and her confidence was so low she felt like an accident waiting to happen. But rather than stop answering the phone, as she had considered, she decided to apply for a transfer back into sales. As a first step, she needed to update her résumé, and this involved pulling together a summary of all her major projects and accomplishments. In the course of doing this, it suddenly dawned on her that she now knew as much or more about marketing than she did sales, and she had the results to prove it. Furthermore, her well-rounded experience in both sales and marketing made her uniquely qualified for what she was doing, while her colleagues in marketing were predominantly one-dimensional.

Once she'd had this insight, Joanne decided to stick things out and give it another try, but this time with greater self-appreciation for what she'd learned and accomplished. She began to feel more at ease with herself and the knowledge she possessed, and during ensuing conversations with marketing, she spoke with the confidence of an accomplished, well-rounded professional. Her transformation was apparent, and within a couple of weeks, it seemed that people were calling not to criticize but to solicit her ideas so they could be migrated to other regions. She developed a renewed appreciation for her work, but before she was able to fully enjoy it, she was promoted to a corporate role where she was given broader marketing responsibilities. It wasn't a coincidence that her résumé had already been updated in time for this opportunity. She had begun to review her accomplishments each quarter and to update her résumé as a way of recognizing her contentment. It was the fuel she'd been missing but didn't realize was always there.

As I've noted throughout the book, career contentment must come from within you. You might try to buy it with a higher-paying job, yet that will be only a temporary solution—especially if that higher pay comes with more stress and less time to enjoy your job. You could also decide to settle for less of what you think you deserve in your job, because this is an easy route to take. But then you risk bitterness and disappointment, which can spill over into both your personal and professional lives. You might also choose to accept and appreciate the job satisfactions you have (money, window office, a great title) and drop any longing for what your employer cannot provide (more creativity, more time off). Yet with all these choices, you'll probably feel like something is missing.

How Do You Recognize Career Contentment?

You can discover your on-the-job contentment from many sources. You might begin to feel it when you sense your confidence rising at the start of a task or when you take pleasure in performing a task—such as when you get lost in your work and lose track of time, when you love what you're doing so much you'd consider doing it for free, or simply when admiring the results of a job well done. You might sense it when you've completed a goal, when you've discovered a bright idea, or when you've recognized the beauty of a simple solution. And you might also sense it when you discover a new skill or when your unique gifts and abilities are recognized for their contribution.

The contentment you intentionally derive from these and other situations gives you a momentary pause and boost in self-appreciation. And when you relive this contentment again and again, it can help to propel you forward and reinforce your strength to endure no matter what happens to your current job. This strength constitutes your contentment at work, though you may not realize it's there or may take it for granted—at least until you need it or intentionally make a point of utilizing it. Here's an example of how this can happen from my notebook.

 RECRUITER'S NOTEBOOK

From Class Clown to Successful Executive: Proving His Guidance Counselor Wrong and Himself Right

Joey grew up in a rural part of the country where the only career role models were laborers and small business owners. He had no concept of having a career, and his parents never went to college, so during his senior year of high school they arranged a meeting with the school guidance counselor to discuss college and career. His grades proved that he'd been the class clown, a distinction he relished with pride. The counselor told his parents that he wouldn't be suited for college unless he entered on a probationary basis and studied something simple. As for a career, she said there was no evidence to suggest that he loved anything but attracting the attention of his fellow students.

This meeting was deeply embarrassing for both Joey and his parents, and he regretted not having applied himself sooner. However, he imagined himself doing great things—the only problem was he didn't have a clue about what that could become or how to go about pursuing it. All he wanted was a job that would allow him to wear a tie and look important.

Joey enrolled in college on a probationary basis and without committing to a major. He struggled through the first year of mandatory courses and just barely managed to earn passing grades. At the start of his second year, he was still on probation but was confident enough to change his major to business. He began to excel based on his newfound enjoyment of studying. Within the next three years, he was on the Dean's List nearly every semester, became an officer of his fraternity, was elected student body president, and graduated.

He went on to complete a master's degree and was recruited by one of the *Fortune* 100s. They put him through a two-year rotation of disciplines that allowed him to explore and settle upon a favorite. He chose marketing because he said it gave him the opportunity to use the skills he had developed in high school as a class clown. He leveraged his love of marketing to swiftly advance through good and bad jobs. He said it didn't really matter as long as he got to do what he liked and could find a way to make a contribution.

Joey changed employers three times, and 25 years later he is the president of his division. Each time he changed jobs, he said he couldn't help but think of the comments made by his high school guidance counselor. Whether or not it was her intention to do so, she gave him the determination to succeed by causing him to focus exclusively on his assets and the possibilities associated with each and every opportunity. He said his circumstances were never as important as his ability to recognize the greatness in whatever he did. He would never again be held back by his own deficits, or the deficits caused by others. He couldn't recall when it happened, but he said that, at some point during his career, he shifted from attempting to prove his guidance counselor wrong to proving himself right. Doing so supplied his contentment, and he relished this as a resource in his ability to succeed.

Your career is shaped by the pursuit of what you believe will supply your contentment. It's why you change jobs or careers, and also why you don't. You reason with yourself: "Can I find it in my current job, or do I have to change jobs to get it?" You experiment with different employers, positions, styles of supervision, and work environments. You suffer through work you dislike, lose track of time, and don't want to stop when doing the work you love. You calibrate your preferences, make choices, and establish routines. You learn that finding your contentment requires doing what you love, as your parents and teachers taught you, but also the courage to follow your heart, the honesty to acknowledge your limitations, and the strength and resiliency to endure despite hardships created by circumstances and other people.

Through the tough times and bad jobs, you find that your contentment is fragile and can't be trusted to any one person or employer, so you develop your ability to succeed through increased self-reliance, and that too becomes a source for your contentment. When your contentment feels threatened, you may leave one job or employer and start over with another. If you don't give up or quit, you can find contentment by locating that agreeable middle ground—ideally without compromising your authenticity, forfeiting your goals, or settling for less.

Doing any of these negative things would lead to discontent, so you instead view your situation as paradoxical and choose to focus more on some dimension of its positive side. For instance, when your job begins to seem intolerable, you could spend a few hours the next morning updating your résumé, and while doing this you could muse about the great new jobs that your current trials are preparing you for—in the spirit of "It's great résumé fodder" and "If it doesn't kill you, it will make you stronger." By finding ways to love what you do, no matter what, you discover your truly secure career contentment: knowing that you can *choose* to be content—come success or setbacks, triumph or tragedy, or anything in between. Muriel's story from my notebook is a particularly vivid example of how true contentment can get you through almost anything (see next page).

Usually, your contentment is at its peak when you feel competent, secure, resourced, encouraged, recognized, and rewarded. And it's generally at its lowest when you believe you're settling for too little or are sacrificing too much, or when you venture too far from what you love doing the most. True, but Muriel's example in the Recruiter's Notebook entry shows how it's still feasible to be content even during the harshest of circumstances—as long as you're predisposed to find meaning in the source of your contentment. Unfortunately, because of

RECRUITER'S NOTEBOOK

Muriel's Contentment: Armor for Tragedies, Source of Courage to Write and Endure

When we met, Muriel had been unemployed for more than 18 months, and her bank was in the process of foreclosing on her mortgage. Despite her circumstances, she had a great sense of humor and told stories in a manner that captured my interest. I couldn't help but wonder how she could appear so content when it seemed her world was crumbling around her. She had been downsized and was struggling to leave her engineering profession to become the writer that she had always wanted to be, and she had one heck of a story to tell.

She had been raised separately from her brothers and sisters, married at a young age, and had twins. Before she was released from the hospital, one of the twins died, and her husband abandoned her. With only $37 to her name, she left the hospital and lived alone with the surviving twin in a car for nearly two years. She worked for food at homeless shelters, and she survived cancer, the death of one brother, and the imprisonment of another. She put herself through college and earned an engineering degree by delivering newspapers in the morning, driving a forklift in the afternoon, and waiting tables at night.

After graduating, Muriel took her first professional engineering position and was eventually able to buy her first home. It burned to the ground during her first business trip. Her career progressed, but not without further incidents—including her recent downsizing and fruitless search for new employment. As these and other tragedies befell her, she grieved but said she still felt somehow uniquely privileged. She believed that God was allowing these things to happen for a reason that was beyond her ability at the time to understand. Rather than dwell on her past or her immediate difficulties, she focused with excitement on discovering the benefits paradoxically linked to each tragedy, and from this she intentionally recognized that her contentment could be rooted in writing about her experiences, and her writing gave her strength to endure.

Muriel persisted with her writing because it was the one thing that gave her contentment. As a result, she became the writer she had always wanted to be. She believes without a doubt that her experiences, as bad as they were, were formative to her ability to write with greater empathy and passion.

their conditioning to value satisfaction and success, not many people are able to do this. The need for and benefits of contentment are overlooked as a factor of true satisfaction and success that you can control no matter what.

Without an orientation to recognize your contentment, you learn through experience that there's a price associated with escaping from or tolerating what causes job dissatisfaction and that this price can be so great at times that even doing what you think you love is not enough. When bad things happen, you inventory your satisfaction and scrutinize your options with the intent of determining whether to look for it elsewhere, or you stick things out in hopes that your satisfaction will follow. Sometimes it doesn't. Let's look at a story from my notebook about how Kathy's eventual contentment helped a job find her.

RECRUITER'S NOTEBOOK

From Fruitless Search to the Job Finding Her

Kathy's career in engineering had evolved through design, applications, and then to sales. The change had been refreshing, because it had given her direct contact with the customer, but this is where her natural abilities fell short. She was not a salesperson. Her supervisor recognized this, but also the fact that she was unsurpassed in her ability to develop innovative designs and quotes. Rather than encourage her to develop new business, as she was supposed to be doing, he exploited her natural abilities to enhance his own quotes and customer relationships. The arrangement worked for nearly a year, until a new vice president was hired to increase profits and sales. His solution would involve eliminating the "dead weight," which in his eyes was what Kathy had become. Things were about to change.

Kathy was now expected to sell and develop new business like everyone else, but she didn't know how, so her work deteriorated. In the months that preceded her inevitable layoff, she'd been separated from the design work she loved doing most and was reaching burnout as a dissatisfied salesperson with no experience. Her short-term memory had deteriorated, and her personal life had become highly disorganized. She couldn't sleep and was having difficulties making decisions. Her detail orientation and concern for quality had slipped away, and she was guilt-stricken as a result. She believed there was no option but to work harder, and despite her best efforts, it seemed the harder she worked the worse things got. She was missing work and couldn't get to the office before 9:00 a.m., even though her co-workers were often starting as early as 7:00 a.m. Even if another job were to be found, she now lacked the confidence and energy to pursue it.

On her way to work one day, Kathy absentmindedly drove through a red light and her car was totaled. Fortunately, there were no serious injuries. When her layoff finally occurred, Kathy felt it was a relief, despite the fact that she had no job. Thus began her quest for another sales position that would give her the job satisfaction she had once experienced in her uniquely customized position. Her search continued for months, and despite interviews with several companies, nothing happened until she realized that what she was looking for didn't exist. She humbled herself to this discovery and took stock of her gifts, strengths, and preferences, and she began again—but this time with a contented, open mind that the right job would find her instead. That's when another design job found her.

Balancing Your Concern for Job Satisfaction with Contentment

Although it's a great idea to focus your job search and career on the potential of achieving job satisfaction, you must realize the chances of this succeeding are never more than 50 percent. This is because you, the job, other people, the employer, the competition, the economy, and any unforeseeable life circumstances are never static. Life-altering changes can occur within days after you start even the most satisfying new job, and these changes may not always be to your satisfaction— leading to regret, disappointment, stress, performance issues, or career instability.

But instead of expecting and looking only for job satisfaction, at the same time you could develop an orientation toward discovering your contentment—an orientation that can help compensate for those unexpected dissatisfactions that are guaranteed to occur during some point during your career. However—and this is important—contentment is not out there waiting for you to find, stumble upon, or grab like the proverbial brass ring. Nor does it depend on any dream employer, new job, pay increase, other people, or even job satisfaction. These things are important, and you'd rather have them than not, but they're secondary in importance to your beliefs about them, and you can choose to believe whatever you like. In other words—as was explained in chapter 6—genuine contentment comes from within, and you can discover it in any situation through your ability to pause, take a second look, and reason to find the acceptable middle ground in any employment or life situation. Thus, contentment is a factor of how you think. Here's a story from my notebook of how I learned to think this way.

RECRUITER'S NOTEBOOK

From Chore to Boon: The Fruits of Changing Your Attitude

One summer during my high school years, I took a part-time job painting an old black iron fence that surrounded a house on the main street of my hometown. At first, I dreaded this job because the fence seemed to be a mile long and was so rusted that it would have to be sanded by hand. It was a tedious and dirty job, and I wasn't particularly excited about the whole town watching me work, but there was no way out since the owners were friends of the family. I had to keep reminding myself that I was doing it for the money, and even that wasn't much.

The job lasted four weeks due to frequent rainstorms, and it turned out to be the most enjoyable part-time job that I was ever paid to do. Things started slowly and then gradually went faster as I began to understand what I was doing and how to do it. Everyone who walked by that fence had something nice to say, like "Big job," "Nice work," "You're making good progress," and "I never saw this old fence look so good."

This feedback certainly helped, and to my surprise, I began to look forward to each day and to the encouragement I received from the people passing by. I knew exactly what to expect each day, what to do next, and how to do it—and, except for the whole town, no one was looking over my shoulder. I found pleasure in seeing the rust come off and the paint go on. I perfected how to clean the brushes at the end of the day so they stayed in good condition for the next day. I made sure there was no trash or tools left in the yard or on the sidewalk. When it rained, I didn't work, but I was concerned how it might affect my new paint. I eventually stopped thinking about the money and instead focused on how the finished product would look and how proud the owner would be.

I didn't realize it at the time, but after the job was done, it occurred to me that I got much more out of that experience than I'd bargained for and that it would last me a lifetime. Not only did I learn a new skill, I learned that I was capable of hard work, and by recognizing and taking pride in my efforts, I was able to keep myself pleased and motivated; otherwise, I'm sure I could never have finished that job. I thought of this each time I went back home and saw that old fence. And I must have done a good job, because it had been left alone for about 15 years and I could tell it was badly in need of a new coat of paint.

Then, during one summer visit, I passed by the house and was glad to see someone finally at work painting the fence. Empathizing with what this young, hardworking fellow was going through, and because I felt the fence created a sort of bond between us, I thought it would be a nice gesture to park a few houses away and walk by and tell him, "Big job, nice work, you're making good progress." I did, and what he said is unsuitable to print. In any case, I knew firsthand that the job would go a lot faster and be a lot more enjoyable if his attitude became a bit more positive. But then again, he was just getting started and had a long way to go.

Your ability to reason and find the satisfactory middle ground makes you the primary source of your own contentment, not anyone or anything else. Because you have this ability, it also makes you the primary source of your own good performance, productivity, and job stability. You can find contentment in any situation and without having to settle for less, make do with what you have, or forfeiting your goals. It's a choice—and now you know.

The Paradox of Job Satisfaction versus Contentment

Do you think you need more contentment because you lack job satisfaction? Leverage your reasoning abilities and paradoxical qualities to think differently about it. Do you dislike your boss or the people you work with? Do the same with all of them. Are you tired of commuting, sick of your work, not earning enough, unable to sleep at night thinking about work, unhappy you didn't get that last promotion, worried sick about the upcoming reorganization, disillusioned by all the office politics, beaten down by the competition, disappointed that more benefits are being taken away, angry that you got no bonus this year? You can choose from three ways to think about each of these things:

♦ You could allow them to take over your peace of mind, affect your judgment, and then see what other problems develop—obviously a negative no-win.

♦ You could leave and find another job where you're likely to find all these same sources of discontent—another no-win.

♦ Or you could use your inner contentment to endure the situation until you can come to terms with it, find a solution, or discover any benefits associated with it—you win no matter what!

Regardless of how bad your situation may be, you'll have a difficult time dealing with it until you finally realize and accept that your contentment comes from within and stems from your ability to think differently about your circumstances. For instance, you may not have received the promotion you wanted, but you still have a job. The commute may not be so good, but the people are great. Let's look at a story from my notebook on the facing page about how John chose fruitful contentment over complaining.

Contentment and Stress

Whether you stay or leave a less-than-satisfactory job situation depends on the beliefs you hold about that situation and the tolerances you've established for dealing with it. If you're uncertain what to look for, start by reviewing the four Ps covered in chapter 4 (the people, the place, the particulars involved, and what's personal to you),

RECRUITER'S NOTEBOOK

Choosing Not to Complain but to Bloom Where You're Planted

Early in his career, John rejected a promotion because it involved relocating from corporate to a plant, and this was despite the fact that without plant experience his future career options would be narrowed. He made it clear that he had no desire to leave the corporate offices. In the meantime, his advancement at corporate was blocked by managers who had been in their positions for a relatively short time. He had no place to go and no idea how long he would have to wait for another opportunity.

Meanwhile, John's peers who worked elsewhere were progressing as he sat still. His managers were aware of the situation but had the opinion that it was his decision to stay rather than move to get the experience he needed, so there was nothing they could do. Rather than complain, John exploited every opportunity his position allowed to keep himself interested and engaged. He was content to stay in this situation because he was divorced and shared joint custody of his daughter, and relocating would have separated him from her. He perfected his craft and created projects to solve problems that no one else would dare attempt.

Over time, John was recognized as the go-to person for matters even outside his scope of responsibility. He never complained, and on the basis of his contributions he was promoted several times without ever relocating. He found contentment in everything he did and believed he was experiencing his life and career on his terms. Had he complained, I'm certain his managers would have facilitated his release so that he could find his contentment elsewhere.

and, as recommended in chapter 6, take note of any unreasonable, negative, or dramatic thoughts, self-talk, or intolerances you have about each. Then recognize any obstacles that these kinds of thoughts and feelings may be imposing on your ability to choose contentment. In other words, be attentive to your beliefs about your situation and, if required, be willing to change how you think about it. You can decide to find the bad in any situation or just as easily decide to find the good, as long as you're thinking responsibly—and that's the tricky part. Look for the acceptable middle ground.

Remember that a discontented mind interferes with your ability to tolerate the things you normally find upsetting, to think clearly, and to make good decisions. So as your work-related challenges arise, your ability to deal with them effectively is suspect to begin with, and this is why some situations go from bad to worse or lead to job dissatisfaction and career instability.

Medical researchers estimate that 60 percent of illness and disease is linked to how you respond to stressors. Work-related strain and dissatisfactions resulting from job changes, relocations, and conflict can last for months at a time and may never get resolved, and therefore they can pose a major threat to your health. Fortunately, research also suggests that you can reduce the risk of a stress-related illness by improving how you respond, and by countering the effects through diet, exercise, hobbies, and the like (Selye 1977; Seligman 1998). This leads you back to a review of your resiliency strengths discussed in chapter 5, but first things first.

Delaying Decisions Until You Achieve a Contented State of Mind

Genuine contentment acknowledges that your life and career are cyclical. There will be periods of consolation when it seems that things are going your way and periods of desolation when it seems nothing goes your way. Instances and even periods of serious discontent are therefore likely during the span of a typical 50-year career, and during those periods, it's advisable to avoid making any major decisions or important changes. Decisions made hastily in response to stressful circumstances can lead to more mistakes, further dissatisfactions, and future regrets. Your best decisions are made with a contented state of mind, because it allows you to function from a position of strength due to increased clarity of thought. Delay the decision until you can achieve a contented state of mind.

A good place to start is by making use of your resiliency strengths and paradoxical qualities that were discussed in chapter 5. Use these natural resources to regain your strength, peace, composure, and clarity of thought to change your thinking and make the right choices. When using these resources, you'll no doubt find the solution you're looking for, or you'll be led to the right resource that will provide a solution. Remember from chapter 6 that your circumstances are seemingly random and meaningless until you assign them a meaning and react. You decide the meaning and can alter your reaction by assigning a meaning that is beneficial to your contentment (Seligman 2002).

You could also try and give things a little time for the cycle to swing back around. But if you can't wait, or things are moving a bit too slowly, you still have options. It's possible in a bad situation to find your contentment elsewhere and then apply its beneficial effects to help you in your current situation. Let's look at a story from my notebook about how you can do this.

RECRUITER'S NOTEBOOK

Surviving the Boss from Hell by Applying Contentment from Elsewhere

Steve was a logistics and supply chain director who had recently returned to the United States from an expatriate assignment in China. It was time to come home, he was willing to take any assignment that would allow his family to be reacquainted with relatives and friends, and his wife was finally looking to get her own career back up and running. Unfortunately, the boss he was about to inherit was someone he would have never chosen to work for under normal circumstances. This boss's world revolved around him—in his office he had no fewer than seven pictures of himself on the walls and desk, none including his family.

As a vice president, this boss was given the power and autonomy to make things happen the way he liked. He built a loyal team beneath him who were willing to accommodate him, laugh at the same jokes he told again and again, and secretly report back to him on things that were happening in the department. Everything went through him, nothing got beyond him, and he took credit for everything while creating the impression that he was magnanimous, flexible, and accommodating. From above, he was perceived as harmless and was appreciated for the results his division achieved. From below and outside his division, he was the subject of jokes and speculation regarding how long before he would retire or how long the organization would tolerate his charade, and the people who worked for him were

Surviving the Boss from Hell by Applying Contentment from Elsewhere (continued)

considered his drones and were therefore undesirable for movement else-where. If you worked for him, it was expected that you would become another of his drones or otherwise he would force you to leave—which is exactly what had happened to Steve's predecessor.

Steve was not a drone, but he had to endure this boss from hell because there was no other job at the time, and if he left, it would have a negative impact on his long-term career plans. He would stick it out, and his boss would have to force him to leave. He estimated it would take about six months before things might become intolerable, and so during those six months Steve began to execute "Plan B," which he and his wife had developed while still in China. Steve performed his duties to the best of his abilities. Like everyone else, he laughed at the same jokes told over and over by his boss; and he agreed to the minor changes made to his memos and reports, even though his boss would claim that he'd come up with the ideas or that the changes he'd made had transformed what would have otherwise been a disaster.

As frustrating as his circumstances became, Steve consistently demonstrated great resiliency because, from his perspective, this was only his day job. On evenings, weekends, and holidays, he devoted himself to assisting his wife in setting up her new business on the Internet—the heart of their Plan B. She was making her hobby, designing and selling craft and scrap-booking prod-ucts, into a full-time job. She had a business plan and had eagerly started to implement it as soon as they returned to the United States. Part of the plan involved using Steve's expertise in logistics, and it was hoped that his new job would allow him to devote some time to the start-up operation.

Under the circumstances, Steve had no desire to hang around the office after hours. Rather than becoming an office drone, he was pursuing another job working with his wife, where his experience would prove invaluable in set-ting up supply chain networks from China, and warehousing and distribution operations in the States. His wife was in charge of finances, sales, and mar-keting, and she had no idea how Steve did what he did. This allowed Steve full authority to do what he thought was best to grow the business, and thanks to Steve it did.

The business was launched at the start of the scrap-booking craze, and it took off as they had hoped. His night duties gave him the distraction he needed from the frustrations of his day job, and rather than wasting his free time feeling sorry for himself or stewing over his boss's personality quirks, he was putting all his gifts, skills, and abilities to use without permission or second-guessing from anyone else. He shared ideas and solutions between the two businesses, so both sides benefited from his contributions, and he was smart enough to recognize that what he was doing was supplying his contentment.

The six months came and went, and after nearly 18 months, his boss seemed just another boss and Steve believed that it was possible the family could make do if he worked full time with his wife. However, Steve's plans also involved probably assuming his boss's job, because it appeared the boss might be retiring within another two years.

Problems with Work Relationships—a Real Challenge for Contentment

Work relationships are the primary source of both delight and dissatisfaction in any workplace, and they also pose the greatest challenge to your ability to recognize your contentment. These relationships are subject to change, and you may not always be given the opportunity to choose your boss or your associates. It's all part of the job, but you expect and would like to believe that you'll get along with others and have the ability to work through your differences. But if you have problems with these relationships, and if you don't have a way to solve them—like Steve's Plan B in the Recruiter's Notebook entry above—you're likely to avoid the other people, keep your interactions to a minimum, or even want to leave. It can be awkward, dysfunctional to the business, and harmful to your ability to recognize contentment unless you can find a solution to these problems.

One very useful solution to problems with work relationships requires a working understanding of the Theory of Interpersonal Relationships, and how to apply it to your new and existing relationships. This theory was developed by the psychologist William Schutz, who contends that people need people, and that your needs with respect to interpersonal relations lie in three specific areas (Schutz 1958):

- *Inclusion*: You need to establish and maintain meaningful connections with others. You want and need to feel accepted, understood, and worthwhile. When this doesn't happen, you feel lonely and unwanted. If you have a high need for inclusion, your contentment is likely to be challenged when you are paired with someone who ignores you.

- *Control*: You need to make the decisions and influence the events and people around you, and at other times you need to submit and allow others to have this control over you. When these things don't happen, you become anxious. If you have a high need to control, your contentment is likely to be challenged when you are paired with someone who insists on controlling. Or if you have a high need to be controlled, your contentment is likely to be challenged when you are paired with someone who expects you to control.

- *Affection*: You need opportunities to express and receive affection. You want and need to establish close ties and relationships, but at other times you also need your privacy. When these things don't happen, you feel unfulfilled and neglected or otherwise exposed and vulnerable. If you have a high need for affection, your contentment is likely to be challenged when you are paired with someone who prefers to keep his or her feelings private. Or if you have a high need for privacy, your contentment is likely to be challenged when you are paired with someone who insists on being affectionate.

Figure 7-1 shows the various aspects of how these three areas cover the phases of relationships, including examples of low and high needs for each and how both your and others' needs come into play.

Let's see how these three areas apply to your work (and other) relationships. You experience your first opportunity for *inclusion* when you are introduced to someone new or reconnect with someone. You are welcomed and invited to exchange contact information, have lunch, get to know each other, and share resources. You feel accepted, included, and worthwhile as a result. Things seem to progress smoothly until

Figure 7-1. How to Keep Your Relationships Moving Forward

Be aware of your needs

To Be Included		To Control		For Affection	
Low Needs	High Needs	Low Needs	High Needs	Low Needs	High Needs
Quiet, self-sufficient, loner	Outgoing, expressive, involving	Follower, reactive, submissive	Leader, decisive, aggressive	Indifferent, serious, focused	Warmth, sensitive, caring

But also be attentive to the needs of *others* (What to do)

To Be Included		To Control		For Affection	
Low Needs	High Needs	Low Needs	High Needs	Low Needs	High Needs
Give space, allow privacy, don't pressure	Invite, involve, inform	Volunteer, initiate, command	Give in, cooperate, comply	Stay focused, professional, serious	Kindness, friendship, concern
To help form and develop the relationship		When the relationship appears stuck		To help repair and maintain the relationship	

suddenly a *control* issue develops. It's inevitable and can be something very minor or serious, depending on the meaning you assign it. Who leads and who follows? The uncertainty and anxiety are uncomfortable. Someone has to make the first move. The outcome may not be to your liking, and you may feel resentful as a result.

The situation eventually gets worked out, and the sense of relief that follows sparks your *affection* (you might say: This is silly, I'm sorry, I've always admired you) and the willingness to forgive, forget, and reunite. You do this through inclusion (Let's get together, here is something I'd like your thoughts on), and the cycle continuously repeats through control (I thought you were supposed to do that, you never told me anything) to affection, and back again to inclusion.

This relationship cycle happens with your co-workers, neighbors, friends, lovers, and every one you meet and with whom you have a purposeful conversation, face-to-face or by phone. It continues in this manner until it is suddenly realized that one of you will be parting for some reason, and then the cycle reverses. So these sequences happen:

- inclusion → control → affection /
- inclusion → control → affection /
- discovery of departure and reverse /
- affection (We're going to miss you) /
- control (Call me; no, you call me) /and
- back to inclusion (Let's stay in touch).

Being content in your relations with other people requires you to be attentive to both your own needs and the needs of others. Schutz's theory gives you the means to anticipate and prepare for the ups and downs that are likely in every relationship. The highs from inclusion, the struggles through control, and the reconciliation through affection are going to happen. He maintains that the most successful relationships develop between people who aren't extreme in their interpersonal needs. It's better to be sociable, adaptable, and willing to include and be included. When control issues arise, it's better to respond democratically. Be flexible in your willingness to submit when it's advisable and worthwhile to do so. Be personable but also prepared to grant others the space and privacy they may need.

If you follow Schutz's theory, you'll know when things are back on track if you're in the midst of one phase and you sense or observe evidence of the next. For example, say you're experiencing a control conflict with a co-worker and you decide to give in and allow him or her to have control just to move things along. If you sense his or her affection as a result, then you know you've helped the relationship. You can also expect some form of inclusion next—and, of course, another control issue in the future. The shift between phases can be slow or fast, depending on how often you interact, and the willingness of either person to move things along. In lieu of anything else, Schutz's theory is a great little resource.

Watching Out for Too Much Contentment

In some situations, your work relationships can be so good, and the contentment so great, that you lose sight of the importance of other dimensions of your career. In other words, is too much contentment bad for your career? Here's an illuminating story about this question from my notebook.

RECRUITER'S NOTEBOOK

The Perils of Too Much Contentment

The industry in which Beth was working started its decline during the early 1980s. The culture in the firm where she worked was defined by a strong team orientation but also by a declining market share, stagnation, and uncertainty about layoffs. There were no promotional opportunities, and to survive, you had to settle for what you had or find ways to make your work interesting. If you didn't like what you were doing, you could leave, and resignations were welcomed as an opportunity to reduce the headcount.

The first layoffs came as a regrettable relief during the late 1980s. Beth and the other survivors felt as if members of their family had died, and they drew closer together to support each other. This enabled them to endure the prospect of even more layoffs in the near future, and as a result, many even resisted the opportunity to leave when it was possible for them to do so. A few companies nearby were actively recruiting—why did Beth and her

The Perils of Too Much Contentment (continued)

co-workers choose to stay with a company that had the potential of stalling their career and income potential? She said they found contentment in the support they received from each other, and in the fact that everyone was stagnating at the same rate of speed; the "up or out" pressures no longer existed, because there was no place to go. They were comfortable with each other, they had good benefits, and their profit sharing was based on the parent company's performance rather than their own, so they were still making good money. They inspired their own contentment by refining their jobs, and they worked with the general belief that it would be difficult to find work or other co-workers quite as good elsewhere.

Not until eight months later, when Beth was transferred to another company within the same corporation, did she finally realize that she had been working under a spell. She said, "I was like the frog sitting contentedly in the pot as the water was slowly reaching its boiling point. We chose to stick it out, while in reality our career progression and development had been stalled. I wish now that I had moved sooner, and despite my telling this to my former co-workers, they don't get it. It's unfortunate, because there are some pretty talented people there, but they're still under the spell."

In the situation of Beth and her colleagues described in the Recruiter's Notebook entry above, contentment was recognized individually and collectively within a group as its members leveraged supportive relationships. This contentment enabled them to endure, make do with what they had, and readjust their sights more realistically. It also caused the careers and earning potential of some talented people to stagnate during the prime of their life—something they may later regret. This raises the question of whether too much contentment can cause you to become inattentive, lazy, or to lose ambition. The answer is: Yes it can, but only if your contentment is based on beliefs that are unrealistic, irresponsible, or without regard to possible future regrets. Otherwise, an abundance of contentment is always a good thing.

Genuine career contentment is not achieved by fooling yourself into enduring a situation that seems illogical, illegal, immoral, or un-ethical. It requires thinking responsibly to determine whether you should stick it out or take your contentment elsewhere. But remember that contentment comes from within and does not depend on any place, people, or particulars. Material things are temporary, they may or may not be available, and eventually you may take them for granted. So by allowing your contentment to depend on things or on other people, you're setting yourself up for future discontent. The ability to recognize your contentment, and to make the most of its beneficial effects, can make the grass greener wherever and whenever you want it to be, in good or bad situations, but it requires that your thinking be responsible and realistic—not like the contented frog about to be boiled. (See Seligman 2002 on happiness.)

Summing Up Contentment

It's your privilege and opportunity to choose not to find contentment in any aspect related to your current situation, or even within you while you're in that situation. You may decide you're better off taking your contentment elsewhere and recognizing it under a different set of circumstances. That you don't leave shows that the timing is not right or that you're content to stay for some reason you've decided is important—and whatever that reason may be, it's enabling you to endure for the time being, you're perfectly content to do nothing, or it's holding you back.

Genuine contentment acknowledges that you have one shot at this life, and getting the most from it requires the courage to act. You can choose to either stay and endure or—if you sincerely believe going elsewhere could enable you to better use your gifts and talents to fulfill your purpose—give serious thought to leaving a situation. Look within yourself for direction, because it's your life and the only thing other people can tell you is "do what you love." Doubts and worries are normal; and if you read part I of this book again, you'll be reminded that those doubts are coming from your controlling five-sixths nonconscious thoughts and are intended to hold you back and in your comfort zone. Remember, your nonconscious mental guardian doesn't care if you don't fulfill your purpose. If you decide to leave a situation, make sure you go when you're in a contented state of mind and your thoughts are clear.

That way, you'll be sure to attract what's looking for you. It all comes back to that balance of thinking contentedly and finding the middle ground—and here's one final notebook story about that.

RECRUITER'S NOTEBOOK

Questions to Evoke a Sense of the Middle Ground

Working as a recruiter and career coach, the calls I receive are from people who are first and foremost interested in their careers. But until I know what the issue is, I don't know if what they need is a coach or recruiter. The start of most conversations goes something like this: "Things are not going as well here as I thought they would, and certainly not as well as I was promised when I took this job. Something's missing, and I get a sense the company is either clueless or headed in the wrong direction. I guess what I'm saying is that I may be in the market for a new job." Now is when my fun begins, by asking this question: "Well then, should I help you as a career coach or as recruiter?" Regardless of their answer, my next question is usually: "Tell me what do you like most about your current job?"

Nine times out of ten, this question causes people to pause, to take a second look, and to reason and find the middle ground in their current situation. They never expect this question, because their thoughts are so intensely focused on finding fault so as to justify their lack of job satisfaction. Sometimes, all people need is to reorient their focus so they can recognize their contentment. If this doesn't work, then we roll up our sleeves and get down to business, and that depends on which direction they want to go.

What's Next

The next chapter presents and explains a model for the flow of your career. This model seeks to make sense of the various phases of your career—from those exciting new beginnings to times when you feel you've achieved true expertise to times when you feel ready to reach out and share what you've learned. Of course, depending on the job changes you go through, these phases can return again and again in new incarnations. But that's what we'll look at in detail.

8

Manage Your Career Contentment with the Career Flow Model

.... In this chapter, you'll learn ....

◆ why you need to do career planning—flexibly

◆ how your career flows, and how your career senses help you go with or change your flow

◆ how you can use the three phases of the career flow model to your advantage

nless you're one of those lucky people who discovers your career and contentment at an early age and manages to stick with it until you retire, you're likely to evolve through several employers and even change careers four or five times. Anything is possible and—despite your best efforts at career planning—you'll end up doing things you never anticipated. This chapter discusses the flow of your career or careers and how important messages from your senses can help you anticipate and influence what might happen—in turn enabling you to find and maintain your contentment.

Why Have a Flexible Career Plan?

Career plans are rarely written down and filed in a drawer. They're etched in your head and heart and follow a flexible path toward a goal or pinnacle within a certain time period. Your retirement date is usually nonspecific, but early enough that you still have time to play around in good health. Then you guide your career in the general direction you want it to go, usually along a specialized track in one discipline or industry. At the same time, you remain flexible to better opportunities along the way, and the possibility of a self-employment period is not unrealistic. It all depends on how things progress. So how will they progress?

No matter what career track you decide to follow, you'd probably like to see some return on your investment in education, even though what you studied in school may not be relevant to your chosen career field. But no matter what shape your career seems to start taking, you don't want it to stagnate, be derailed, or guided by anyone but you. What you hope for is stability and progressive increases in income and expertise, and advancement through increasingly higher levels of responsibility and authority. However, lateral moves and the occasional steps backward do occur, as well as the corresponding changes in income. Of course, that's because your career is the result not only of your desires and choices but also fluctuations in employment caused by unpredictable changes—ups and downs in the economy, competition, technology, climate, family, health, war, terrorism, and so on. You need to be flexible in response to these kinds of changes or you'll waste time and energy longing for the could've been, should've been, would've been.

Because you can't predict what might happen or in which direction you may need to guide your career, as challenges occur along the way, you'll need to make concessions. You can

- ◆ stick things out
- ◆ get more training and education
- ◆ go where the jobs are
- ◆ adapt to fit the jobs that are available
- ◆ create your own job

- take whatever job pays the bills until you get your career back on track
- do some combination of all these things, as long as it puts food on the table.

Then, in the midst of all these struggles, one day you realize that five, 10, 15, or 20 years have passed, and you wonder: "Am I doing what I'm supposed to be doing?" In effect, this "wondering thinking" is a moment of career crisis, which may happen again and again.

The Chinese word for "crisis" is made up of two characters, one meaning danger and the other opportunity. So you have a choice: give in to the danger of dwelling on a career slump, or look for an opportunity. And the opportunity here is to learn to do this kind of thinking about your career in advance—before all that time has passed—and that's essentially what career planning is all about. So how do you begin to plan? The first step is to realize that your career has a flow and that you can anticipate, if not control, the kinds of changes you'll probably face as part of this flow. And once you've imagined these probabilities, you can plan for what you'd do, depending on alternative possible outcomes and the other contingencies (Csikszentmihalyi 1990).

How Your Career Flows

Your career is a dynamic reality. It can take many twists and turns—it doesn't progress in a straight line. And because it will probably last for a long time, and be subject to many unknown variables that you cannot plan for, you'll never be 100 percent certain 100 percent of the time. So it's no wonder that career plans are maintained inside your head informally, because doing so allows you to remain flexible and to minimize your own internal bureaucracy.

This informal planning isn't a problem as long as you believe you're using your talents, fulfilling your purpose, and not wasting time on the wrong career track or with the wrong employer. But if you reach a moment of career crisis and start to doubt that what you're doing is accomplishing these things, you'll sense the need to alter your plans and guide your career into new directions. The fact is, you'll work as long as you want to work or have to work, and although your career is subject to unpredictable forces, you'll keep it moving forward—if only because of three constant, basic forces:

- your time in a job
- your developing expertise
- your desire for contentment.

These three basic forces are more within your ability to control than those unpredictable events mentioned above, and when you pay attention to these forces, they can help shape your career and enable you to understand how it flows, what to anticipate, and how to plan. Thus, they establish your career flow.

As your career flows, the path it takes is documented by your résumé. And as it keeps on flowing, your career constantly recycles through three distinct phases that are shaped by the three basic forces of time, expertise, and your pursuit of contentment. Your flow can be viewed from two perspectives: your overall career, which is less specific; and your incremental career flow or choices. This chapter focuses primarily on your incremental career flow.

The Three Phases of Career Flow

Your incremental career flow refers to where you think your career is in relation to the three phases of the career flow model (see figure 8-1):

- First, you could be the "seeker" involved in exploring new options and choices—you're at the *orientation* phase and are focused on developing your expertise.
- Second, you could be the "go-to person" who is settled in and down to business—you're at the *acceleration* phase and are focused on making things happen, on leveraging your expertise.
- Third, you could be the "guru" who has done it all—you're at the *actualization* phase and are ready to share your expertise with others.

Figure 8-1. The Three Career Flow Phases

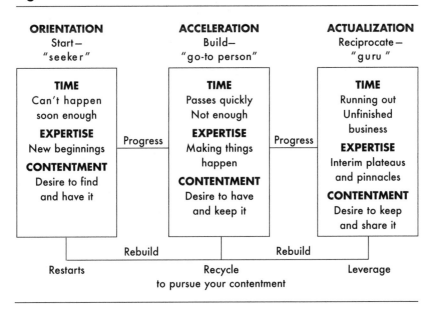

Figure 8-1 shows the flow of these three career phases. This simple diagram depicts more about your career and what to anticipate than you could possibly imagine at first glance. The contents of the three boxes in the figure describe the three phases of your career flow (orientation, acceleration, and actualization), and above each box is given your designation within each (seeker, go-to person, and guru). The three forces influencing your flow within and between each phase (time, expertise, and contentment) are likewise described in each box. Your evolution is shown by the lines connecting the boxes, as you "progress" to the next phase or "recycle," "rebuild," and so on and then begin again. The flow never stops until you stop working.

We'll be looking at the three phases of this model below in detail. For now, it suffices to observe that reasonable estimates suggest that—before retiring—up to 20 percent of your overall career time will be spent in and out of the orientation phase, up to 60 percent in acceleration, and up to 20 percent in actualization (author's calculations). At any given moment, it's your call where you think your career is, and the rest of this chapter seeks to provide you with the perspective of this career flow model to enable you to make these calls and act with your contentment as you decide what to do next.

Your Senses Tell You When to Move to the Next Phase or Recycle

Your incremental career flow or choices involve your evolution and development within each position you take as you move to the next phase of the career flow model, and the changes that occur between positions, employers, and careers. Your flow occurs one position at a time, and the progression from phase to phase is not announced or celebrated. You simply sense that it is happening based on clues gathered from around you. For example, if your boss has been unusually solicitous about your accomplishments recently, it may be time to let her know that you'd be willing to take your turn presenting the monthly "Lessons I've Learned" meeting—you've become a guru!

As you apply yourself to your job, your senses will also suggest when it's time to move from one career flow phase to the next; drop out of a phase and recycle; or start over with another position, employer, or career. At the orientation phase, you sense right away by your creative confusion that you're the seeker who needs to get started, explore options, and adjust to your new work environment. Then you can rely on your senses to let you know when you've developed enough expertise to get antsy just performing your duties and need to move on to the acceleration phase, where you settle in, get down to business, and become the go-to person. And finally, you'll sense when you've mastered your job and reached the actualization phase, where you become the guru who has done it all and can share it with others.

Even without any celebrations by your co-workers or employer, you can still appreciate it when others acknowledge your progress to the next phase, because this confirms and demonstrates that your career senses are working and that your career is evolving in the direction you want it to go. Thus, when your co-workers begin to drop into your office all the time for pointers, it's safe to assume that you've reached the acceleration phase and possibly the actualization phase.

In any phase, you won't want to stagnate, be held back, or be blocked, because such lags would keep you from fulfilling your goals and challenge your contentment. However, the actual time spent at each phase of the career flow model varies from person to person and is determined by how long it takes you to become integrated in your new position and to develop and master your expertise, as well as by whether or not you're able to recognize your contentment.

Problems arise when your sense of where you are in your career flow, or where you want to be, doesn't match your employer's perceptions. They can also crop up when you attempt to function below or beyond the phase that's most appropriate to your level of expertise. Depending on the situation, you may stagnate or get ahead of yourself, and somewhere in between is where you'll recognize your contentment.

Your senses will also tell you when it's time to recycle back to the orientation phase by making a change of positions, employers, or careers, and you can do this starting from either of the other two phases. You'll sense it's time for something to happen—when you're not getting what you want, are desiring more, think you can get it elsewhere, or no longer have a sense of the contentment you seek. If you don't heed your senses or answer these callings, you may lose opportunities or tolerate less-than-desirable career situations. Answering the wrong calling can also lead you to take the wrong job and more regrets. You'll have to make the call, and you'll be able to do this by once again relying on your senses.

Recycling also occurs as the result of unplanned promotions or forced job changes due to job loss or termination. In either situation, recycling enables you to manage your flow by exploring new opportunities, building upon and leveraging what you've already learned, and actively pursuing the contentment you seek somewhere else besides your day job. Recycling is a tool—when you know how to use it.

By now it should be obvious that your career and choices *really* depend on your senses. They are calibrated in keeping with your discernments or what you believe is good timing for you, your level of expertise, and what you think will make your contentment possible. Because you arrived on Earth without a user's manual, it's a good idea throughout your entire career to keep your senses keen with the help of trusted friends, mentors, and advisers. And you'll find that the most helpful people are usually at the same overall career flow phase as you, or the next higher one.

Maximizing Your Career Senses

Your *career senses* are the mature version of the senses you developed while growing up. You know, the senses that helped you in a wide variety of crucial situations:

- to stay out of trouble
- to pick your friends
- to identify the bullies
- to know right from wrong
- to decide what's best for you
- to know when to get things done and to what level of quality
- to keep on track and maintain pace and direction
- to stay ahead of the game.

In some ways, your abilities to do these things are products of intuition as well as your senses—although you use your eyes and ears and other physical senses to discern them, you also use that deepening sixth, intuitive sense that undergirds all your other senses and really is the fruit of all your experiences.

Let's assume you've done a good job developing your six senses for these kinds of life situations. Now you instinctively know that what has worked in one situation may not work in another, so you'll be constantly recalibrating your career senses whenever your situation changes. Thus, in a tight situation, you'll seek to understand the rules and spot the "wiggle room," in the event you might need it. You'll identify the authority figures and learn quickly what they like and don't like, so you can walk the straight and narrow. You'll size up the competition and determine your corresponding strengths and weaknesses—and theirs. And you'll look for the people you can and cannot trust and identify the opportunities where you can make a difference.

All this can happen within minutes, hours, or days, depending on how keen your career senses are, and then you'll test and refine them before fully trusting them—and the funny thing is, you may not even realize you're doing this. When they're working, your career senses will alert you when something is about to happen; when it's time for you to make a move, duck, or dodge; and when something is or isn't best for you. You'll sense that something is lost or missing; that you're not getting what you want; that there might be something better elsewhere; or that it's simply time for a break, change of pace, or new scenery.

However, before acting on your career senses, you'll once again test them by looking for the clues that confirm whether you're right or wrong. Even then, you'll admit that these senses are not always perfect—but they're usually all you've got. Because you rely so much on your senses, and you can't afford to have them fail, you care for them by taking vacations and getting away from your routines so they can rest, recharge, and recalibrate based on what you believe is currently and, in the long run, most important for you, your career, and your contentment.

As always, the biggest risk to your career senses is whether they are based on your intentions or those of your nonconscious mental guardian. This is important because the primary concern of your nonconscious guardian is not your career or contentment but holding you back and keeping you safe in your comfort zone. It's your life and career, and only you'll know for sure whether your senses are working for you or against you. Let's look at a story from my Recruiter's Notebook on listening to those hunches that are really powerful messages from your senses.

RECRUITER'S NOTEBOOK

I Have a Hunch: Wise Pointers from Ken

Have you ever had a boss who genuinely cared about you and was courageous enough to tell you what you needed to know? I've had two, and fortunately, one of them appeared very early during my career. His name was Ken, and his education was in clinical psychology. One day, he said to me, "You have good hunches, but I've noticed that you don't always act on them. You need to develop the habit of listening to your hunches."

I Have a Hunch: Wise Pointers from Ken (continued)

No one had told me anything like this before. I thought he was probably smoking something illegal during breaks. He always moved slowly and was very contemplative and considerate. I was in my late twenties, and life could not move fast enough. Already, I was thinking how could I sidestep him and move up the ladder. And then a funny thing happened. I heard a clear voice in my head telling me to slow down and pay attention. For the next two days, I thought deeply about what Ken had said to me, and then I went back to him for a more detailed explanation.

He said I had gotten to where I am not by accident but because it was something I wanted and felt compelled to do. He was right. I was on a mission to learn as much as I could about employment and selection. He told me those same hunches that had gotten me here were still active and could be relied on to guide me and keep me out of trouble. As my experience deepened, those hunches would come more frequently. Here's what he said:

"Hunches are the same as intuition—an inner wisdom that considers the past, present, and probable future and may be experienced as a gut feeling, a flash of insight, a picture or memory, a dream, an idea, or a burst of energy"—or a voice like I'd experienced. "When you learn to capture and dissect your hunches," he said, "you can almost play it out in your mind like a movie to visualize how a particular situation might evolve." In either case, he said, "when your hunches are combined with common sense and knowledge from practical experience, *they can help to foster emotional well-being, keep you connected to what you think is most important, and can also provide insight when you need to make a decision.* However, none of this can happen unless you develop the habit of paying attention to your hunches."

And then he gave me five practical suggestions:

First, reduce noise. You can't hope to think clearly or pick up on your hunches if you're plagued by noise and distractions due to phones, pagers, calendars, computers, meetings, and so on. Even your own self-talk is capable of drowning out any thoughts you'd like to have. Make time during each day to hold a private meeting with yourself and where you do the listening. Just a few minutes is enough to "switch off" and listen to your hunches. Breathe slowly and try to center yourself, and when you feel sufficiently relaxed, ask yourself a question about any important issues on your mind: "Should I stay in this job, or do I apply for the promotion?" If you're not used to listening to yourself, you may not get an answer. Keep practicing.

Second, increase trust. As you begin to develop your listening expertise, you must also learn to trust your own advice. Keep in mind the fact that you don't just act on your hunches, you reason with them in relation to your common sense and practical experience. Use your intuition as a resource, and always be mindful of any counterintuitive effects created by your nonconscious guardian that has a tendency to hold you back and keep you in your comfort zone.

Third, feel energized. Each of us represents a form of energy. We create and release energy through our thinking and emotions, and we also capture and apply it in the same way. When you're listening to your hunches, you're looking for emotions that lift you up and cheer you on, including joy, optimism, excitement, enthusiasm, and gratitude. Your hunches can also serve to warn you—if they create a less-than-favorable mood or tend to sap your strength, it may be a warning to avoid certain people or situations that may be harmful to you or your career.

Fourth, make connections. As you continue to practice with your hunches, you may be surprised at just how insightful and accurate they are. You won't know unless you track them, and by that I mean remember that you had the hunch and then make the connection to what happened. The more you recognize this, the more efficient and reliable your hunches will actually become. Even the hunches that prove wrong are beneficial, because they help you to improve their effectiveness.

Fifth, develop the right mindset. Intuition is a good thing, but your capacity for hunches can be impaired by thoughts and feelings that are pessimistic to begin with. Pessimistic attitudes are more likely to produce pessimistic hunches, whereas optimistic attitudes offer a far better chance not only for better hunches but also better outcomes—regardless of your hunches. Keep your mindset positively oriented and free of any debilitating thoughts and feelings. Replace them with positive affirmations that help you to view your life and circumstances more positively.

We all have hunches, but few of us actually develop this ability and use it intentionally. My hat's off to Ken for introducing me to this important topic. Had I not developed this ability, I could have easily missed out on a wealth of free advice and ended up someplace other than where I wanted to be.

The Two Dimensions of Career Flow

Beyond the importance of using finely honed senses, the career flow model emphasizes that your career doesn't stop flowing until you decide to stop or run out of time. It recycles constantly, which means that your career is always in a state of transition—not just when you're unemployed. Unemployment implies reemployment at some point, which means you're in the orientation phase of career flow. In the meantime, your overall career will be still very much progressing, and because of the potential benefits of recycling, when you're unemployed you'll sometimes be in a better position to guide your career than when employed. It's all a matter of perspective, but if you think your career is not transitioning, it's because you're unaware of the phases, not in tune with your senses, or both. Your senses will confirm that your career is always in motion due to forces seen and unseen.

To illustrate the two dimensions of career flow, and how your senses come into play, let's say you're 10 years into your career and already in your third position. Your senses are telling you that you've chosen the right employer and career field, and with only 10 down and 35 years to go, your *overall* career is probably in the *acceleration* phase, and you think that's good and on target with your contentment.

However, your senses are also telling you the timing is right for another move. Your *current* position is going well, and your expertise has evolved to the *actualization* phase, but there's still something missing. You realize that to accelerate your career, you need more well-rounded experience, include supervisory training. You know you can't get it where you are, so you suspect it's time to recycle a fourth time to get it, and you believe doing so would give your career a greater sense of contentment.

You now have to decide whether to do this recycling and get a different job elsewhere, and if so, where to go and when. Do your senses suggest staying with the same employer or moving to another? Are your senses on target in assuming you're in the right career field, or is it time to explore another before you become "typecast" in one discipline or field? Are you sure you're not running from something, or are you running toward a calling? To help show how to answer questions like these, let's look at the career flow model in more detail.

The Career Flow Model

When it comes to your career, you and your senses are the judge and jury. Of course, your employer has an opinion, and you may need their cooperation. But in the end, it's your life and career. You control the flow, and you're accountable for what you seek and your results. Chapter 9 discusses how to control your flow in more detail. The rest of this chapter gives more insights into each of the three phases of career flow—again, orientation, acceleration, and actualization—to help you boost the power of your career senses.

The Orientation Phase

You're in the orientation phase of career flow if you're at the beginning of your career, in transition between employers, or embarking on a restart of some sort (position, career, employer, and so on). This phase is the launching point for each and every new or different position you'll occupy throughout your career. It's the foundation that you'll build on and refer back to when you need to rethink, revise, or revitalize your career plans. And you'll need to do these things again and again, which explains why you'll never forget your first career position and every first position with a new employer. First impressions always last the longest—you're fresh, perhaps confused, and your career senses are charged with adrenaline.

This is the "find and have" phase associated with your contentment. The sense associated with this phase is that a change is imminent or in progress. You feel a calling to something new or different, and there's often a sense of urgency that suggests it can't happen soon enough. It's up to you to clarify your desires and do what it takes. And when any fears you may have are exceeded by what you believe is the potential to recognize you contentment, you'll make it happen. Otherwise, your senses will tell you it really wasn't meant to be. It should be a very exciting time, and if it isn't, that should tell your senses something.

Once you're in the orientation phase, it serves as a testing ground to confirm your senses and whether you've made the right decision. Are you as good as you thought you were, and is the employer as good as you want them to be? Considerable time is usually spent during the first two months in a new job questioning whether you're on the right track to fulfill your plan, meet your goals, and realize your contentment. This happens regardless of whether you're a beginner or veteran. At the same time, you're trying to learn new things, think differently, adapt, and make adjustments. As you do, your doubts and uncertainties should be fading and are likely to disappear by the six-month mark. Then you'll be preoccupied with dreaming, clarifying, and planning what you hope to achieve in that position and in the future, with and even without your current employer.

If, after six months or so in this phase, your doubts and uncertainties fail to disappear, your senses will be trying to decide whether this position and employer will enable you to recognize your contentment. Your answer is important, because it establishes a belief about your situation that you'll use when deciding from this point forward whether your experience with this position and employer will be good or bad. By intentionally monitoring and controlling your beliefs, you can positively influence not only your senses but also your experiences during this phase—and whether and how soon you should move to the next phase and the one after that. You're responsible for your own contentment, and this is where it begins.

This is not to suggest that you try to make an obviously bad situation good. You could, but, as was pointed out in chapters 6 and 7, genuine contentment is based on beliefs that are responsible and realistic. If your senses suggest that your decision to take this position was a bad one or that the employer has engaged in any inflations or misrepresentations about the opportunity, and you have no doubts about this matter, then pay close attention to your senses and what they suggest you do. Just be sure that your beliefs and senses are positive to support your intentions in this position and with your employer and are not the result of your mental guardian's nonconscious intentions to hold you back or keep you safe in your comfort zone. Let's look at another story from my notebook on learning to trust your career senses.

RECRUITER'S NOTEBOOK

Disaster or Challenging Opportunity? Learning to Trust What Your Senses Tell You

Leslie was only four months into her job with a new employer, and already she was feeling at home and no longer like the new kid on the block. She had accepted this position in the good faith that it was everything she thought it would be, and it almost was. The people were great, the pay and benefits were better than anything she'd experienced before, and, most important, she felt she was valued for her gifts and was being enabled to use them to make a difference.

And use them she did. Leslie was beginning to sense that she was a bit overloaded for someone who hadn't had this experience before. For some reason, the second position that was open when she interviewed for her job had still not been filled. She had even recommended one of her former co-workers for the opportunity, but apparently things didn't work out, and she never followed up to find out why. Consequently, she was rapidly becoming the go-to person for not one but two positions.

At first, this was not an issue, because Leslie's adrenaline as she started her position was pumping and it was her intention to demonstrate her worthiness. She did, and now her senses were advising her that she was beginning to demonstrate her willingness to accept abuse. Averaging 10 to 12 hours a day would be difficult to maintain, and unless that second position was filled, this would evolve to become one of the worst mistakes she'd made thus far in her career. Her supervisor explained that their budgets were temporarily frozen and the decision had been made to suspend some of the hiring.

Because things were also falling through the cracks in areas of the firm other than Leslie's, the decision was made to not fill the second opening in her department, and no one thought to inform her of this. It was unknown how long the situation would last, but she was told by her manager that "you're doing a fantastic job and I want you to keep up the good work." There it was. Leslie was now in a situation where her superhuman gifts and abilities could be applied, recognized, and leveraged in a desperate situation to accelerate her career to new heights.

However, the last thing Leslie wanted to do was kill herself for an employer who didn't care enough about her to let her know the position she was counting on

Disaster or Challenging Opportunity? Learning to Trust What Your Senses Tell You (continued)

being filled would instead be dumped on her without any adjustment in pay. She tried, but after another month without any relief in sight, her senses were screaming that she was being abused and should cut her losses and run.

Leslie's biggest challenge now was how to explain leaving an employer after only five months. Her job search files were still relatively fresh, so it was just a matter of rediscovering the trails that had grown a bit cool and warming them up. She estimated she could easily have another job in her sights within two months if she applied herself, and this meant she would focus only on doing just her basic job duties—the rest would have to slide. She was on her way out and needed those hours to accomplish other things. She stuck to this plan while remaining her positive and professional self, and she was also much more optimistic because her job search was looking good.

Within only three weeks, and thanks to Leslie sticking to her plan, her employer discovered they didn't have enough people to go to and informed her that the second position would now be filled, and it would be her responsibility to fill it because her manager had just announced his decision to leave the company. Leslie was being offered her manager's position within six months after she had started and was already contemplating leaving herself. Her first question was, "Do I have authorization to fill my old position as well?"

The answer was yes, and Leslie complied with her senses by telling her employer that she would talk with her husband and think about it overnight. She also sensed it would be a good idea to seek out and speak with her former manager to get the lowdown on what was really going on. She did, and her senses pleaded with her to decline the opportunity. But rather than comply with her senses this time, she went back to her employer the next day and negotiated what she felt were acceptable expectations for members of her department. She had nothing to lose and everything to gain. She sensed the problems were not so much due to her employer as to her manager who had left, and her employer had pretty much confirmed this.

Leslie realized, of course, that she was in a very challenging situation. Although she initially sensed a disaster, she felt up to the challenges because she also sensed the potential for contentment in this situation, and her adrenaline had already started to pump again.

There are five major scenarios you're likely to encounter during the orientation phase; the beliefs you hold about each and the choices you make among them will affect your potential for progressing to the next phase of your career flow, or perhaps leaving to try something else:

1. This position was meant to be, and I confirm the assessments I made earlier regarding the people, place, particulars, and my own personal preferences related to them (see chapter 5). Otherwise, this is what I need for the time being, and I am willing to make concessions.

2. I am unaware of any inflations or projections related to this situation that were caused by me or by the employer (see chapter 3). It is a genuine fit, and there is no possibility that I may be fooling myself into doing something that is not good for my career or for me.

3. My abilities and potential related to this situation are good, and I thus have a heightened sense of awareness regarding my gifts, their relevance to this opportunity, and my ability to use them to fulfill my purpose, make a contribution, and ultimately recognize my contentment.

4. I can envision my success or needs being fulfilled within this position and how this experience is likely to benefit me in the future by furthering my development, providing new skills and abilities, bolstering my self-confidence, and even enhancing my marketability for future opportunities.

5. This is time well spent, and once I've made the adjustment, I can imagine progressing fairly quickly to become the go-to person for my chosen area of expertise. I want this because this is the right time and place for me.

The choices you make in dealing with these five scenarios—and others—will be influenced by whether your senses confirm that your potential for contentment is feasible within a period of time that you determine is reasonable. And if you choose the fifth scenario, you'll be moving toward the acceleration phase.

The Acceleration Phase

You're in the acceleration phase of career flow because you've become acclimated to your new position and sense that it's time to be recognized as more than just the new person. Rather than just passing through, you've made the commitment to stay for the time being, and now it's time to build, grow, and make a contribution. This phase is the central point from which you can make things happen in your job by mastering your craft and advancing or maintaining your level of competence, expertise, and contributions. You've evolved to become the go-to person for one or more aspects of your job, and it feels good in relation to your contentment.

This is the "have and keep it" phase associated with your contentment. The sense associated with this phase is that you're on the right track to realizing your goals but that time is passing fast or there's never enough of it. That's because you're into the flow. You've settled in and gotten down to business, and there's a lot more to learn. If you play your cards right, you believe there exists a chance to grow, succeed, and realize a return on your investments—that is, all your earlier related experiences and hard work that got you to this point. You've earned the right to be here, and now you have to keep it.

Once in the acceleration phase, you encounter a different sort of testing ground. The honeymoon is over, and it's time to confirm whether you have what it takes to succeed by mastering your job and all the relationships that come along with it. How long this may take poses yet another test related to your endurance. You're trained to do a job, and the employer probably won't be too anxious to lose their go-to person to another position or employer anytime soon. They want a return on their investment just as much as you do on yours. They want to know whether you'll stay and deliver through good times and bad; and, if so, they want you around long enough to benefit from having to correct some of your own mistakes.

This acceleration phase may last years, and to make the best use of this time, you'll want to do your job but also involve yourself in refining your career plans and developing the tactics and contingencies that will later help to catapult you in the direction you want your career to go.

This includes identifying and removing any barriers, building relationships and alliances, and getting the necessary training and experiences that will ensure your ongoing competitive advantage for opportunities in your current firm or elsewhere.

As your career evolves through this phase, your senses will realize soon enough that this phase has the potential to last the longest compared with any other phase—and it should. Otherwise, you've chosen a job that may be insufficiently challenging. If not, your senses have been hard at work trying to decide whether it's best for your career to recycle or stay and progress to the next phase and become a guru. The forces at play are once again related to time, expertise, and contentment, but you're unlikely to find contentment if you believe you're wasting time by staying and not learning anything new.

However, when considering your future from within this phase, you now have to weigh the risks associated with forfeiting the equity you've built within a known situation, the time and challenges involved in starting over elsewhere, the possibility of being viewed as a job hopper, and, of course, the "golden handcuffs" or loss of any financial incentives due to leaving. These are tough issues with which your senses must grapple, and it doesn't make things any easier when at the same time you're being recruited for positions elsewhere—and why not, because you're one of the go-to people for your employer. That's who recruiters are looking for.

What becomes obvious during the acceleration phase is that the longer you stay in a position, the higher are the stakes associated with leaving. Do you stick it out or cut your losses and run? This is usually a non-issue if your senses suggest it's worth your while to stay. However, if your senses have suggested that you leave but you've managed to talk yourself out of it, make sure that this is your best-considered decision and not just the work of your nonconscious guardian attempting to hold you back.

Anytime your situation gets to this point, there's at least a 50/50 chance that your employer feels it might be a good idea if you did leave. They may not tell you this, however, hoping that you'll just go.

This is usually a hard fact for most people to accept at any level. But if this is true, what you think is your comfort zone could become a battle zone. Give your senses the benefit of a second thought in situations like this. You'll be glad you did.

Proactive or involuntary recycling out of acceleration or any other phase of the career flow model can be frightening but also liberating, when the situation warrants it. Recycling has enabled the salvation and rejuvenation of many stalled or troubled careers, because it creates the opportunity to start over, forgive and forget, answer your callings, follow your passions, add to your portfolio of experiences, and accelerate not laterally to guru status but outward in new directions. This also applies to the recycling that occurs when returning from sabbaticals or working as an entrepreneur or stay-at-home spouse. Any form of recycling is best accomplished with an opportunity mindset, because—while your incremental flow is temporarily disrupted—your overall flow is still progressing and senses the opportunities afforded by a change on the horizon. So should you.

However, if you're faced with the possibility of losing what you have and your career senses suggest that you stay and turn things around, this acceleration phase could involve learning more about yourself and human nature than you ever thought possible. As such, your objective in this or any type of "probationary" situation should be to come out of it wiser and stronger than before, whether or not you keep the job. Of course, you want the job, and as odd as this may sound, you're usually better off in this situation detaching yourself from wanting or needing it and instead developing a greater sense of self-confidence and self-reliance to get things done. Thus, when the test is over, and regardless of the employer's decision, you come out of it more resilient and stronger than before, and still in control of your own career flow because it will continue, with or without the existing employer.

In other words, the bigger picture here far exceeds your imagined need or dependence on any one employer. During the acceleration phase, it's easy to lose sight of this fact, because your identity can become so intertwined with your employer's that it's hard to imagine yourself somewhere else. But regardless of this potential for mistaken identity, you'll find that your contentment remains aligned with you and your efforts to do what you believe is right—as long as you choose to recognize it and leverage its beneficial effects so that you can endure. (See an illustrative story from my notebook.)

RECRUITER'S NOTEBOOK

The Seven-Year Itch

That point of restlessness when you're simultaneously tired of what you have but can't imagine being without it is referred to as the "seven-year itch." It's real, and it doesn't pertain exclusively to your spousal relations. It occurred for James right before his seven-year mark with his firm, and it was related to his employer. He had been with this same employer for just over six years and was two years into his fourth position. On the surface, everything seemed to be going OK, but he couldn't put his finger on what was bothering him. His performance appraisals were positive, and he was aware of being on the succession plans for bigger and better opportunities. He had good relations within his team, boss, senior management, and the departments with which he interacted. He had more than enough to keep himself busy, and he could also envision good things for himself. Things were going quite well at home, so it seemed there should be no reason to be feeling so blue. He was unhappy and didn't know why. He'd worked for two previous employers, and nothing like this had ever occurred.

During lunch one day, one of James's close colleagues decided to inquire whether everything was OK or if there were problems at home. He pointed out that it seemed as if James was not himself and been uptight and irritable for almost a month, and people were talking about it. He recounted three instances where others had observed the same thing, and it was suspected in the department that James was having marriage problems or there might be an issue with one of his children or his health. James indicated that it was nothing at all like that but that something was wrong and he wasn't sure what it was.

Now James was even more worried because his moods had become an issue among the people he worked with, and this meant his boss had to be aware that something was wrong. He decided to speak with his former boss, whom he trusted and with whom he was developing a mentoring

The Seven-Year Itch (continued)

relationship. The conversation got right to the point because his former boss had been noticing the same curious behaviors of irritability, short temper, and low tolerance for routine problems. James confided that he was toying with the possibility of leaving, even though he had no place to go and his job really wasn't creating problems.

After they had talked for about 20 minutes, it occurred to James's former boss to ask, "So how long have you been working here now, James?" Almost as soon as James indicated he was coming up on seven years, his former boss started to chuckle and suggested, "It's the seven-year itch." James recalled the movie by that name in which Marilyn Monroe's skirt blew upward over the street grate. Other than this, he admitted knowing nothing about it. That evening, he talked at length with his wife about this because she had also noticed he wasn't happy. They briefly researched the topic, and the results were mixed but tended to confirm that a period of restlessness does occur within the seventh year and is heightened when there are younger children in the home.

James began to piece things together and realized this was the first time he'd spent more than five years in any one place. Up until this point in his life, everything had been marked by periods of fewer than four years—high school, college, the military, graduate school, three years with his first employer, four years with his second employer, five years being married, two children beneath the age of five. But now, for the first time in his life, he was going on more than four years—seven years!—with his employer.

Could it be? It was inconclusive, but right then and there, James and his wife committed to proactively working to prevent any seven-year-itch problems with their marriage. They kept their research and referred to it several times, and it influenced their taking dance classes and the decision to purchase a pop-up camper. As for James, his problems at work disappeared within two weeks after talking with his former boss.

No matter how long the acceleration phase lasts, there's much to do and learn. This is true even if you're viewing this phase as your last before recycling. Here are seven major scenarios you're likely to encounter during the acceleration phase; once again, the beliefs you hold about each and the choices you make among them are guaranteed to influence your senses and ultimately your choices in the future:

1. I am maximizing the use of my time by mastering my craft and developing my resourcefulness and creativity, and I am therefore recognized as one of the reliable go-to people in my chosen area of expertise.

2. I am becoming the person I want to be. I'm hitting my stride, enhancing my professional image, increasing my earning power, and conquering any fears, while simultaneously increasing my resiliency, adaptability, acceptance, and ability to endure.

3. I am developing practical career management skills, taking on increased responsibilities, developing relationships and alliances, improving my competitive advantage, and overcoming resistances and roadblocks.

4. I am motivated, enthusiastic, and persistent and at the same time I am conscious that challenges are inevitable. I am therefore maintaining my work and life balance by using my organization, prioritization, and self-discipline skills.

5. I can identify with this position and employer but at the same time I have not lost sight of my own identity, the fact that my career flows without a dependence on any one employer, or my integrity in doing what I sense is best for my employer, me, and my career.

6. I appreciate the importance of building and maintaining equity with one employer and the risks and rewards associated with giving it up to start over with another. What matters most is having the sense to decide, the courage to act, and the contentment for having done either.

7. I understand that while the potential exists in any employment situation that a job could be lost, my overall career is still very much progressing and within my control to rejuvenate by recycling in the directions I choose.

The Actualization Phase

You're in the actualization phase of career flow because you've mastered all the elements of your position, you've fulfilled the demands and expectations of your employer, and you've conquered the challenges and distractions associated with making it to an interim plateau or pinnacle without falling off. You've arrived and are now a guru of sorts in your area of responsibility, and although it feels good and reinforces your contentment, you're already wondering "What's next?" That's because your senses may be telling you there are miles to go before you sleep and that it doesn't have to end here.

This is the "have and share it" phase associated with your contentment. The sense associated with this phase is that you've made it or you've done it all in relation to your position, and you're grateful. You've acknowledged this by looking for ways to share what you've learned, and by reciprocating or giving back to others who can benefit from your knowledge and experience. However, your senses are also suggesting that you'll have to start thinking soon about how long being a guru should last and how to leverage this into something bigger and better—or, otherwise, how to endure until something else comes along.

Once in the actualization phase, you'll encounter yet another sort of testing ground. Because your progression to this phase was not the subject of a formal announcement, this makes your status as a guru self-proclaimed and therefore vulnerable to challenges from other gurus and even aspiring gurus or go-to people. This is the phase where challenges to your credibility are likely, and you'll have to decide which if any of these challenges are worth confronting. Some will be unavoidable because you feel it's necessary to protect your legacy and good works.

Another test within this phase is the ongoing discovery that the tactics and resources you once relied on are probably changing, leaving the wisdom you have to offer as a guru in the dust. Defending the way things used to be only draws attention to the fact you're an outdated guru. To remain a guru in good standing, you've to get up to speed and stay there—or recycle. Similarly, it's in this phase that you deal more frequently with the expression "What have you done for me lately?"

Your previous accomplishments are yesterday's news, particularly when go-to people are doing all they can to become gurus just like you. Thus, in this phase you begin to sense there's unfinished business ahead and that time is running out or pressing you to find another pinnacle.

Progressing beyond the actualization phase can become interesting and creative, largely because you eventually reach a point where it becomes obvious that something has to be done either to keep you engaged or onboard with the company. Some gurus are transformed into super-gurus by being promoted in place. This is accomplished by adding new responsibilities to a person's position, including supervisory responsibilities, and this can occur again and again.

Another solution involves a lateral move to a similar position where, due to special privileges, the benefits of being a guru don't have to be forfeited and yet you're in a position where you'll have the opportunity to continue learning new things. Beyond this point, and depending on the tolerances and intentions of the guru, the only other options are to do nothing or recycle to a uniquely different position, department, or employer. A concern for those in the actualization phase is their unfamiliarity with the employment process and current job market. It's probably been a while since they've updated their résumé or had to look for work.

If you choose to do so, recycling from the actualization phase is best initiated with the mindset that you have nothing to lose and everything to gain. However, this is easier said than done. Your senses keep reminding you that a "bird in the hand is worth two in the bush." There's no guarantee that your next move will be successful. That's why each time you recycle externally, the same risks and anxieties you felt at the very start of your career come rushing back to greet you, including: "How do I make a living, find what I want, know where to look?" "Am I doing what I'm supposed to be doing, how long will it take to get back on top, and will I be OK?" These concerns can humble even the greatest gurus—and sometimes that's exactly why it's beneficial to consider the possibility of recycling, if not actually going through the process. Here's an example from my notebook of how recycling and actualization work.

RECRUITER'S NOTEBOOK

Sometimes You Have to Get Fired to Recycle and Actualize

Janice had advanced to vice president of marketing at a large cosmetics firm in New York City. Her employer was an industry leader that sold products worldwide, and this promotion represented to her a major pinnacle within her career. She had achieved her goal. Her employer was well respected for its marketing, and it consistently had the best advertising. Each time one of its products made a splash, the credit went directly to marketing. But rather than bask in the glory related to something she had worked on months before, Janice was already working on next year's successes. She was a workaholic, her life revolved around making things happen, and she was good at it—with the exception on one very important thing.

During the three years Janice had been in her new position, she'd stayed as forward focused on the business as the day she accepted the promotion. Beyond this, she hadn't made it a priority to establish links with peers or other companies within her industry, or among consultants, advertising agencies, and vendors. She was always working behind the scenes, and even within her company she hadn't seen fit to reciprocate to the people who'd helped her climb the ladder. It wasn't that she was rude so much as she was always too busy. She was a marketing genius, and she was convinced her only job was to drive marketing to generate sales. On this dimension, she'd done a good job. But recently, market share had begun to slip. Janice was on top of it as usual, but she hadn't thought to involve anyone else.

Janice had become an enigma to the people with whom she worked. Unless you were on her agenda, your calls and emails seemed to disappear into a black hole and were never returned. This happened often enough that people began to interact more frequently with her staff, and even they had stopped creating excuses for Janice. In fact, they were beginning to model some of her reclusive characteristics. Marketing was slowly becoming inapproachable, and the competition was encroaching more aggressively on its share of the market. It seemed that Janice was being sucked deeper and deeper into the black hole she'd created, and she was clearly in the dark regarding what was about to happen.

Because of Janice's earlier track record and his favorable relationship with her, the CEO decided to give her the benefit of the doubt rather than simply let her go. He engaged the services of consulting firm to explore options to improve efficiencies in distribution, sales, and marketing. The black hole was identified as an impediment to the direction where the company was now headed. Despite Janice's unquestionably hard work ethic, expertise as a marketing guru, and all her previous contributions, the company believed greater synergies linked with marketing were required, and the current team seemed incapable of this. Janice was let go, along with three of those who reported directly to her.

Six months later, Janice's replacement had already made significant inroads in reestablishing trade relations, repositioning several of the firm's existing product categories, and laying the groundwork for the introduction of multiple new brands in cooperation with sales and distribution. It was as if the dam had been opened and creativity allowed to flow full force. The company was intent on reclaiming what had been lost. As for Janice, she was as pleased as everyone else, because her newly formed consulting firm had been hired to execute several of the marketing plans developed by the new team.

Not until she left did Janice realize how she'd dropped the ball on over 50 percent of her overall responsibilities. She'd neglected the importance of giving back or reciprocating, building alliances, and identifying and leveraging new innovations that would've preserved or extended her employer's share of the market. Once apart from all the noise and confusion, she had time to get reacquainted with who she was and what she wanted. She reasoned that all her earlier successes had been derived from her ability to plan and execute, and she'd continued to favor this dimension in lieu of anything else. She'd stopped growing. She realized that once she achieved the vice presidential level, it was as if she had no more mountains to climb other than to start her own business.

However, she was too busy to start a business while serving as vice president, and doing so seemed impractical at the time, so she was dragging her feet, not realizing that the rest of her body was dragging as well. Without realizing it, Janet had resigned on the job and all she needed was a nudge to recycle. Fortunately for her, the CEO proposed to Janice that she consider continuing her relationship with the company as a consultant. Had it not been for her termination, Janice might have missed the next and perhaps most exciting phase of her career.

Here are seven major scenarios that you'll face during the actualization phase; once again, the beliefs you hold about each and the choices you make among them will influence your senses as you progress into your future:

1. I can acknowledge having reached one of the top plateaus within my position, and also the obligation to reciprocate or assist others to do the same by sharing what I've learned.

2. I embrace the challenges and obligations associated with remaining proficient within my chosen career field, including always being open and flexible to the ongoing discovery and acceptance of new ideas and solutions.

3. I understand that reaching a plateau within any position raises the possibility of someday having to consider new challenges and opportunities within the same position, in a new position, or with a different employer.

4. I recognize the ongoing value and importance to my career of maintaining an up-to-date résumé, knowledge of the employment marketplace, and strategies for improving and leveraging my marketability.

5. I understand the dynamics associated with each phase of career flow and the forces of time, developing expertise, and the pursuit of contentment as influencing the progression and recycling between each phase.

6. I accept responsibility for ensuring that my career senses are consistently reliable and unencumbered by faulty beliefs that could hold me back or prevent me from having an enjoyable career or the career I choose.

7. I am responsible for sensing my own contentment and for leveraging its beneficial effects throughout my career to enable me to endure, and my contentment is recognizable by my ability to pause and reason to find the acceptable middle ground in any situation.

Summing Up the Career Flow Model

The career flow model reminds you that if something doesn't feel right, you'll be able to find the explanation by discerning where you are in the flow and then examining three basic forces:

- *Time*: Are you moving too fast, too slow, or not at all?
- *Expertise*: Are you no longer learning what you need or want to learn, or are you in a rut, learning the same old things, and feeling bored?
- *Contentment*: Are you doing what you love and loving what you do, or are you being called to something more meaningful elsewhere?

The answers to these questions may not be immediately obvious, but if you're paying close attention to your senses—which ultimately are telling you the direction of the energy that's propelling your career flow—then you'll soon know whether you're about to progress, recycle, or do nothing, in keeping with the career flow model. Most important, by using this model, you'll be able to know what to expect either way. And thus you'll have no excuse for not planning the strategy that will enable you to have and enjoy the career you desire. Your final decision should reveal your calling and purpose and may not have anything to do with those satisfactions provided by your employer.

What's Next

The next chapter will look at how you make the most of your career contentment once you've "arrived"—you have a full set of assets, and now the challenge is to maintain them and continue to make the most of them. We'll look at how to balance your application of your total assets and your power to use them.

9

Maximize Your Career Contentment by Controlling Your Career Flow

······················· **In this chapter, you'll learn** ·······················

- ◆ how to use all your assets to make the most of your life and career
- ◆ how to use your sovereign power to control your career flow
- ◆ how to balance the use of your total assets and sovereign power

elieve it or not, the simplest, most effective strategy for having the career you desire, on your terms, involves two simple but very challenging steps. First, clarify your intentions, get what it takes to make it happen, and then make an unwavering commitment to achieving it—as if you already have it. You can do this anytime, starting right now. The best examples that come to mind are individuals who believe unconditionally that what they want is possible, despite what anyone says—Noah building his ark, Joan of Arc, the Wright brothers, Henry Ford, Charles Lindbergh, Howard Hughes, and Mother Teresa, to name just a few. Closer to home, it's your friend who despite his meekness suddenly decides to quit his job to pursue a field of study that will qualify him for another career. He's on a mission, and without asking permission, he begins making progress as he pursues it, and he may even burn his bridges to ensure that there's no turning back.

The second step is to boldly relay your intentions to everyone who has any direct or indirect impact on your career, and then never stop reminding them of your desires and commitments—you might call it hypernetworking. Human resources professionals see this played out every day by the individuals who believe they're pursuing their calling. The serious ones appear single-minded—willing to stretch the boundaries of their comfort zone by reaching out to allies and links to allies not once but several times to let them know they're serious and will do what it takes. Everyone they contact becomes a participant, cheerleader, blocker, or observer on the stage of their life. "Help me or get out of the way" becomes their mantra, and the humility of defeat is a possibility they don't wish to consider.

After you've taken these two steps, and everybody realizes you're seriously committed, they usually won't bother you with things that don't conform to your plans and goals. In fact, when it appears you're getting off course from your plans, they'll ask "What're you thinking?" as if you're violating some master plan they're now a part of. They'll challenge and test your resolve, of course, but they'll also try to keep you on your course, encourage you, and cheer you on. When it's obvious you're this committed, most people who know you will want to see you win, because it helps them imagine they can, too. So why don't you do this? Why doesn't everybody take these two key steps? Let's look at a story from my Recruiter's Notebook about one man who did (see notebook on next page).

What Rudy did is a theoretically workable strategy, but most people aren't willing to make that same indomitable commitment. You're not as resolved, you could be held accountable for doing what you said, you don't want to fail, something better might come along, you think you don't have what it takes, there are too many variables beyond your control, you have a family to consider, you really didn't want to work

RECRUITER'S NOTEBOOK

Rudy's Story: Impossible Goal? Not on the Notre Dame Field!

Among the top five movies voted most likely to make you cry is *Rudy*, made in 1993 about the life of Daniel E. "Rudy" Ruettiger. Rudy's goal was to play football at Notre Dame, despite his small size and lack of athletic ability, and it was a question to begin with whether he could even get into Notre Dame. Rudy told everyone about his goal, and he never stopped reminding them until everyone he knew was cheering him on—despite their doubts and disbeliefs.

Rudy struggled and, amazingly, he managed to get accepted by Notre Dame. His next hurdle was to get a spot on the football team. Incredibly, he made it onto the practice team, but after two years of getting trampled by much bigger players, it appeared certain he'd never be allowed to play, let alone live to remember it. He was heartbroken that his goal might not be reached. But at the point when he was about to give up, people wouldn't allow him to, and a former player told him: "You're 5 foot nothin', 100 and nothin', and you have barely a speck of athletic ability. And you hung in there with the best college football players in the land for two years. And you're gonna walk outta here with a degree from the University of Notre Dame. In this life, you don't have to prove nothin' to nobody but yourself. Am I making myself clear?"

Rudy was once again inspired, he put himself back on course, and, at one point, fans began demanding that he be given the opportunity to at least go onto the field. Captain: "Rudy, are you ready for this, champ? Rudy: "I've been ready for this my whole life!" Captain: "Then you take us out on the field." Only because another player had been injured, Rudy was reluctantly placed into the final seconds of the final game of his final year, and he was so dwarfed by all the other players that it was comical—but not to the people who knew him. His playing experience lasted seconds, but he had achieved his goal, and everyone seemed just as excited as he was. It was clear that only because of the power of his will and commitment, and despite his lack of assets and all the doubts and disbeliefs of others, Rudy had achieved his goal.

that hard anyway, so forth and so on—and it's all coming from your good old mental guardian, the five-sixths nonconscious part of your brain that, despite your intentions, intends to hold you back and keep you safe in your comfort zone. Instead of energizing your beliefs, you reduce your desires, and then you push away from shore and allow the flow to take you. You influence what you can, flex where you should, hope for the best, and see what happens. This isn't exactly commanding, but it's not career roulette either, so you still feel in control.

The fact is—and this is true whether you take Rudy's approach or not—you still have to say "yes" to job offers, promotions, and lateral transfers. Always consider this as having 51 percent of the vote—and why not? It's your life and career! However, and just as a reminder, don't forget the two irrevocable parameters pertaining to career contentment discussed in earlier chapters: You are who you are but also who you're paid to be; and your employer's primary purpose is to make a profit, not please you. But even within these parameters, it's still very much within your area of ongoing responsibility to control your career flow.

The foundation for purposefully managing your career, and to have it on your terms as much as possible, is a balanced application of your total assets and your sovereign power to use them. The operative word here is "balanced," and we'll discuss what this means after first reviewing your assets, and the relevance of the term "sovereignty" to your career.

Using the Assets of Your Life and Career

Your assets are what you possess, develop, protect, and use to benefit your life and career. Your assets are both visible and hidden; there are really too many of them to mention, and all of them are useful for your career in some form or another. For example, just to see, hear, walk, talk, laugh, and love are assets for many people's careers. But what we're looking for here are the assets that distinguish you and your ability to have the career of your choice and control its flow. The principal categories of these distinguishing career assets include

- empowering, deeply held beliefs
- guiding purposes and dreams

- enabling unique gifts and abilities
- inspiring faith and imagination
- confirming professional and personal credentials
- sustaining contentment and resiliency.

These kinds of career assets are your tools, which you've developed through long, hard experience, proving that you know what you want and how to get it. In other words, the assets you've intentionally accumulated and on which you rely point to what you do or want to do; otherwise, why would you have them—except for the possibility that you might be working with the wrong tools? You own your assets, you have the power and authority to use and further develop them, and you can even acquire more of them as you see fit throughout the course of your career. So let's see what distinguishing assets you have to work with. We'll expand on the categories listed above, and you decide whether you have or need them.

Empowering Assets

The distinguishing assets that empower you are your beliefs and how you've conditioned them to support you. Your beliefs empower your intentions. Everything you want to do, whether you do it, and how well you do it are completely contingent on the beliefs you hold about yourself, your capabilities, your purpose here on Earth, the contributions you hope to make, and the accomplishments you envision.

How often—or have you ever—inventoried your beliefs about these things? Listing them or putting them on a spreadsheet can reveal where you're headed and whether or not you'll get there. If what you believe is not conditioned to empower you, then you'll know where to spend time energizing your beliefs. If you fail to do so, that guarantees you'll shrink your desires to match your weakened beliefs. What do you believe you can do? What do you believe you're supposed to do? Do you believe you can do it? What distinguishes you is the strength of your empowering beliefs and how you act on them to control your flow.

Guiding Assets

The distinguishing assets that guide you and your career are your purpose and dreams. Everyone has both, but they're not all the same. It might not be to play football at Notre Dame, as Rudy did in the Recruiter's Notebook entry above, but there's a movie about how great your life could be that's been playing inside your head since you can remember. That's because your brain converts words to pictures.

So what does "your movie" have you doing, with whom, and where—and are you enjoying it? As the director of your movie, have your senses led you to living out this role, or are you denying yourself the starring role of your lifetime? Controlling your flow involves synchronizing your life with your movie to fulfill your purpose, or otherwise you've shrunk your desires to match your weakened beliefs and you're playing a different role, often close to what you really want. That's OK, because only you can see the real movie or what it could be, and only you can decide whether a supporting role is acceptable.

However, your character may be so strong and believable that the people who know you will even suggest you're playing the wrong role: "You should be doing this!" Or "You should be that!" Are you listening to your audience? How much of your quality time have you devoted to watching your movie, and to fine-tuning the picture until you can really see the possibilities? What distinguishes you are your purpose and dreams, and how they're guiding your flow.

Enabling Assets

The distinguishing assets that enable you are your unique gifts and abilities and how you've developed and used them. If you haven't read the book *Whistle While You Work* by Leider and Shapiro (2002), do so, because it provides a list of 52 distinguishing gifts that people possess to varying degrees. Leider and Shapiro present these gifts without definitions, so they can mean different things to people. I've recently identified my own five gifts as "writing things, seeing possibilities, awakening spirit, starting things, and bringing out potential." Leider and Shapiro's book suggests that these gifts define my career and help to fulfill my purpose. The book also cross-references the 52 gifts to the Holland Career Test, which in my case tells me that my personality and work types are "artistic" and "enterprising," suggesting that I'd have an enjoyable career as a journalist or financial planner. However, the last time I experimented with this exercise, it told me that I'd have an enjoyable career as a therapist or teacher. So the results vary, but they do provide valuable insights for you to consider.

As you review the 52 gifts and top five gifts, you'll know it's your gift if, when using it, you feel fully engaged in what you're doing and lose track of time—and it can be so enjoyable that you're willing to use it for free or without expecting a paycheck. The focused utilization of your gifts enables you to recognize your contentment, even during periods of job dissatisfaction. What distinguishes you are your unique gifts and abilities, and how you're using them to define your career and control its flow.

Inspiring Assets

The distinguishing assets that inspire you are your faith and imagination. Faith is the belief in things unseen, including whatever you choose to imagine and believe. Because there are no limitations to your imagination, and if your faith is strong enough, logic suggests that anything you can imagine and believe is possible. When I say possible, I don't mean probable. But imaginative faith can give you the inspiration to pursue something that might seem impossible but that you really desire, and this inspiration can fit with a motivation—such as needing to earn more money from your small business to cover the mortgage. Then, in tandem, this inspiration to create a really exciting and marketable service—which will, by the way, exponentially increase your income—can pull you forward while the motivation pushes you.

We're talking imagination now, so don't spoil this beautiful idea of faith moving mountains by allowing your party-pooper five-sixths nonconscious guardian to interrupt and caution you about what is or isn't within reason. This cautiousness is always a factor, and that's precisely why your faith in overcoming this persistent obstacle is an asset. Other people, things, and events will inspire you to imagine endless possibilities, including for your career. And faith the size of a mustard seed—which, though tiny, grows into a mighty plant—can make sensible even the most seemingly unreasonable possibilities. So what distinguishes you is what you imagine might happen and your faith that it will happen—and both will inspire how you control your flow.

Confirming Assets

The distinguishing assets that help to confirm you are your credentials. These are your more tangible assets that allow you bragging rights— not that you would, but with these you could. They confirm who you are and where you've been, and they may imply or confirm where you're headed. They include all the things you're inclined to put on your résumé—your academic achievements, certifications, member- ships, sports, hobbies, interests, who you know, where you've worked and for how long, what you've done and accomplished. In chapter 2, we looked at the résumé somewhat less obsessively than many books on career guidance; the point is to do your best but realize that a résumé is in the end simply a glorified calling card—the employer hires you, not a piece of paper!

Your credentials usually reflect what's most important to you. In other words, you've accumulated your credentials for the purpose of leverag- ing them to get what you want, including your career and the direction in which you want it to go. Even if one or more of your credentials conflict with or disconfirm your choices, there's always another one or two you can point to that do confirm your choices; and if they don't, you'll go get another credential if you believe it'll help. What individ- ually distinguishes and confirms you are your credentials and how you use them to control your flow.

Sustaining Assets

The distinguishing assets that sustain you during the tough times are your contentment and resiliency strengths. Actually, you're sustained by all your assets, distinguishable or otherwise, but when problems occur or you temporarily lose control of your flow, the assets you grab first are those that reinforce your resiliency and ability to endure until you can solve the problem or regain control. Chapter 5 highlights the seven resiliency strengths that you automatically rely on or may intentionally activate when needed (see sidebar). For example, you're sustained during the tough times by your meaningful relationships, ability to find humor, creative expression, initiative, and desire to get away from it all. These genuine assets sustain you and allow you to "go with the flow" when that might be your only option. To these, you can add an eighth resiliency strength: contentment.

Yet, with regard to the assets that sustain you, contentment is, of course, not an add-on but the essence of sustenance. By your ability to reason and intentionally focus on the things that are going right as opposed to everything that's going wrong, you can rec-

Seven Resiliency Strengths

- insight
- independence
- relationships
- initiative
- creativity
- humor
- morality

ognize and leverage the beneficial effects of your contentment to think and see things more clearly, and to identify and focus upon what you believe is really most important in the scheme of things. What distinguishes and sustains your ability to endure and control your flow are your resiliency strengths—particularly contentment.

Summing Up Your Assets

These empowering, guiding, enabling, inspiring, confirming, and sustaining assets are not all your assets, just the ones that help to distinguish you and your career. They represent the fact that you know what you want or that your intentions are to have the career you want and control its flow. You own them, they are yours to use and further develop, and you have the power to acquire more of them throughout the course of your career. Whether or not you choose to use them is another matter— for that, you need to claim your sovereign power, our next topic after the next installment from my notebook, on how to realistically build up your assets.

 RECRUITER'S NOTEBOOK
. . . .

Envisioning Your Career, Question by Question, Year by Year

When I provide career coaching to people who seem uncertain of their career direction, or they feel stuck in a particular career flow phase, I like to ask them "By what age do you plan to retire?" Most people don't have a clue, and their answers range from "as early as possible" to "I'll probably work until I die." I'll press them until I get something more specific, and it's usually age 55 to 60 years.

Next I ask their age and allow them to do a quick mental calculation to realize how many years they have to work with. Say they're 35 and plan to retire by 60; this leaves 25 years. For some people, the relief is visible in that they still have time to play around. But for others it provides a wake-up call, and they realize they need to get busy, and fast. Let's discuss the 35-year-old. Next I ask "What is it you expect to be doing by the time you retire, and for how long would you like to enjoy that position?" In this example, the person says "I'd like to be vice president and hold that job for at least five years before retiring."

OK, now we're down to 20 years, and the next question is, "What will you be doing before then, and for how long?" They say, "I hope to be a director of a large division, and probably hold that position for maybe 10 years." Now we're down to 10 years, and I ask, "What about before then, and for how long?" They say, "I'd like to be a manager of a major department, perhaps for five years." Now we're down to five years, and then I ask, "What tools do you need and what do you feel you have to learn and experience to qualify for that manager's position within the next five years?"

As this conversation progresses, you can often watch the fog lift, and they get it. They have a vision of what they must do to pursue a career and create the assets they need, or at least it's become clearer than before. The rest of the conversation probes the elements of their five-year plan, and they often already have it in their head, but it all seemed too overwhelming to voice before. Beginning with the end in mind, and then working backward, pinnacle by pinnacle, allows them to also consider their career flow phases for each position as well as the importance of pacing to build expertise.

Sovereignty: Your Power to Use Your Tools

"Sovereignty" is one of those old-fashioned words referring to the power of royalty over territories. But it also refers to the power over oneself—self-ownership, or the "sovereign individual," as suggested by the philosopher Friedrich Nietzsche. Though rarely used today, this term says precisely what it means and applies quite well to the control of your career flow.

Your career is your territory, and you have the power and authority over its control. Others can claim parts of your territory as theirs or try to interfere and influence your authority, and it's up to you to claim what's yours and to defend it when required, and you can count on your control being challenged. It's up to you how much and on what matters you're willing to share control. And if you abdicate control, it's assured that somebody else will claim it. This is usually your employer, life circumstances, or your five-sixths nonconscious guardian, who prefers to see you not on your throne but locked securely in your comfort zone. You inherited your career sovereignty, and you'll pass it on to your children—provided you act on your sovereignty and teach them how to use theirs, possibly as your parents taught you.

The main categories of this sovereignty are

- efficacy power—when you use mind over matter to overpower your nonconscious guardian
- personal power—for self-control and the like
- knowledge power—to be curious and learn
- decision power—to decide and change your decision
- command power—to take charge of all your assets and powers to pursue your career
- immunity power—to protect and enforce.

Just below, we'll look at these categories in detail. But first, a few caveats about the limits and possibilities of sovereignty.

Your sovereign control is not supreme, because it's always within the two irrevocable parameters discussed in earlier chapters—you are who you are, but also who you're paid to be, and the primary purpose of your employer is not to please you but make a profit. Nor is your control absolute or exclusive, because if you have a family, you will no doubt involve them in decisions that may have an impact on them. So within the parameters created by your employer and family, what you have is more along the lines of "popular sovereignty" or closer to a democracy. Even then, it's still your career, and having it on your terms depends on the optional resolve and force you claim and maintain to function with greater reliance on you rather than on your employer, other people, or your circumstances.

Your sovereignty is, therefore, not without limitations and constraints. But beyond the two employer and family parameters, it's limited only to the territory of your career, not anybody else's. Similarly, how you rule can affect the ability of others to rule their life and career, and also their willingness to get along with you. As such, your power to control comes with responsibilities and obligations, not only to yourself and your career but also to others, including not infringing on their sovereignty. Despite these limitations, maintaining sovereign control of your flow is better than simply going along with it, or allowing others to control it for you and later regretting that you never had the career you wanted. So let's review some of the powers associated with your sovereign control, so you'll know what your options are.

Efficacy Power

Efficacy power is your mind-over-matter power to perform, to produce results, to create your own reality, and to recognize your contentment (see chapter 6 for the concept of efficacy beliefs and the power they create). For example, you can inspire yourself to overcome the internal resistance to procrastinate by thinking not of the challenges but the benefits of getting something done that's hanging over your head. With this efficacy power, your beliefs, thoughts, and emotions will be kept positively conditioned and aligned with your intentions. In other words, this is your power to overpower your five-sixths nonconscious guardian and to have the career you want and to do what you determine is best for it.

You'll use this efficacy power to assign meanings to your circumstances that will prevent them from overpowering you, or to respond confidently and endure. This is your mind-over-matter power to self-motivate as a means of overcoming instances of self-pity or periods of apathy and listlessness, and to put hope back into seemingly hopeless situations. You'll use this power to experience all your emotions without allowing them to control you—from anger and grieving to joy and celebration—and to leverage the fuel from your intentional emotions to inspire actions, to jump out of bed each day, and to think nonnegatively with an opportunity mindset under any circumstances. This is your sovereign power to control your thoughts and emotions as a means of controlling your career.

Personal Power

Your personal power entails self-control and self-management. For example, in the course of pursuing the career you desire, you'll inevitably encounter distractions, diversions, obstacles, resistance, and the contrary advice of others. But you can navigate these matters to get what you desire through your power of self-control, which will enable you to manage yourself and thus control your career—by choosing, negotiating, or changing the content or location of your work to ensure that you reach the highest levels of performance and productivity.

Your personal power also includes the use of your efficacy power as well as your ability to leverage all your assets as you need them to perform, meet deadlines, and deliver results that are on time and on target. It's your power and courage to be your authentic self along with who you're paid to be. You'll use this power to be self-reliant and also to fit in and be a team player when the situation requires. It's your power of integrity to fulfill your promises, demonstrate a solid work ethic, and achieve what you envision.

Finally, your personal power is your clout, muscle, force, and guts to do what it takes to compete and win—or to get up and do it again with greater resolve when temporarily defeated. It's the same power that says you have the good sense and restraint under some circumstances to submit, but without completely abdicating your power to control your career. Likewise, it's your power to admit weaknesses, training needs, and performance deficits, and the will and courage to do something about them. You'll use this power to fuel your passions and willingness to make a commitment, to make and fulfill your goals and obligations, to reach pinnacles, and to endure. It's your sovereign power of self-control and discipline that enables you to control your career.

Knowledge Power

Your knowledge power derives from curiosity and continuous learning. For example, to have and enjoy the career you desire, sometimes you may have to open new doors and explore uncharted territory. This is more likely to happen when your curiosity leads you to investigate and learn new things, and thereafter you'll have the insight or knowledge to do what you must.

You can use this knowledge power to gather information, make observations, experiment and explore, and build self-awareness. Without knowledge, you're vulnerable and may lack purpose or direction. But when used properly, the knowledge you gather and maintain benefits your efforts at self-improvement—to develop your expertise and master your craft; to enhance your life, career, and circumstances; and to make the most of your competitive abilities and potential.

You use your knowledge power to expand and develop new and more reliable sources of information as your situations evolve, to keep your mental databases updated and accurate to support you, to keep the pulse on what's happening around you, and to minimize the surprises that could affect your career. Your resulting and accumulating knowledge keeps your career senses sharpened and gives you an edge or the advantage of foresight so that you can anticipate, make the right choices, be flexible in response to demands, make changes, alter your thinking, and endure based on what you know. The knowledge you gather and maintain also contributes to your ability to make the choices and decisions that are right for you and your career. It's your sovereign power of knowledge, and it can enable you to control your career.

Decision Power

You use your power to decide—including the power to reverse a decision if you think it's necessary—to develop your options and to select from among them what you believe is the best course of action for your career. This power reflects your willingness to take responsibility for your decisions and, thus, for your actions. Indecision implies that you don't know what you want or don't know how to get it—which opens the door to others making your decisions for you. Unless you take a stand, you're vulnerable to having only the career that someone else wants you to have, not the one you desire.

Making the most of this power requires self-confidence and courage, the ability to think clearly and to act with resolve, sometimes contrary to the wishes of your employer, family, and even your five-sixths non-conscious self. Your decision power does not depend on your circumstances or other people but on all your assets and powers to use them to do what it takes and get what you want. You have the power to choose the career you want and for the choices in relation to your incremental positions. You reserve the right to choose and be chosen—and to either adapt, change yourself, influence your situation, or otherwise move on if you believe it's in your best interest.

You also reserve the right to involve whomever you want in your decisions. This works only if you're able to maintain your identity and livelihood independent of any one employer. Anything you wish to start, change, or achieve during your career depends on your conscious ability or intentions to progress through your career flow or recycle (see chapter 8) and to capitalize on the potential benefits of an unplanned career transition. These are your decisions, not anyone else's. It's your sovereign power to make decisions that will control your career.

Command Power

Your command power enables you to have, develop, and use your career assets and all your powers as resources—that is, to have each asset and power at your command to use them when you need them. Throughout your career, of course, no one will be more concerned about your assets and powers than you are, so you have the obligation to acquire and care for them and not make excuses for not having what you need. Imagine a general entering battle without an arsenal, an inventory of assets, or the means to substitute or replenish his assets as the battle progresses. Why try, unless you're relying on a miracle? No one should be more concerned about your career than you.

With regard to the assets you were born with, it's your responsibility to develop them in a manner so that they can be relied on to benefit you. Similarly, you have the power to acquire and develop any new assets that will enable you to pursue and control your career.

If you fail to develop or use your assets, they may atrophy or be lost—it's the same principle that applies to muscles in the human body. So it's very important to stretch your assets and challenge them. And if you abuse or rely too much on a particular asset, you may exhaust or strain its effectiveness, and so it's also within your power to ensure its balanced use and maintenance. You also have the right to expect that in exchange for meeting your employer' demands, you may ask for and be given the resources you need to perform your duties. It's your sovereign power to acquire and use the necessary resources to control your career.

Immunity Power

Immunity power is your ability to say no and to defend yourself when it seems appropriate for your career. Your job is not exactly a field of battle where your boss can threaten you with consequences for "disobeying a direct order"—particularly if what your boss is asking you to do is something he or she wouldn't do or is even illegal, immoral, or unethical. Beyond just "picking your battles," it's important for you to understand what you're getting yourself into and to always know your options so that you can get out without causing your career too much damage.

You have rights and privileges afforded by the laws, policies, and procedures of the jurisdictions under which you work—country, state, employer, association, union. Your immunity power relies on your knowledge of these rights and privileges along with your understanding of the employer's culture, because ignorance of these matters may not be an excuse. Depending on your situation, you're likely to have the power to expect an equitable income and benefits, equal employment opportunity, safe and secure working conditions, and due process when resolving disputes. In some situations, you have the power to put your foot down about these things—particularly if you believe you need to for the sake of controlling your career.

Similarly, you have the power to defend yourself from complaints and criticisms regarding performance, particularly when you're put into nonconsensual situations, given duties that are beyond your scope to perform, or encouraged to take responsible risks or make mistakes for the purpose of benefiting the business. With these powers comes the obligation to take responsibility for your actions. It's your sovereign power to leverage the immunities and protections available to you to control your career.

Summing Up Sovereign Powers

The powers described here are not all of your sovereign powers, of course, but only the ones that help distinguish you and enable you to control your career. As you recognize that you possess these powers and use them, you'll show that you're willing to do what it takes to have the career you want and to control its flow. You own these powers, they're yours to use and further develop, and you can acquire more of them throughout your career.

In other words, if you lack one or more of these sovereign powers, go get it and build upon what you already have—or as the old U.S. Army commercials used to say, "Be all you can be." This can't happen if you simply wish for these powers. You need to constantly monitor your inventory of sovereign powers and expand your powers as you see the need for new ones—especially when you change jobs and careers.

After you gain all the powers you need, your next challenge is to ensure that you don't underuse or overuse them to your detriment. Remember, your powers are not supreme but democratic, so you need to consider their impact on others as well as on yourself. Thus, to have the career you desire, you need to apply your assets and powers in a balanced way, rather than an overrelying on one asset or power.

Balancing Your Application of Assets and Sovereignty

Your assets represent your potential to become your honest best self, and your sovereign powers represent your potential to do your honest best. Both support your ability to manage your career flow so that you can pursue and enjoy the career you desire. However, your assets and powers won't mean anything until you put them to work, and if you rely too much on just one asset or power to compensate for some deficit elsewhere, you'll create problems that may have a negative impact on your potential for career contentment.

What this means is that your career flow relies on the balanced application of both your assets and powers. You still have to convert your inspirations into realities, or they accomplish nothing. Your good looks and sweet personality can only take you so far, particularly if your job requires technical know-how and you don't have it. Your degree from an Ivy League institution matters little if one of your co-workers with a lesser degree or no degree is running circles around you. An overbearing personality or intimidation works only a few times before other people begin to complain.

The so-called one-trick pony relies on the one thing he or she does best to get ahead; but in a complex, constantly changing world, that person soon reaches his or her limits and has difficulty advancing further. We all have our limits, but we can get around them through our adroitness and dexterity in drawing on our multiple assets and powers when we need them the most.

Problems typically arise when your tricks or abilities rely on just your assets or just your powers, rather than a balanced application of each. When this happens, you can sense the strain as you compensate for some deficit that could have a negative impact on your success. A deficit in your ability to control could result in putting more emphasis on one of your assets, or vice versa. Say your employer values MBAs and you don't happen to have one. To compensate, you rely more heavily on other assets or you exert more control than the situation requires. Over time, this wears on you and can become annoying to other people.

Psychology has referred to this situation as an inferiority or Napoleon complex (Hoffman 1994). This is best described as a person driven to extremes to compensate for some psychological need or shortcoming, and in the case of Napoleon, it was his short height compared with other men. Though the "short-man syndrome" has since been disproved by a recent study conducted at the University of Central Lancashire in Britain (http://www.uclan.ac.uk/news/2007/web041 .html), our drive to get what we want may still result in our compensating for some deficit by overtaxing one particular asset or power.

As I've stated throughout this book, the optimum condition for career contentment is when your work is meaningful in relation to your talents and purpose. If your job requires talents you don't have or are not motivated to use, or if you are inhibited from using your motivated talents, your discontentment is likely to fester. It, therefore, stands to reason that if you lack the required assets and powers to have and enjoy the career you desire, you're going to have problems. It's a good thing to rely on your best assets—but not to the extent of exhausting their effectiveness to compensate for some deficit that you should instead be working on transforming into an asset or power.

To illustrate further, imagine your assets and sovereignty each as a separate pillar that supports and keeps your career flow balanced (see figure 9-1). Whenever you rely too heavily on one pillar versus the others, it creates an imbalance or area of vulnerability that puts an unnecessary strain on the resource, on you, on your career flow, on your employer, and on other people. And unless you prevent this from happening, any extended imbalances are guaranteed to create problems. The problem is enhanced if that overreliance on one pillar is to compensate for a deficit in another. For example, a heavier reliance on assets suggests that you may have what it takes and know what you want but lack the power to get it. But a heavier reliance on powers suggests that you're willing to do what it takes but lack the tools or don't know what you want.

Say your job requires specific assets like vision, innovation, problem solving, patience, endurance, and directly related academic training and work experience. It's never enough just to have these assets; you must exercise your various powers to ensure that they produce the desired results. And your powers are enhanced by the command you exercise over your clarity of thought, self-control, knowledge proficiency, and decisiveness.

Figure 9-1. The Support and Control of Career Flow

ORIENTATION	ACCELERATION	ACTUALIZATION
Find It / **Have It**	**Have It** / **Keep It**	**Keep It** / **Share It**

Have What It Takes	CAREER ASSETS AND TOOLS		SOVEREIGN POWERS	Do What It Takes
		Empower	Efficacy	
Balanced		Guide	Personal	**Balanced**
Underused		Enable	Knowledge	Underused
Undeveloped		Inspire	Decision	Undeveloped
		Confirm	Command	
Developed and utilized assets		Sustain	Immunities	Developed and utilized powers

BALANCED APPLICATION

Have What It Takes	CAREER ASSETS AND TOOLS		SOVEREIGN POWERS	AREA OF VULNERABILITY — Do What It Takes
		Empower		
Imbalanced		Guide	Efficacy	Underused
Overused		Enable	Personal	Undeveloped
Undeveloped		Inspire	Knowledge	
		Confirm	Decision	
Compensating for lack of power		Sustain	Command / Immunities	Underused or weakened power

IMBALANCED APPLICATION

Have What It Takes	AREA OF VULNERABILITY — CAREER ASSETS AND TOOLS		SOVEREIGN POWERS	AREA OF VULNERABILITY — Do What It Takes
		Empower	Efficacy	
	Undeveloped	Guide	Personal	Underused
		Enable	Knowledge	Undeveloped
		Inspire	Decision	
Undeveloped or weakened assets		Confirm	Command	Weakened power and compensating for lack of assets
		Sustain	Immunities	

Let's assume a problem arises that requires more innovation and problem-solving skills than your current assets allow. To compensate for these deficits, you'll need to exercise your appropriate powers to expand your assets or determine which other assets you can rely on more heavily. Unless you're occasionally relieved of this extra burden, your overutilized assets may contribute to feelings of job stress, leading to burnout. Or, to prevent this from happening, you could exert your personal and knowledge power to ignore the need for more innovation and problem solving—or to bully others into helping you. But unless you're relieved of the burdens caused by this negative behavior, you'll eventually experience the same job stress and burnout.

Now let's look at this from another angle. Say you possess the necessary assets to perform your job but lack the needed powers to make them work, or that you're inhibited from using your assets and powers to the degree necessary. You might be lacking confidence, you might not be sufficiently engaged to make things happen, or you might have a controlling boss who ignores or underutilizes the assets and powers you feel most compelled to use. Unless relieved of this opposite burden, you'll once again experience the same job stress leading to burnout.

The solution to these kinds of situations that leads to greater career contentment involves knowing what you want and having the tools to get it (that is, developing all your assets and applying them in a balanced way) and doing what's needed to make it happen (that is, developing all your powers and applying them in a balanced way). Otherwise, you may discover that you're in the wrong job, or this may be an indication or warning that it's time to recycle to something more within your range of talents and means to keep them developed. Let's look at one last notebook entry illustrating the need for the asset–power balance.

RECRUITER'S NOTEBOOK

Assets, All Present and Accounted For; Power, Missing in Action

Ron had achieved considerable success in his work as a chemical research scientist, but he felt disillusioned because his dreams of taking a drug to market had not yet been realized after 14 years. He realized the impossibility of

Assets, All Present and Accounted For; Power, Missing in Action (continued)

instant gratification when he chose his profession, and so he learned to find contentment in other areas of his work—specifically in publishing a variety of insightful research papers and proposals. When his periods of frustration surfaced, his managers were very good in allowing him to explore alternative positions within his division. But after 14 years, he felt he'd tried almost everything within his area of specialty. He sensed it was time during his career to try something new or different, and he wasn't sure what that was.

Ron used his research skills to investigate alternative career choices, focusing on the professions that would make good use of his analytical and quantitative skills and at the same time allow him a bit more instant gratification for his efforts. To the surprise of some who knew him, he decided to explore the area of sales and business development, and within his same company. From his perspective, he would be able to leverage his technical knowledge of products and components to sell and his analytical skills to design and deliver technical sales proposals; and, at the same time, he would have the gratification of closing sales as often as he wanted.

After discussing his ideas with his wife, Ron's uncertainty was so high that he even felt compelled to ask his nine-year old son, "What do you think of daddy becoming a salesman some day? Can you see me doing that?" After what seemed like an eternity to him, but was really only two weeks, he decided to meet with his boss to explore his ideas of transferring into sales. He told his boss what was on his mind and asked, "What do you think of getting my feet wet in sales?" His boss felt that after 14 solid years of performance, and the fact he'd demonstrated his abilities in more than one position already, Ron deserved a shot, if that's what he really wanted. His boss would contact his counterpart in sales to explore whether they would be willing to look at Ron's résumé and give him an exploratory interview. The answer was yes, the reason being the factors that Ron had anticipated, including his technical product knowledge and analytical skills to develop and present sales proposals.

Ron was given the go-ahead to call and make the interview appointment, and he did. In preparation for his interview, he tried to imagine himself in the role so that he could more easily interview as he thought a salesperson would. With only three days to go before his scheduled interview, the feet he'd wanted to get wet were starting to get cold, and he wasn't so sure about his new direction. However, he had cast the dice, and he decided he'd see it through—at least to the interview phase. It was apparent during the interview that the sales director was quite impressed with Ron's depth of product knowledge and obviously strong analytical skills but, even more so, with his ability to think on his feet and his personality to establish rapport and relations. The director sensed that Ron had the potential to make a smooth transition to sales, if that's what he wanted, so the balance of the interview was spent allowing Ron to ask whatever questions he had. He was hoping that Ron would ask for the job.

By the time the interview concluded, though, the sales director was no longer certain that Ron could make the transition. Ron had spent the majority of his time asking the sales director for career advice: "What do you think I should do?" "Do you think I have what it takes?" "Do you think this is best for me?" "Do you see me as a salesman?" "Will I succeed?" The director advised Ron: "Talk with Human Resources and come back when you figure out what you want to do when you grow up."

Ron expressed his appreciation for the advice and interview but also realized that the director's "advice" had been an insult. Ron had blown his opportunity. Not only had he not closed the deal as a salesperson might, he'd demonstrated his uncertainties and lack of resolve. He was embarrassed, even recalling the fact that he'd asked his nine-year-old son for career advice—"What was I thinking?" Ron had most of the obvious assets for a sales career, but he lacked the necessary power to direct his flow in that direction. Maybe it just wasn't meant to be, but if he ever did want to move, Ron had learned that he'd have to be more powerful than before.

Summing Up Assets and Powers

As you can imagine, any severe or prolonged imbalances in either your assets or powers can have a direct effect on you and your ability to control your career flow. The strain it causes contributes to instances of career indecision, and potentially an overreliance on others for direction during your career. Unless you're careful on this point, you can inadvertently find yourself doing things you really don't want to or you may later regret. This is one of the primary reasons for false starts and career instability. Therefore, it's crucial for you to think continuously of how to balance your application of assets and powers as you use them to pursue what you believe will provide your career with its greatest contentment.

What's Next

In the final chapter, we'll review and distill the lessons about career contentment we've explored in this book. We'll look at 10 handy indicators of career contentment, and I'll provide you with some tools to help you discern and maintain your own career contentment.

Becoming Comfortable with Career Contentment

········· **In this chapter, you'll learn** ·········

◆ the essential aspects of career contentment—a review

◆ why, again, it's important to pursue your career contentment

◆ how to recognize and maintain career contentment— with 10 handy indicators

Wouldn't it be grand going to work each day with the thought of constantly recognizing the contentment in what you're doing? To believe you're using your gifts to fulfill your purpose and make a contribution, and it feels like it was meant to be? To automatically choose not to look for problems or not complain about what somebody did or didn't do, what you have or don't have, or even with or for whom you work? But do you perhaps think this is an unattainable career nirvana for some workplaces?

That would be totally wrong! Want proof? Just watch one of those TV programs that highlights the most dangerous or dirtiest jobs on Earth. After getting a sense of why those jobs rank among the worst, ask yourself why those people are doing them. Even if they chose to be there, you have to wonder how they do it. Why are they smiling and willing to be televised? It starts with what you choose to do, and thereafter it depends on how you choose to view it. And before you read this book, you thought it was all about job satisfaction. The fact is, you can't be paid enough to do some jobs, but even within the least satisfying jobs on Earth, it's still possible to recognize your contentment, and that's far more important.

The Essential Aspects of Career Contentment

Throughout this book, you've learned how to recognize your career contentment—your ability to intentionally pause during your busy life, take a second look, and admire and derive pleasure from the use of your gifts to fulfill your purpose and make a contribution. When you do these things, you experience a peaceful, contented state of mind that enhances your effectiveness to think more clearly, make decisions, and endure through periods of stress and job dissatisfaction. And your ability to find this state of mind at will doesn't depend on whether you're happy or satisfied, on other people, or on material things, but on your innate ability to reason and find the acceptable middle ground in any situation. This contented state of mind is a gift, and your supply of this contentment is constant while your jobs, employers, careers, and even your purpose are all subject to change. For a particularly vivid example of how powerful contentment can be under the worst conditions, let's turn to this story from my Recruiter's Notebook on the facing page.

Your contentment is an indispensable resource and resiliency strength that costs you nothing, and you use it every day without realizing it. For instance, when things don't seem to be going your way, you can still recognize contentment in the few things that are nevertheless going your way, you can bring contentment into the situation from other areas of your life that are faring better, or you can simply recognize contentment in the fact that you're looking so hard to find it. You can even recognize contentment in being discontent. You can recognize it anywhere you choose to reason and recognize the agreeable middle ground. And once recognized, it gives you that momentary pause and peace of mind that gets you through and beyond.

RECRUITER'S NOTEBOOK

How People Find Meaning Beyond the Worst Suffering, and Applying the Principles to Careers

Back in 1991, I was given a gift of a copy of the book *Man's Search for Meaning* by Viktor Frankl (1977), the psychiatrist and concentration camp survivor. I had heard about this book for years but never had the courage to read it because I didn't want my mind filled with what I knew was the misery and suffering of millions. I had read other books about the Holocaust, seen the movies, and even visited the museum in Washington, so I preferred to focus my mind on more positive thoughts and ideas, never realizing I had in my possession a book that would help me to help others recognize their contentment.

It was 10 years later that I finally decided to read the book. Thankfully, Frankl avoids discussing all the Holocaust atrocities and focuses instead on explaining how people endured when they weren't sure they would live or die within the next hour. I was curious to learn if there would be insights that could be applied to helping employees find contentment during periods of job dissatisfaction—albeit a substantially lesser condition than life or death, but still important to many people. Frankl says that even in the most barren conditions, after everything has been taken away, you still have the right to choose your attitude and your own way, and the call to an unfinished meaning or purpose gives reason to endure, more so than mere gratification or satisfaction.

So there it was, distilled from some of the most "dissatisfying" conditions possible to imagine. What matters most to your contentment is not so much what the employer does or doesn't supply but rather your ability to reason and to pursue the fulfillment of your purpose. To translate this into practical advice for the person who seeks to improve his or her career contentment, particularly during periods of job dissatisfaction: Apply yourself to meaningful work that fulfills your calling and purpose, and reason to recognize the good in this rather than expecting satisfaction based on other people or material things.

Recall our discussion in chapter 7 of etymology and the Latin roots of the words "contentment" and "satisfy." The former originates in "contain," suggesting that the contented person holds herself or himself together with a calmness protected by self-sufficiency. The latter originates in "sad" and "factitious," suggesting that you're always dependent on someone or something else to make you satisfied—and that it's rare for you to ever be completely satisfied. Stated another way, you can think in such as way as to begin to feel content any time, but you must wait to be made satisfied, and you can only hope that it happens.

You've learned that when intentionally recognized or allowed to possess your thoughts, your contentment enables you to appreciate what you have, to accept what you don't have, and to endure what you choose to believe is less than satisfying. It could be your job, income, or achievement level, just as easily as it could be your weight and appearance, your marriage and spouse, your residence, or the car you drive. You're not changing jobs every week, getting married to a new person every month, driving a new car every calendar quarter, or getting plastic surgery and liposuctions every year. Maybe you wish you could, but you don't.

Instead, you reason to recognize and appreciate the acceptable middle ground, and you realize that it's not about tolerating or doing without so much as simply pausing to appreciate what is. You bring a halt to your mind's continuous rambling—what could've been, should've been, might've been, what you did or didn't do, and so on and so forth. You pause, stop thinking, and just look, listen, and appreciate, and the peace that comes over you is experienced as contentment, and it feels good. You enjoy a cup of coffee; a sip of beer; a walk through the park; the sound of water, music, or laughter; the feel of soft fabric; the smell of a flower; the touch of a loved one, how they smile; the pride of accomplishment or just the effort, recognizing your self-sufficiency—and then you get up renewed and do it again, more content than before.

You've also learned that if your contentment depends on anything, it depends on you and on whether you think the right way and whether you prevent yourself from thinking the wrong way. You've learned how to improve and recondition the way you've been taught to think as a way of enhancing your effectiveness. You have to think hard to think correctly, and this involves making sure that what you believe supports and enables what you intend to do and achieve. This is crucial, because what you believe determines how you feel, and these emotions fuel your actions and therefore your results—and also your ability to recognize your contentment. If what you believe contradicts or opposes your intentions, then your intentions lose momentum and will not be fulfilled. That's because your tendency is to scale back on your intentions, not recondition or energize your beliefs, and this leads to problems and dissatisfactions that your contentment would rather you not experience.

You've learned to evaluate and keep your beliefs strengthened to support your intentions, to think about opportunity nonnegatively, and then to make sure that your actions are guided by your intentions, not your self-limiting nonconscious mental guardian's automatic thoughts that want to hold you back and keep you safe in your comfort zone. You now realize that managing your thoughts to achieve what you desire will be your greatest challenge throughout your career, and you can refer to this book time and again for solutions that will help you to accomplish this.

How you think not only allows you to fulfill your goals and recognize your contentment but also shows you how to attract meaningful work, which is the foundation for your career-related contentment. In part I, you learned the process of attracting meaningful work, how to convert interviews into offers, how to make the best choices, and how to endure all the frustrations and challenges during the job search process—long after you've accepted a position.

Considering the universal law of cause and effect, or what we know about physics at the quantum level, you've learned that thinking about meaningful work causes it to exist as potential energy. By developing the job seeker's mindset described in this book, you've become able to convert this energy into reality and then attract and claim it as yours. Thus, in effect, you reserve your future jobs by imagining having something new or different, and they seek you out—which explains why it often feels as if a job finds you.

When it feels as if a job finds you, you can actually sense the tug or calling, and thanks to how you think and your ongoing pursuit of contentment, this happens again and again, thereby causing your career to flow and evolve. Can this be proven? Probably not; but we do know that employers prefer to hire people with the attitudes that closely resemble the job seeker's mindset, and so you've got nothing to lose but the job you want, and everything to gain by trying. You're more likely to get the job when you believe you will, and when those beliefs empower and support your intentions. In other words, ask and you'll receive what your faith expects.

However, because you get what you think about most, you must detach yourself from needing or wanting a job and think instead as if you already have it. This is not self-delusion but just using your inspiring assets of faith and imagination. It's like the old Broadway song—you've got to have a dream if you want to have a dream come true. Otherwise, by focusing on your needs and wants, what you attract is not the job but more needs and wants. That's the universal law of cause and effect, and it works every time, whether you want it to or not—just like gravity.

You've also learned about the importance of serendipity and synchronicity—how they play a huge role in discovering and attracting meaningful work, and how you can develop this as a talent to use during job searches. And you've learned how the employment etiquette models provided in part I will help you to eliminate or minimize the anxieties associated with the process of employment and will allow you to focus instead on creating the impressions that will demonstrate your chemistry and fit with your target employer. Job seekers who use these tools to master the process and etiquette of employment claim they're able to sense more about what's going on during the process—sometimes even more than the employer. This gives you the edge you need to connect with your calling and convert more interviews into offers.

Also, as for further minimizing anxiety, you've learned in part II how your career flows or progresses through phases based on the forces of time in job, your developing expertise, and your pursuit of contentment. Understanding how your career flows through these phases allows you to pace yourself, to anticipate what may happen during your career, and to sense the changes or when it's time to move to another phase or recycle by starting over to pursue your callings and purpose. You've learned how to use your distinguishing career assets and sovereign powers to control your flow to ensure that you have the career you want, not the career somebody else thinks you should have. Your career will flow until you decide to stop working or run out of time—and even then, you'll continue to look for ways to enable your contentment, and you'll know how to find it.

Why It's Important to Recognize Your Career Contentment

In this book, you've learned that it's important to recognize your career contentment because you work for the contentment that's derived from using your gifts to make a contribution and to fulfill your goals and purpose. And thank goodness it's for more than just a paycheck, benefits, job security, good supervision, accommodating work hours, promotional opportunities, or even the people you work with, because all these things, though important, are transient. They satisfy one day and disappoint the next, or there's never enough. Your career can last a long time and the allure of satisfaction is persistent.

Before you learned about the value of contentment, you relied on these transient things because your thinking about careers, passed down for generations, was conditioned to make you want to find what you'd love—which mostly was determined by what might provide job satisfaction. You were conditioned to expect a return on your investment of time and talents, so what satisfied came with a price tag, and either you had it or you lacked job satisfaction. Even if seven out of 10 things were going superbly well, you would've found a way to claim dissatisfaction because of the missing three things. By golly, you worked for it, you deserved it, it was your turn, you'd fight for it, you'd take it out of something else or you'd leave—and nowhere in this mess of conditioned thinking was there room to consider your contentment. That's because what little career training you had probably didn't involve an understanding of contentment. So you're forgiven, but now you can rectify this situation.

You've learned that contentment involves doing what you love but also finding ways to love what you do, and it's feasible with or without a price tag or dependence on other people, material things, or whether or not you have job satisfaction. It requires looking beyond these things to find the good in all things. It's not about making do or settling for less but rather about becoming your honest best self and achieving your honest best, despite the presence or absence of things, and about continuously pausing to appreciate your efforts and results. You've learned this is possible because your contentment comes from within, and you take it with you wherever you go and however your purpose evolves. It's free and based on how you think and reason to find the agreeable middle ground in all things, even in the absence of things. This is important because even within the jobs you love and are satisfied with, you'll still experience dissatisfactions. It's your conditioned nature to do so.

Although it may seem to you that you're living in response to your good or bad circumstances and other people, you've learned that how you think creates your reality. In other words, your circumstances are random and meaningless until you assign them meanings and, therefore, determine how you will react and how others will respond to you. As such, your life and career are the result of how you choose to think, and if you can keep this in mind and make it work to your advantage, you can choose to reason and recognize your contentment in any situation, even the most extreme—as the next excerpt from my notebook shows.

Last Thoughts

In closing, it's important to remember that what you believe and how you think create the workplace experience and your career, and thus determine whether it's good or bad. This applies wherever you work, regardless of whom you work with or for, and no matter what you're given or not given—as long as you have something meaningful to hold onto—and like the guy on the wire in the Recruiter's Notebook entry above, it's your contentment. Satisfaction comes and goes, but your contentment is always present because it comes from within you and is

RECRUITER'S NOTEBOOK

Fearing a Fall from Ninety Feet or Electrocution?

Public TV recently featured a program on helicopters. One segment focused on the utility of these machines to facilitate our work. It began with a man in a white hat and jumpsuit sitting precariously on a small platform attached to the side of the helicopter. As his legs were dangling from the side, the helicopter flew over trees, houses, and rivers, and he seemed to be enjoying the ride. Then, as the helicopter approached a series of high-tension electrical wires, you began to hear a recording the man had made to describe his work. As he spoke, the helicopter was hovering 90 feet above the ground, slowly inching its way to within a foot of the electrical wires.

The man used a small rod to discharge the electricity so he could touch the wire without electrocuting himself or the helicopter. You could watch as the current sparked, jumped, and then formed a bridge between the helicopter and wires. He then used a safety strap to connect himself to the electrical wires before crawling slowly from the helicopter. Next, he disconnected his other safety strap from the helicopter, using his rod once again to discharge and prevent electrocution. The helicopter backed away safely, leaving the man balancing on his hands and knees 90 feet above the ground on two thin, highly charged electrical wires.

The man's job was to scoot along on all fours making repairs. If he fell, it was hoped that a thin strap attached to the wire would fully leave him dangling above the ground. All I could think about was whether I could do this without someone pointing a gun to my head. I didn't think so, but to this guy, it was just another day in the office. Yet what thoughts must've gone through his mind the first time he tried it? Watching this from a camera inside the helicopter, you could see other workers all scooting along those thin wires doing the same thing, giving the appearance of a strange aerial dance you might see performed by Cirque du Soleil.

Even more amazing is what the man said while this was happening. He loved his work and believed that it served an important purpose in supplying electricity to homes and offices. He believed he was good at what he did and it gave him pride and pleasure, so much so that he couldn't imagine doing anything else. But to perform his work, he had to get beyond his two biggest fears: heights and electricity. He did so by holding onto a strap— and also to his career contentment.

based not on material things or other people but on how you think. Thus, just like your faith and imagination, your supply of contentment can be endless as your career and purpose evolve.

Contentment is something you usually don't think about intentionally, at least until you realize it's been taken away or threatened. Unexpected, tragic events linked with war, terrorism, uncontrollable weather, the impact of disease, or the effects of a weak economy cause us to realize and appreciate a previous state of mind or the way things used to be. Then, as if by magic, those thoughts of earlier contentment help give you the resiliency to endure. We recall unfinished purposes and discover new ones, and through our best and honest efforts, we recognize our contentment—but this time, we try to make the adjustments to our lives that may help to prevent our losing it again.

You can watch as this happens every night on the evening TV news. You don't find contentment in disaster, but from within, when you have no choice but to reach down and find hope based on new purposes and recollections of how you've managed before. Doing so helps to fuel your faith and endurance. You may not be satisfied under the circumstances, but you can find contentment in the belief that "I can do this, things are going to be alright, we'll be OK, I can see the silver lining, there's hope and a light at the end of the tunnel." Sometimes hope is your only source of contentment.

Perhaps it's time in your beautiful and simultaneously busy and threatening world to divert just some of your attention away from a dependence on things that supply temporary job satisfaction and to focus intentionally on the more lasting, meaningful rewards of contentment that stem from using your gifts to fulfill your purpose. When you do, that's when it seems the real rewards appear.

You work for what you think you deserve, but you've also learned the importance of working in gratitude for what you don't deserve. The former motive reflects your paradoxical quality of pride, and the latter its paradoxical opposite, humility. Both are extremely important to keep in play and balanced if you plan to succeed and get along during your career.

When you work exclusively for what you think you deserve, what you get is the sum of your deeds minus the sum of your debts, and like everybody, you tend not to think of your debts as part of the equation. Working from this motive means you need to have someone evaluate what you've done and decide whether you're getting what you deserve. It also raises the potential for disputes and dissatisfactions, and in the midst of all this wrangling, you lose sight of your potential for contentment.

In contrast, when you counterbalance your motives by working in gratitude for what you don't deserve, there's no need for an evaluation by anyone because you haven't demanded or expected anything. You're just grateful to be doing your thing. Also, by not imposing any limitations, you could receive not only what you deserve—the door is open to receiving more without limitation. How's that for supplying your contentment?

To optimally maintain your contentment, you need to find the balance between working exclusively for what you think you deserve and working in gratitude for what you don't deserve. This process is illustrated in figure 10-1. If you can control your thoughts, emotions, reasoning, talents, and choices—as portrayed in the figure—you can find the point on the "meter" where they are in balance and the arrow points straight up, where you can maintain your contentment.

Let's look at how figure 10-1 can be helpful. It's really about the paradox of humility versus pride, and getting what you desire. First, look at the left side of the figure: *When you work for what you think you deserve,* you receive the sum of your credits minus the sum of your debts. You tend to forget your debts, of course, and so your pride causes you to doubt that you're being treated fairly or getting what you think you deserve. Without the benefit of humility to oppose your pride, your doubt would progress to intolerance and the belief that you can't take it anymore. Without the benefit of forbearance to oppose your intolerance, you'd become frustrated and lose hope... unless, of course, you oppose this by using another paradoxical quality to help you bounce back.

Now, let's look at the right side of the figure: *When you work in gratitude for what you don't deserve,* you receive without expectation or

Figure 10-1. Finding the Balance to Maintain Your Contentment

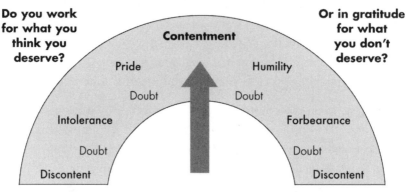

Do you work for what you think you deserve?

Contentment

Or in gratitude for what you don't deserve?

Pride   Humility

Doubt   Doubt

Intolerance   Forbearance

Doubt   Doubt

Discontent   Discontent

Control of thoughts, Emotions, Reasoning, Talents, and Choices

limitation, and your humility enables you to appreciate what you receive but also makes you sometimes doubt that you're being assertive enough to get what you need. Without the benefit of pride to oppose your humility, your doubt would progress to forbearance or to the decision to stick things out even though you might not be getting what you need. If your situation doesn't improve, you'll begin to feel exploited or taken advantage of. Without the benefit of intolerance to oppose your forbearance, you'll progress to being frustrated and losing hope … unless, of course, you oppose this by using another paradoxical quality, and life goes on, continuously balanced by your paradoxical qualities—as shown in figure 10-1, where the arrow points straight up toward your continuing and unassailable contentment.

Employers assume that you're doing what you love. Otherwise, why would you be doing it if not for the pay, benefits, and the like? So their focus is on continuing to make sure you have job satisfaction, and they assume that will make you content. But now you know that it won't. If it appears that you lack contentment, they'll try and fix your satisfaction. And now you know that's not likely to work, either. If you appear content, they'll conclude you're satisfied, even though you may not be. And if you appear to be really, really content, they may assume you expect little more than just the opportunity to do your work, and they'll do less to enable your satisfaction. That's not good either. So now what do you do?

Although your contentment will enable you to endure situations without job satisfaction, you're likely to leave if you can't recognize your contentment, and it doesn't matter if you were previously satisfied. Unless you work exclusively on a mercenary basis, there aren't enough salaries or benefits out there to prevent you from forfeiting your gifts or fulfilling your purpose. So if you're serious about your career, focus first and always on attracting and putting yourself into situations where you're most likely to recognize your contentment by the grateful use of your gifts to fulfill your purpose. When you do, your need for job satisfaction is more likely to be attended to, whether or not you think you deserve it.

You are who you are, but also who you're paid to be, and employers really want both. They want your pride and your humility, and whether they get you really depends on your 51 percent of the vote. If they don't want you, it just confirms that it's not what you've reserved or attracted. Keep looking, but with the courage to control your beliefs and intentions to find and do what you love, to love what you do, and to have the good sense to look beyond mere satisfaction by sometimes valuing all of what you have, even if it's not everything you want.

You become your honest best self and do your honest best not only in exchange for the material things that supply your satisfaction but also for the joy of using your gifts to fulfill your evolving purpose. With this as your intention, you'll attract meaningful work and receive more than you imagined from each new job, career, and employer. And, by your choice, you'll be recognizing and celebrating your career contentment—no matter what.

Last Tools

That's enough deep thinking for now. Here are two last tools as you pursue your career contentment: a visual model of career contentment and 10 indicators to help you recognize and maintain your contentment.

Visualizing Career Contentment—and Playing a Little Game

Now that we've discussed all the aspects of career contentment in detail, it's time to pull all this information together into a visual model of career contentment. You're thinking, "Why didn't you show me this earlier in the book?" Well, at that point, it would have been too much information, as they say. You needed more of a foundation to understand it—but now that you have that foundation, let's play a little game.

The model given in figure 10-2 can help to expand your knowledge about contentment versus satisfaction. Notice the four rectangular boxes surrounding the four inner squares. They represent the control you can exercise over your career by using your thoughts, emotions, reasoning, and career choices to fulfill your calling and purpose.

Now, here's the game: Answer the following questions about your current or last job; and as you answer them, physically point to your answer on the model shown in figure 10-2:

1. Are your *thoughts and emotions* favorable to support the fulfillment of your intentions to have and enjoy the career you desire, or are they unfavorable and causing you grief?
2. Are you *reasoning* to recognize the middle ground in any situation, or are you expecting to be made satisfied and either have job satisfaction or not have it?
3. Is your *choice of work* meaningful to the use of your talents and the fulfillment of your calling and purpose, or does your work lack meaning and purpose?
4. As for the *control* of your career, are you codependent on your employer to make you satisfied, or are you self-reliant to pursue your own career contentment?

As you look at the model in figure 10-2 while answering these questions, I hope you'll have some actual revelations:

♦ Notice that career contentment is feasible with or without job satisfaction based on favorable emotions, middle-ground reasoning, career self-reliance, and work that is meaningful to your talents and purposes for working.

Figure 10-2. A Visual Model of Career Contentment

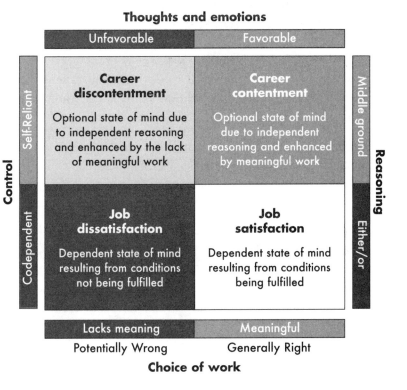

- Also notice that job satisfaction is always based on either/or reasoning (either you have it or don't) and is codependent on your hard work in exchange for the satisfactions offered by employers.
- Career discontentment results from a lack of meaningful work but also from a lack of favorable thoughts and emotional control. Fortunately, you have the option at any time to change your thoughts and to choose different work to achieve career contentment.
- Finally, the optimum situation is to have both job satisfaction and career contentment, but realize that you have no control over employers or the jobs and satisfactions they may choose to provide or take away. Fortunately, you still do have control

over your thoughts, emotions, reasoning, and career choices so that you can recognize your career contentment—and thus have and enjoy the career you desire.

Ten Indicators of Career Contentment

If the exercise above with the visual model didn't enlighten you, then it might help to review these 10 indicators of whether you have career contentment (see sidebar).

A Personal Note—and What's Next

My objective in writing this book, first mentioned in the preface, was to find a solution that would help people overcome the dissatisfactions associated with looking for work so they can have and enjoy the career they desire. Never could I have imagined that the solution already existed within each of us, regardless of where we live or what we do to make a living. It was obscured by semantics but discoverable when you recognize the different meanings of "satisfaction" and "contentment."

To quote one of the first editors to review this book: "It's so simple it's profound." In our quest to be made satisfied, we'd overlooked or forgotten an important lesson from our youth. We are never completely satisfied, but we can always recognize our contentment to endure as we work toward our goals.

What we seek—and what empowers us as we seek it—is not the transient job satisfactions provided by employers but the contentment derived from work made meaningful as we use our talents to fulfill our calling and purpose. It's when we're content with our work that we can appreciate the satisfactions; otherwise, we're restless and keep looking, regardless of efforts to keep us satisfied.

Having read this book, you now know what career contentment is— but this is only the beginning. Still to come in the pages that follow are several more tools to help you pursue what we've explored in this book. First, there's an epilogue about moving toward a new paradigm of career contentment and about an effort to help others recognize

10 Indicators of Career Contentment

1. Love what you do, and your actions demonstrate your passion for what you do even when you are frustrated or angry.

2. Accept that no job or career is perfect. In fact, your acceptance of this inherent imperfection is what helps drive your personal and professional success.

3. Recognize that it is your employer's job to make you satisfied but that contentment has to come from within you.

4. Be completely in touch with why you enjoy your current job or career, so any decision to change is driven by a need for more meaningful work and not transient job satisfactions (like a corner office with a window or even more money).

5. Understand that complaining is a worthless, destructive activity and that a better use of your time is to imagine and work toward a contented job or career situation.

6. Appreciate and applaud your employer's success, but do not base your contentment on how well your company treats you or the incentives it offers to keep you from leaving. You realize that any career decision always comes back to contentment.

7. Keep meaningful work at the forefront of every career decision, no matter what incentive you are offered to continue on your current career path.

8. Push beyond the boundaries of your career because your contented mindset allows you to imagine and expect career doors to be open.

9. Continue to be content even when you know it is time to leave your job but must wait until the time is right to make your move.

10. Be an absolute convert to the idea of career contentment and fully appreciate that it is more important than any traditional, measurable criterion of job satisfaction like salary or responsibilities that can be reduced, taken away, stolen, downsized, restructured, or poorly managed.

their career contentment: the Campaign to Retire Job Dissatisfaction. Second, you'll find two appendixes: a self-assessment to help you home in on the details of your career contentment, and a self-assessment to help you make a decision to leave a particular job. And third, you'll find a list of the references cited above and of books and articles for further reading.

Epilogue:
Toward a New Paradigm
of Career Contentment

What's happened since this book was written? A lot!

Looking back over the years at the effort to solve the problem of job dissatisfaction, we can see that it has persisted for decades, consumed billions of dollars, fueled the growth of industries like self-help and coaching, and preoccupied the careers of countless experts. By now, you'd think we'd have the solution nailed, but we still can't even agree on the problem's scope and severity—or even if there *is* a problem.

For example, after I finished writing this book, in February 2007 the Conference Board released a study indicating that more than 60 percent of the people who work in the United States are dissatisfied with their jobs, and this study wasn't alone in reporting this statistic. Yet, just four months later, the Society for Human Resources Management issued a report indicating that 80 percent of employees are *satisfied* with their jobs.

Then, in August 2007, a study released by the National Opinion Research Center at the University of Chicago, *Job Satisfaction in America: Trends and Socio-Demographic Correlates*, stated that 86 percent of the people interviewed between 1972 and 2006 said they were satisfied with their jobs, and that only 4 percent reported being very dissatisfied. This report suggests that these levels have remained essentially unchanged over the last four decades. Which report do you believe?

I don't think any of these highly credible reporting entities is wrong. I suspect that a large proportion of employees are content in their job and career. But I also suspect that another large proportion may be dissatisfied with their employer-provided job satisfactions. We really won't know until we finally separate "job satisfaction" from "career contentment." Until then, I believe the uncertainty and confusion will persist for another few decades.

In the meantime, writers, theorists, and bloggers still randomly refer to job satisfaction as contentment, and my Google alerts keep spewing forth daily feeds about how bad job dissatisfaction is and how to fix it—when apparently we're not even clear on whether a problem exists or what we should be fixing. What's happening is a travesty.

The Old Paradigm

So what's the solution to this travesty? Interestingly enough, the favored solution—although we've proved it hasn't worked—is to fix job dissatisfaction with new and improved job satisfaction: communication, involvement, training, supervision, incentives, teams, flex schedules, flex benefits, business casual dress, job sharing, telecommuting, enrichment, engagement, gain sharing—you name it.

Although these improvements are all important, worthwhile, and viable tactics that can achieve incremental successes, so far none have proven able to sustain job satisfaction, and they probably won't, unless employees are content and in the right job to begin with. Also, the more we're given, the more we want, and, thus, the problems simply persist at a higher level of expectation: What have you done for me lately? This raises doubts about whether we can fully satisfy one, let alone all, employees all the time. It's impossible to do this—and it makes no sense to continue thinking that more tactics to achieve satisfaction are the solution while employers are taking costs out of the business. Who are we fooling? It's sad and factitious, if you know what I mean.

To quote Christopher Peterson: "Career contentment trumps job satisfaction." Not only do we need to distinguish job satisfaction from career contentment, we need to initiate an assertive, determined effort to teach people how to recognize their career contentment. It's time to shift from the old job satisfaction paradigm:

> *Do what you love—and then, in exchange for your hard work, time, and talents, the employer will reciprocate by helping to make you satisfied.*

This old paradigm seems fair, but it has been used to train employees to expect employers to make them satisfied, and it limits job satisfaction to an either/or proposition. Either you have it or you don't, and you can either stagnate or leave unless the employer provides satisfaction. There is no middle ground.

Furthermore, the old paradigm fails to adequately address the employee part of the equation—their power to exercise control, as we've discussed it in this book. Because the focus of control is on the employer, the old paradigm overlooks the control that employees can and already do exercise over their thoughts, emotions, reasoning, talents, and choices to achieve career contentment.

The New Paradigm

So what's the new paradigm—what's beyond job satisfaction? Here's a draft:

> *Along with doing what you love, look for ways to love what you do. Your career is the pursuit of contentment rooted in meaningful work that fulfills your calling and purpose—not in the pursuit of transient satisfactions that lead to complaints and keep you dependent on employers.*

As we've discussed in the book, I believe we can all agree that employers are concerned first with the needs of their business and only second with their commitments made to employees, and that employees are concerned first with the fulfillment of their career and life purposes and only second with their commitments made to employers. It's hoped that everyone's efforts will favorably influence the satisfaction of the other, but there are no guarantees.

The employer and the employee each view the other as interchangeable to suit their evolving needs and purposes. Employers change employees, just as employees change jobs, careers, and employers. An employee who is content in his or her work is likely to stay even if not entirely satisfied, but an employee who is misplaced or discontent will leave despite your best efforts to keep him or her satisfied. Those employees can't be paid enough to ignore or waste their talents—or at least it won't last too long, because contentment trumps satisfaction.

In the future, it will be essential for employers to continue to provide for the basic job satisfaction of employees but also to reorient employees to recognize their own career contentment. So it would be a good idea for us to end the confusion by keeping these terms forever separate—until the next problem arises. Remember, nothing is perfect.

It's to the advantage of employers to have employees who are genuinely content, doing what they love and loving what they do, rather than not knowing what they want, accepting the wrong job for the incentives, or dissatisfied and waiting for more. Likewise, it's to the advantage of employees to learn to recognize their career contentment and choose to pursue it rather than suffer the harmful effects of poor performance, job stress, burnout, or unwanted terminations.

Key Aspects of Career Contentment

With this new paradigm as the foundation, employers and human resource departments need to consider five key aspects of career contentment:

First, career contentment is not a program but an optional state of mind demonstrated by each employee. It cannot be imposed or required but can be recognized intentionally as the agreeable middle ground. This is feasible when developed as a predisposition or mindset about careers. However, using this mindset represents a change in how employees normally respond to their circumstances, what they expect from themselves and employers, and the control they exercise to pursue and enjoy the career they desire. It's easier to complain about dissatisfaction, but doing so keeps employees dependent on employers and delays employees in fulfilling their goals.

Second, it is mutually beneficial for everyone to have contented employees on board, in jobs they desire and in which they are most productive and willing to endure, despite the inevitable dissatisfactions posed by an imperfect world. As such, beyond employers' efforts to keep employees satisfied—which they still should make—employers should emphasize matching employees with meaningful work and training them to recognize their own career contentment. Likewise, beyond employees' efforts to keep employers satisfied—which they still should make—employees should emphasize recognizing and pursuing their own career contentment rather than expecting employers to make them satisfied.

Third, employees who are content in their work should develop the predisposition to endure by learning to recognize the agreeable middle ground when circumstances challenge their job satisfaction. Similarly, they should develop the resolve to take their contentment elsewhere if their job suddenly lacks meaning or does not fulfill their calling or purpose. Callings and purposes change unexpectedly.

Fourth, employees who are truly discontent in their work are probably in the wrong job or have not developed a predisposition to recognize their contentment. If, despite their efforts and the employer's assistance, they cannot recognize their contentment, they should consider changing jobs or careers if their intention is to fulfill their calling and purpose. It serves no purpose to complain when they can endure or leave.

Fifth, compromises are essential in any human endeavor, and running a business is no exception. You are who you are but also who you're paid to be. Occasions will arise where the employer or employee is challenged to endure despite the absence of satisfaction or the ability to quickly do something about it. Regardless of the situation, it is still feasible to use your reason and recognize some agreeable middle ground, and from there, to work toward doing what's required or most appropriate to the fulfillment of your purpose. A little bit of old-fashioned contentment can go a long way. And with that, let's look at one final, bonus Recruiter's Notebook entry.

RECRUITER'S NOTEBOOK

Look Mom, I'm on the Radio!

It feels silly to admit this, but years ago, while at the Renaissance Faire in Bristol, Wisconsin, I visited a psychic. But it's what she *didn't* say that has affected my life most profoundly.

No one predicted that I would one day host my own talk radio program, or that one of my interview guests would be one of the world's most cited psychologists, who cofounded the new positive psychology. Even if this had been predicted, I'd have never taken the prediction seriously.

After writing this book, I began working on the supplemental guidebooks and instructional audios that would apply the book's principles down at the "how-to" level for trainers, coaches, individuals, and human resources departments. For help in designing the learning exercises, I relied on the very able and innovative Michelle Filicicchia, a top trainer and curriculum designer who came highly recommended by our local ASTD chapter president, Ken Phillips.

As the main book, the guidebooks, and the audios were all being readied for publication, I began preparing myself for the task of marketing. Never having written a book before, I put myself through training offered by the book marketing expert Steve Harrison, and I attended his 2007 National Publicity Summit in New York City.

This exhausting event enabled me to pitch my book 75 times to members of the media. Imagine trying to explain this book within two minutes to editors and producers for leading magazines, syndicated radio programs, *Good Morning America*, *The View*, CNBC, and ABC News. It was so fast and hectic most people couldn't think beyond job satisfaction. They kindly suggested I contact them again after the book was published.

One of the media mavens who specializes in career information suggested that the topic of career contentment seemed important enough that I should consider starting my own radio program. Rather than chasing down the media and convincing them to interview me, I could have authors and experts come to me. This made sense, and all I'd have to do was find a radio station willing to take a chance on a yet-unpublished author.

I submitted proposals to a few radio stations discussing my mission and my Campaign to Retire Job Dissatisfaction, and the greatest interest was shown by Melissa Schmitz and Jeff Spenard, the executive producer and president of VoiceAmerica.com. They're nice people, I liked the professionalism of their Business Channel, and their programs are accessible worldwide on the Internet. Perfect! But before proceeding, they wanted to know who I planned to interview on the program. I hadn't thought of that.

One thing I observed at the National Publicity Summit is how becoming a "radio personality" opens doors. It gives you a reason to speak with people with whom you might otherwise not get a chance to speak, provided they have something to discuss that other people might want to hear. I made a list of all the people I'd like to know more about, starting with the people from whom I learned the most while writing this book.

Due credit is given in this book to the works of Martin Seligman and Christopher Peterson for paving the way for others like me to better understand the psychology of happiness, optimism, and thinking nonnegatively. Without their pioneering efforts, it would have been difficult for me to understand contentment. Who better to have as an interview guest than the author of *A Primer in Positive Psychology*, Chris Peterson?

I put on my "radio personality" hat and was about to call Chris from my converted-bedroom radio studio when it occurred to me that he knows tons about happiness, satisfaction, and optimism, but in all his works I saw only a few references to contentment, and it was always in the context of satisfaction. At this point, none of my materials had been published, so I assembled several of my articles and sent them to him in an email indicating that I would call him after he'd had a chance to review them. My stated objective was to interview him on a radio program called *The Positive Psychology of Career Contentment*. That sounded important enough.

A few days later, I called Chris and we discussed the articles and the relevance of positive psychology to career contentment. He was intrigued, liked what he'd read, and said it seemed we were on the same path and that he'd

Look Mom, I'm on the Radio! (continued)

do the program after he returned from vacation. Fantastic! In the meantime, I told him I'd develop the program outline and prepare a few questions we could discuss later.

When Chris returned, we resumed our conversations. He wanted clarification on how I defined "satisfaction" and "contentment," because, from his perspective, they were terms he thought meant the same thing. Here we go again. I persisted in explaining the difference and provided a few examples. He said he was good to go, and it was now 48 hours to showtime.

On the morning of the radio interview, I had a hunch Chris might appreciate looking at an excerpt from this book in which I discussed the etymology of the words "satisfy" and "content" (see chapter 7). I emailed him the document, hoping he'd read it before the program.

It's now five minutes to showtime. Chris and I have each called the station engineer to begin the live program. We're chatting as we wait for the countdown. Crossing my fingers, I casually ask Chris if he's had a chance to read my last email. He said yes. The etymology helped him to finally resolve the difference between contentment and satisfaction, and he also said it's been overlooked that contentment trumps satisfaction. At this point, I was literally jumping up and down with joy as the engineer was counting in one of my ears, "5, 4, 3, 2 and..." "Welcome to Career Contentment Radio. I'm your host, Jeff Garton."

Look Mom, I'm on live radio. It's my own program, and I'm interviewing one of the world's most influential psychologists. And as I'm having fun experimenting with my new radio voice, it occurs to me that I forgot to tell Chris this was my first program.

The author's efforts to implement career contentment begin with the end in mind, with the Campaign to Retire Job Dissatisfaction mentioned in the final Recruiter's Notebook entry above. Information about this global campaign can be found online at www.career contentment.com, where you'll also find several how-to resources that were developed based on the contents of this book. And for introductory information about the campaign, as well as a conversational review of the essence of this book, simply continue reading the following highlights from an interview with the author.

Career Contentment and the Campaign to Retire Job Dissatisfaction: Highlights from an Interview with the Author

On August 8, 2007, the author was interviewed by Beth Erickson, a psychologist and the host of the radio show *Mirrors of the Soul* on HealthyLife.net. The one-hour program can be downloaded from www.careercontentment.com. The following highlights from this interview provide a good overview of career contentment and the goals of the Campaign to Retire Job Dissatisfaction.

What is the Campaign to Retire Job Dissatisfaction? The campaign is a grassroots marketing effort featured on www.careercontentment.com. This website serves as a one-stop site with a collection of free articles and audio downloads, podcast feeds, and an opportunity to participate in a blog that allows the public to learn more about career contentment and share experiences without releasing company or individual names.

The campaign issues a wakeup call by reminding people that not everything is perfect or within their ability to control, and how it's unrealistic to expect employers to satisfy everyone, but you can always recognize your own career contentment.

Starting in February 2008, this website will be featuring all the new career contentment self-help resources and learning materials for use by individuals, employers, and human resources departments as well as trainers and career coaches. We're very excited by these one-of-a-kind resources.

How do you define career contentment? Career contentment is the peace derived from work made meaningful by the use of your talents to fulfill your calling and purpose. I view contentment as a state of mind and resiliency strength that the individuals control by their ability to reason and recognize the acceptable middle ground. It's neither dependent nor conditional on other people or material things, which is why you can be content even if you're not happy or satisfied.

Is contentment the same as complacency? No. Complacency may get you fired. Don't confuse contentment with being laid-back or settling for less. Realize that nothing in this world is absolutely perfect, completely satisfying, or always goes your way. For instance, you may not be happy or satisfied with your weight, finances, car, house, job, boss, or spouse, but you don't jump off a bridge or upgrade these things every week. You reason to recognize the acceptable middle ground and build from there to improve your situation. Contentment proves you can live without satisfaction, but not without your ability to reason and endure thanks to your contentment.

What does career contentment enable people to do? A contented state of mind is somewhat comparable to happiness, in that it is beneficial to your effectiveness and ability to endure. A peaceful mind thinks clearly, makes better choices, and more easily tolerates things that are upsetting. The opposite, a discontented state of mind, is comparable to driving a car filled with noisy kids while trying to navigate with notes on a napkin, tuning in your favorite radio station, and then noticing that the gas tank is practically empty and you forgot your cellphone and wallet. How can you function?

Career contentment relies on the control you exercise over your thoughts, emotions, reasoning, talents, and choices to fulfill your calling and purpose. It's your pursuit of career contentment that helps to reveal your deep interests and purposes for working.

You say that career contentment is liberating and empowering. How so? Contentment is based on reasoning that is independent of other people and material things. Right now, by using your imagination and visioning, you can experience the contented emotions to be derived from your next vacation. If you choose, those feelings of contentment can benefit your mood the rest of today, tomorrow, and for as long as you like. You can't say that about satisfaction, until you get what makes you satisfied. Contentment is more powerful than most people realize.

What contributes to career contentment? It helps if your work is meaningful and you believe you're on the right track to fulfill your calling and purpose. It also helps if you don't expect everything to be perfect or always go your way, and you're resilient enough to cope with the inevitable job dissatisfactions that come with every job. Getting to this point relies on the control you exercise over your thoughts, emotions, reasoning, talents, and choices. Otherwise, you can live in response to your circumstances, or allow others to control your career. I believe you can help to create a better life and career for yourself by improving how you think, feel, and act.

Are employers concerned about your career contentment? Should they be? Employers seem curious and optimistic about career contentment. After all, they've been struggling for decades to keep employees satisfied, and obviously it's not working.

Any experienced human resources person will tell you an employee in the wrong job or who lacks meaningful work will leave, and it doesn't matter how hard you try to keep them satisfied. But an employee who is content in the right job is more likely to stay even if they're not entirely satisfied. This means that career contentment is potentially less expensive but yet far more valuable to employers than job satisfaction. The problem is that we've overlooked the importance of training employees how to recognize their contentment. As a result, we live and work expecting employers to make us satisfied, and realistically that's not always possible. It's no wonder we haven't been able to resolve job dissatisfaction. My daughter is experiencing the same dissatisfactions my grandmother experienced when she was an intern, and the same dissatisfactions experienced by me and my parents as well.

We're always going to need the employer-provided satisfactions, but it's time we learned to recognize our own career contentment as well. If you lack job satisfaction, it's because you haven't learned how to recognize your contentment or you're in the wrong job. There's no reason to complain if and when you take the appropriate actions to have the career you desire.

Is it possible to have both career contentment and job satisfaction? Yes, it's the optimum situation to have both job satisfaction and career contentment. But you can also have one without the other. Let's say you've got an enviable job with excellent pay and benefits, a good boss, and opportunity for advancement. You have job satisfaction, but this doesn't guarantee that you have career contentment. Not if you're sitting there thinking you're in the wrong job, or being called to something or someplace else closer to your deepest interests. You have job satisfaction but lack career contentment. You're restless and are likely to leave.

Now let's say you're in a job you absolutely love that fulfills your deepest interests and purposes for working. You have career contentment, but this doesn't guarantee that you have job satisfaction. Not if your employer-provided satisfactions are less than what you expect due to a bad boss, low pay, unreasonable hours, or unfriendly co-workers. You might stay but simultaneously resent what's happening.

Do you see the difference and the significance of separating job satisfaction from career contentment? But don't think that we already make this distinction with "intrinsic" satisfaction. You can't have intrinsic satisfaction without the job supplied by the employer, and the mere job satisfactions used to attract, motivate, and retain you have very little to do with whether or not you fulfill your career calling and purpose. You can be content with or without job satisfaction, but only you can make that decision.

What is the role of feelings in career contentment? Contentment is a feeling, and because we tend to act in response to our feelings, I'd think operating with a contented mind enhances one's performance. It's better than functioning with a mind that is preoccupied with fear, worry, doubt, or envy. The example I like to use is you can think to feel rich without owning a dime. Empires have been built starting from nothing but just the power of this contented feeling. So why not apply this beneficial feeling to your work and career?

You talk about recognizing a middle ground. What do you mean? Dissatisfaction is the result of an expectation that's not been fulfilled. Either you have satisfaction or you don't. There's no middle ground. Yet it's possible to create the middle ground by reasoning to recognize contentment, something satisfaction doesn't allow. You didn't get that last job, but you really didn't like them either. You don't drive a Porsche, but your Toyota gets you around just fine. You don't live in the White House, but your house is a step up from the dorm room you had in college. You reason to recognize a middle ground.

What are some outcomes of finding career contentment? Career contentment isn't found. It's recognized wherever you choose to recognize it, thanks to your reasoning that occurs independently of other people and material things. You need this independence to pursue what gives you career contentment. Your callings, if you choose to pursue them, may not always be with the same career or employer. So the biggest outcome might be looking back on your career with the peace of mind that you did what you were supposed to do rather than regretting not doing what you wanted. That's career contentment.

Does career contentment relate to purpose or meaning? Yes. Career is the pursuit of the contentment derived from work that is meaningful to the fulfillment of your calling and purpose. We really don't know what a calling is, except to say that it may not be what you do best but rather what you have a deep interest in doing most. Your purpose is personal and related to why you work and what contributions you wish to make. Both your calling and purpose may change as you age and your interests evolve. This is why career is the pursuit of contentment, and why employer-provided satisfactions sometimes lag behind what you're looking for today.

In one survey I saw quoted on your website, you say that the United States ranks fourth in the world in whining and dissatisfaction. What do you make of that? France, Sweden, and the United Kingdom are supposed to be the biggest whiners. It's a symptom indicating that expectations were not fulfilled. Employers aren't fulfilling their part of the bargain, or employees are expecting too much, or both. As I see it, employees have been trained to expect satisfaction, and yet it's impossible to expect employers to satisfy everyone all the time. Something's got to give.

We shouldn't be too surprised when, for the last 20 years, employers have been intent on taking costs out of the business and expecting more output from fewer employees who are less satisfied due to longer hours and reduced benefits. It's business, and I think we've missed the boat by not teaching employees how to recognize their career contentment. We're stuck on a paradigm that says: Do what you love, and in exchange for your hard work, employers will make you satisfied. It's not happening, and more important, it's taken our eyes off the contentment of working for the pleasure of using our talents.

Why do you think we're seeing the trend of people changing jobs much more frequently than people did even a generation ago? What contributes to this? Beyond the fact that there's been a resurgence of layoffs, the trend toward free agency and voluntary job and career changes tends to confirm the reports about job dissatisfaction, but it also hints at a growing sense of disillusionment and discontent.

Employer-employee loyalty was gone long ago, so more recently I think people have been searching for greater meaning as to why they're working. Contributing to this have been terrorism, war, the economy, natural disasters, the loss of jobs to outsourcing and to cheaper labor overseas, new and seemingly uncontrollable diseases—many things. We're drawn to reality TV programs in record numbers for distraction and to see how other people are coping in real time.

All the while this is going on, the only thing employees have to cling to but don't have—and all they've been taught, know, and understand—is job satisfaction. It's time to begin teaching people how to depend less on employers for their satisfaction and how to recognize their own career contentment. They do it anyway, but if done the right way, I suspect we'd see a lot less turnover. By this I mean that many who complain about dissatisfaction may occupy jobs they love and shouldn't have to leave. We're not helping them recognize their contentment.

How can there be career contentment when fewer employees have to work harder for less? Remember, career contentment is neither dependent nor conditional—except on how you think. It exists as a peaceful state of mind—not in response to circumstances but in response to how you think about those circumstances. Look for the acceptable middle ground.

The idea for career contentment was based in part on *Man's Search for Meaning*, by Viktor Frankl, the Austrian psychiatrist who survived to write about his experience in multiple Nazi concentration camps. If, by reasoning, he could endure some of the most despicable conditions on Earth, certainly we can endure our job dissatisfactions for the sake of pursuing the opportunity to fulfill our calling and purpose.

Is career contentment related to getting what you deserve? Not exactly. Feeling that you're entitled to or deserve something implies there's an expectation to be fulfilled, which is more related to pride and satisfaction. You can be content regardless of whether you get what you deserve or what others think you deserve, and this is more related to gratitude and humility. You need a little of both pride and humility.

Can career contentment be earned? Yes, and it's easier to earn than happiness or satisfaction. It's earned by the independent control you exercise over your thoughts, emotions, reasoning, talents, and choices to fulfill your calling and purpose. No other person or employer holds the key to your career contentment. It's personal, whereas happiness and satisfaction are codependent on you and others to fulfill some condition or expectation. Contentment can exist anytime you say it exists, without depending on others. But you still have to ensure that your work is meaningful to your purpose.

You seem to place a negative spin on job satisfaction. Am I reading you right? Yes, but it's the result of my own impatience. People's minds are locked on job satisfaction and completely miss the limitations and problems it creates. They are not yet aware of career contentment to the extent I am as a result of writing my book.

Job satisfaction is so confusing that right now two highly credible reporting entities in the United States can't agree on how many workers are dissatisfied, which means they can't even agree on what job satisfaction is. It's not just a little disagreement, it's huge. In February of this year, one entity reported that 60 percent of U.S. workers are dissatisfied. Then, four months later, another entity reported that 80 percent of workers are satisfied. Who's right?

"Job satisfaction" lacks a consistent meaning. It refers simultaneously to people, things, and events, and they could be intrinsic or extrinsic, and you never know if that means to the job or to the employee. It's generally assumed that everyone will be satisfied by the same things and that people's needs remain constant or don't change as we age. One size does not fit all.

It still remains that you can't have job satisfaction—intrinsic or extrinsic—without a job that is provided and controlled by employers. Also, you can't promote yourself, give yourself a pay raise, a bigger bonus, or a vacation, and you can't trade in your boss and co-workers when they make you dissatisfied. Job satisfaction is always employer provided and controlled.

We've ignored what the employee controls, which is not the job, employer, or satisfaction, but their thoughts, emotions, reasoning, talents, and choices that enable their career contentment. You need both satisfaction and contentment, but you control only one. You control contentment, and employers control satisfaction.

Do employers and managers have any obligation to contribute to career contentment? No. Employers are obligated to the business, which includes fulfillment of their commitments made to employees. Employees are obligated to the fulfillment of their life purposes but also to the commitments they make to employers. It's up to each how they choose to satisfy the other, and they can only hope that what they do influences the other's contentment. Each will do what they have to do—that's their obligation. In this regard, employers view employees as interchangeable, just as employees view jobs, careers, and employers as interchangeable. It's a matter of what each perceives as necessary to fulfill their purpose. Job satisfactions are important but secondary— unless the employee is in it just for the money.

Would they be wise to contribute to career contentment? Yes. If employers would like to improve employee retention and performance, and reduce job dissatisfaction complaints, they would be wise to train employees how to recognize their own career contentment rather than always depend on them for more, new, and improved satisfactions. Over the last three decades, we've proved that you cannot fix job dissatisfaction with more satisfaction. Also, no one benefits from having the wrong person in the wrong job or complaining about dissatisfaction.

Getting to where you are today proves that you can make do without satisfaction, but you couldn't have endured without the ability to reason and build upon your contentment. Career contentment trumps necessary but transient and unreliable job satisfactions.

Appendix A: Career Contentment— Self-Assessment

Based on the premise that contentment is a relaxed state of mind and that nothing is perfect, to what extent do you experience career contentment today? Take this assessment and find out. Don't labor over your responses. Instead, go with your first response. For each section, tally your scores and fill in the numbers at the end of the assessment. Finally, calculate the percentage of yes, no, and N/A responses.

Do you agree with these statements?
Checkmark Yes, No, Not Applicable (NA)

A. Enjoyment and contentment	Yes	No	NA
1. You are doing what you love and you are you happy			
2. You are fulfilling your ambitions and life's purpose			
3. You feel challenged and your strengths are fully utilized			
4. You work hard and enjoy what you do			
5. You feel passionate, engaged, and energized			
6. You find yourself "in the zone" and lose track of time			
7. You are motivated by what you do			
8. You can't see yourself doing anything else			
9. Money is important, but not a deal breaker because you love what you do			
10. You feel a sense of fulfillment			

	Yes	No	NA
11. You can envision a career path for yourself			
12. Your personal and professional lives are balanced			
13. You know how to relax, have fun, and make friends			
14. You make health and fitness a priority			
15. Vacations and holidays are planned and taken			
Subtotal			
B. Environment and team	**Yes**	**No**	**NA**
16. You complement the team and feel a positive chemistry with them			
17. You can be yourself without worrying about what others think			
18. You feel that you're in the right position, at the right time, with the right people			
19. You feel minimal levels of doubt, fear, and uncertainties			
20. You are confident and know what you are doing			
21. You can change career directions if you need to and/or want to			
22. You know what to do without being told			
23. Your contribution makes a difference and is valued			
Subtotal			
C. Resources, recognition, and accomplishments	**Yes**	**No**	**NA**
24. You are recognized for your unique abilities			
25. You feel empowered to utilize your gifts			
26. You perceive feedback as positive and constructive			
27. You feel the environment is safe to make mistakes and learn from them			
28. You believe that procedures and bureaucracy are not insurmountable			
29. You experience contentment in spite of barriers that come with the job			
30. You think that the compensation you want and need is adequate			
31. Your "above and beyond efforts" are acknowledged			
32. You accomplish goals that you set			
33. You have pride associated with what you do			

		Yes	No	NA
34.	You are trusted and respected by your boss			
35.	You are trusted and respected by your co-workers and/or direct reports			
	Subtotal			
D.	**Hope and optimism**	**Yes**	**No**	**NA**
36.	You feel hopeful and optimistic with regard to your career path			
37.	You recognize the position that you're in isn't ideal, but it works for now			
	Subtotal			
E.	**Career path**	**Yes**	**No**	**NA**
38.	You have a career plan that you are excited about			
39.	You know what you want and you are making strides with your career			
40.	You are willing and able to make things happen to "do what it takes"			
41.	You are decisive and sure about career specific situations			
42.	You are able to identify the acceptable middle ground with all things			
43.	You already experience career contentment in your life			
	Subtotal			
F.	**Support network**	**Yes**	**No**	**NA**
44.	You have a mentor or coach to assist you			
45.	Your friends are supportive and affirm your career and/or direction			
46.	Your spouse is supportive and affirms your career and/or direction			
47.	You have a network of professionals that you can tap into			
48.	You are a member of organizations that support your goals and aspirations			
	Subtotal			
G.	**Sense of control**	**Yes**	**No**	**NA**
49.	You exercise control over the decisions regarding your career			
50.	You are able to market yourself and gain employment			
51.	You are certain regarding your direction and purpose			
	Subtotal			

Career contentment scoring	Yes	No	NA
A. Enjoyment and contentment			
B. Environment and team			
C. Resources, recognition, and accomplishments			
D. Hope and optimism			
E. Career path			
F. Support network			
G. Sense of control			
Totals			
Divide by 51			
Percentage of total			

Appendix B: Self-Assessing Your Decisions to Leave

Career intention statement:

It is within your control to fulfill or modify your career intentions.

In the space below, restate your career intention (goal, dreams, and purposes):

_____

_____

_____

	Checkmark Answers
Does your current decision help to fulfill your career intention?	☐ Yes ☐ No
Will your decision prolong the fulfillment of your career intention?	☐ Yes ☐ No
Will your decision change your career intention?	☐ Yes ☐ No

If so, what is your revised career intention, goal, dream, or purpose?

_____

_____

_____

Career senses:

It is within your control to interpret events and others as you see fit.	Checkmark Answers
Are you making this decision without pressure from others?	☐ Yes ☐ No
Can you sense joy, optimism, excitement, and enthusiasm linked with the decision?	☐ Yes ☐ No
Does this decision reflect your best option at this point?	☐ Yes ☐ No

Are you sensing this decision is best for you and your career?	☐ Yes	☐ No
Are you simply taking the easy way out?	☐ Yes	☐ No
Can you see yourself succeeding as a result of this decision?	☐ Yes	☐ No
Will this decision reflect the love you have for what you do?	☐ Yes	☐ No
Have you confirmed or validated your hunches and intuition on this matter?	☐ Yes	☐ No
Do you anticipate any regrets for having made this decision?	☐ Yes	☐ No

Career contentment balance:

It is within your control to bounce back from adversity and to endure or leave.

Are you making this decision with a contented state of mind?	☐ Yes	☐ No
Is your decision influenced by unchecked feelings of pride or entitlement?	☐ Yes	☐ No
Is your decision influenced by unchecked feelings of humility?	☐ Yes	☐ No
Have you checked for any excess feelings of intolerance?	☐ Yes	☐ No
Have you checked for any excess feelings of forebearance?	☐ Yes	☐ No
Do you have doubts or reservations you might have overlooked?	☐ Yes	☐ No
Have you reached a point of genuine discontentment?	☐ Yes	☐ No

Career contentment model:

It is within your control to think, feel, reason, choose, and change.

Is the current decision within your control?	☐ Yes	☐ No
Is your thinking realistic, optimistic, and opportunistic?	☐ Yes	☐ No
Is your thinking influenced by anger, fears, or doubts?	☐ Yes	☐ No
Have you assigned favorable meanings to your circumstances?	☐ Yes	☐ No
Are you responding in the most favorable manner?	☐ Yes	☐ No
Have you reasoned to recognize the agreeable middle ground?	☐ Yes	☐ No
Are you expecting complete satisfaction, or that everything will go your way?	☐ Yes	☐ No
Did you make a mistake in choosing work that is not meaningful?	☐ Yes	☐ No
Has your job since changed so that it is no longer meaningful?	☐ Yes	☐ No
Are you prohibited in any way from making best use of your talents?	☐ Yes	☐ No
Are you attracted to an opportunity that is more meaningful?	☐ Yes	☐ No
Will the new opportunity make better use of your motivated talents?	☐ Yes	☐ No

Do you assume complete control over your career intentions?	☐ Yes	☐ No
Have you abdicated control of your career?	☐ Yes	☐ No

Career flow model:

It is within your control to progress or recycle to have the career you desire.

Will this decision result in your pursuit of a career calling?	☐ Yes	☐ No
Have you weighed the advantages of both progressing and recycling?	☐ Yes	☐ No
Do you understand the effects (good and bad) related to progressing?	☐ Yes	☐ No
Do you understand the effects (good and bad) related to recycling?	☐ Yes	☐ No
Have you used this model to anticipate what to expect in the orientation phase?	☐ Yes	☐ No
Is the current decision influenced by the force of "time in job"?	☐ Yes	☐ No
Or by the force of "developing expertise"?	☐ Yes	☐ No
Or by the force of "career contentment"?	☐ Yes	☐ No
Do you have a contingency or backup plan?	☐ Yes	☐ No
Are you guiding your flow in the direction of your career intentions?	☐ Yes	☐ No

Balanced assets and sovereign powers:

It is within your control to develop, use, and acquire new assets.

Does this decision reflect best use of your assets?	☐ Yes	☐ No
Does this decision reflect best use of your sovereign powers?	☐ Yes	☐ No
Will the decision result in putting an unnecessary strain on either?	☐ Yes	☐ No
Will the decision optimize, benefit, or enhance your assets in any way?	☐ Yes	☐ No
Will the decision impair, limit, or restrain your sovereign powers in any way?	☐ Yes	☐ No

Re-evaluate your decision related to any boxes that are checkmarked.

References and
Further Reading

Amen, D. G. 1999. *Change Your Brain, Change Your Life: The Breakthrough Program for Conquering Anxiety, Depression, Obsessiveness, Anger, and Impulsiveness.* New York: Three Rivers Press.

Anthony, R. 2005. *Beyond Positive Thinking: A No-Nonsense Formula for Getting the Results You Want.* New York: Morgan James Publishing.

Argyle, Michael. 2002. *The Psychology of Happiness*, 2nd ed. New York: Routledge.

Badaracco, Joseph L., Jr. 2002. *Leading Quietly.* Boston: Harvard Business School Press.

Bandura, Albert. 1997. *Self-Efficacy: The Exercise of Control.* New York: Freeman.

Bateson, Mary Catherine. 1990. *Composing a Life.* New York: Plume.

Batstone, David. 2003. *Saving the Corporate Soul.* New York: Wiley.

Bench, Marcia. 2002. *An Insider's Guide to Career Coaching.* Lake Havasu City, AZ: High Flight Press.

Boldt, Laurence G. 1999. *Zen and the Art of Making a Living: A Practical Guide to Creative Career Design.* New York: Arkana.

Bolles, Richard. 1991. *How to Find Your Mission in Life.* Berkeley, CA: Ten Speed Press.

———. 1997. *What Color Is Your Parachute?* Berkeley, CA: Ten Speed Press.

Book, Howard E., and Steven J. Stein. 2002. *The EQ Edge: Emotional Intelligence and Your Success.* Toronto: Stoddart Publishing.

Bouffard-Bouchard, T. 1990. "Influence of Self-Efficacy on Performance in a Cognitive Task." *Journal of Social Psychology 130*: 353–63.

Bragdon, A. D., and D. Gamon. 2003. *Use It or Lose It! How to Protect Your Most Valuable Possession.* New York: Walker.

Bridges, William. 1980. *Transitions.* Reading, MA: Addison-Wesley.

Buckingham, Marcus, and Donald O. Clifton. 2001. *Now, Discover Your Strengths.* New York: Free Press.

Caple, John. 1993. *Finding the Hat That Fits: How to Turn Your Heart's Desire into Your Life's Work.* New York: Dutton.

Cloke, K., and J. Goldsmith. 2002. *The End of Management and the Rise of Organizational Democracy.* San Francisco: Jossey-Bass.

Collins, Jim. 2001. *Good to Great.* New York: HarperCollins.

Combs, A., and M. Holland. 1995. *Synchronicity: Science, Myth and the Trickster.* New York: Marlowe & Co.

Csikszentmihalyi, Mihalyi. 1990. *Flow: The Psychology of Optimal Experience.* New York: Harper & Row.

Dewey, J. 1933. *How We Think.* Boston: D. C. Heath.

Dispenza, J. 2007. *Evolve Your Brain: The Science of Changing Your Mind.* Deerfield Beach, FL: HCI.

Edelman, Marion. 1993. *The Measure of Our Success.* New York: HarperPerennial.

Erikson, E. 1980. *Identity and the Life Cycle.* New York: W. W. Norton. Orig. pub. 1959.

Fox, Matthew. 1995. *The Re-Invention of Work: A New Vision of Livelihood for Our Time.* New York: HarperCollins.

Frankl, Viktor. 1977. *Man's Search for Meaning.* New York: Pocket Books.

Fromm, Eric. 1976. *To Have or to Be.* New York: Harper & Row.

Gardner, Howard. 2004. *Changing Minds: The Art and Science of Changing Our Own and Other People's Minds.* Boston: Harvard Business School Press.

Gillham, J. E., ed. 2000. *The Science of Optimism and Hope: Research Essays in Honor of Martin E. P. Seligman.* Radnor, PA: Templeton Foundation Press.

Goldman, Daniel, et al. 2002. *Primal Leadership.* Boston: Harvard Business School Press.

Goleman, Daniel. 2000. *Working with Emotional Intelligence.* New York: Bantam Doubleday.

Hackett, G. 1995. Self-Efficacy in Career Choice and Development. In *Self-Efficacy in Changing Societies,* ed. A. Bandura. New York: Cambridge University Press.

Hassin, R. R., J. S. Uleman, and J. A. Bargh. 2006. *The New Unconscious: Social Cognition and Social Neuroscience.* New York: Oxford University Press.

Hawley, Jack. 1993. *Reawakening the Spirit in Work.* San Francisco: Berrett-Koehler.

Hillman, James. 1996. *The Soul's Code: In Search of Character and Calling.* New York: Random House.

Hoffman, E. 1994. *The Drive for Self: Alfred Adler and the Founding of Individual Psychology.* New York: Addison-Wesley.

Hudson, Fredric M. 1991. *The Adult Years: Mastering the Art of Self-Renewal.* San Francisco: Jossey-Bass.

Hudson, Fredric M., and Pamela D. McLean. 1995. *Life Launch: A Passionate Guide to the Rest of Your Life.* Santa Barbara, CA: Hudson Institute Press.

Huettel, S. A., and A. W. Song. 2004. *Functional Magnetic Resonance Imaging.* Sunderland, MA: Sinauer Associates.

James, William. 1950. *The Principles of Psychology*, vol. 1. New York: Dover Publications.

———. 1975. *Pragmatism.* Cambridge, MA: Harvard University Press. Orig. pub. 1885.

———. 1985. *Psychology: The Briefer Course (Works of William James).* Notre Dame, IN: University of Notre Dame Press. Orig. pub. 1892.

———. 2005. *Pragmatism and the Meaning of Truth (The Works of William James)*; introduction by A. J. Ayer. Cambridge, MA: Harvard University Press.

Jung, Carl. 1998. *Jung on Synchronicity and the Paranormal.* Princeton, NJ: Princeton University Press.

Kaye, Beverly. 1997. *Up Is Not the Only Way*, 2nd ed. Palo Alto, CA: Davies-Black.

Keeney, Bradford. 1996. *Everyday Soul: Awakening the Spirit in Daily Life.* New York: Riverhead Books.

Leider, Richard J., and David Shapiro. 1995. *Repacking Your Bags: Lighten Your Load for the Rest of Your Life.* San Francisco: Berrett-Koehler.

———. 2002. *Whistle While You Work.* San Francisco: Berrett-Koehler.

Lent, R. W., and G. Hackett. 1987. "Career Self-Efficacy: Empirical Status and Future Directions." *Journal of Vocational Behavior 30:* 347–82.

Loehr, Jim, and Tony Schwartz. 2003. *The Power of Full Engagement: Managing Energy, Not Time, Is the Key to High Performance and Personal Renewal.* New York: Free Press.

Lykken, David. 2000. *Happiness: The Nature and Nurture of Joy and Contentment.* New York: St. Martin's Griffin.

Mason, Marilyn. 1997. *Seven Mountains: The Inner Climb to Commitment and Caring.* New York: Dutton.

May, S. 2002. *Nietzsche's Ethics and His War on "Morality."* New York: Oxford University Press.

McKenna, Patrick J., and David Maister. 2002. *First among Equals: How to Manage a Group of Professionals*. New York: Free Press.

Murphy, Pat, and William Neill. 1993. *By Nature's Design*. San Francisco: Chronicle Books.

Myers, David. 1993. *Pursuit of Happiness*. New York: Avon Books.

Niven, David. 2000. *The 100 Simple Secrets of Happy People: What Scientists Have Learned and How You can Use It*. San Francisco: HarperSanFrancisco.

Noer, David. 1996. *Breaking Free*. San Francisco: Jossey-Bass.

North, Carolyn. 1994. *Synchronicity: The Anatomy of Coincidence*. Oakland, CA: Regent Press.

Peterson, Christopher. 2006. *A Primer in Positive Psychology*. New York: Oxford University Press.

Peterson, Christopher, and Martin E. P. Seligman. 2004. *Character Strengths and Virtues: A Handbook and Classification*. Washington and New York: American Psychiatric Association Press and Oxford University Press.

Redfield, J. 1996. *The Celestine Prophecy*. New York: Bantam Books.

Reivich, K. J., and A. Shatte. 2003. *The Resiliency Factor: Seven Keys to Finding Your Inner Strength and Overcoming Life's Obstacles*. New York: Random House.

Rokeach, M. 1968. *Beliefs, Attitudes, and Values: A Theory of Organization and Change*. San Francisco: Jossey-Bass.

Sapolsky, R. M. 2004. *Why Zebras Don't Get Ulcers*, 3rd ed. New York: Owl Books.

Scheinfeld, R., and R. G. Allen. 2003. *The 11th Element: The Key to Unlocking Your Master Blueprint for Wealth and Success*. New York: Wiley.

Schunk, D. H. 1984. "Self-Efficacy Perspective on Achievement Behavior." *Educational Psychologist 19:* 48–58.

Schutz, W. C. 1958. *FIRO: A Three-Dimensional Theory of Interpersonal Behavior*. New York: Holt, Rinehart & Winston.

Segal, Jeanne. 1997. *Raising Your Emotional Intelligence: A Practical Guide*. New York: Henry Holt.

Seibert, Al. 1996. *The Survivor Personality*, rev. ed. New York: Perigee.

Seligman, Martin E. P. 1998. *Learned Optimism: How to Change Your Mind and Your Life*. New York: Pocket Books.

———. 2002. *Authentic Happiness: Using the New Positive Psychology to Realize Your Potential for Lasting Fulfillment*. New York: Free Press.

Seligman, M. E. P., K. Reivich, L. Jaycox, and J. Gillham. 1996. *The Optimistic Child*. New York: HarperCollins.

Selye, H. 1977. *The Stress of My Life: A Scientist's Memoirs.* Toronto: McClelland and Stewart.

Shinoda Bolen, Jean. 1979. *The Tao of Psychology: Synchronicity and the Self.* New York: Harper & Row.

Stephan, Naomi. 1994. *Fulfill Your Soul's Purpose.* Walpole, NH: Stillpoint.

Vaughan, Allan. 1989. *Incredible Coincidence: The Baffling World of Synchronicity.* New York: Ballantine Books.

Wolin, Steven J., and Sybil Wolin. 1993. *The Resilient Self: How Survivors of Troubled Families Rise Above Adversity.* New York: Villard.

Zaidel, Dahlia. 2005. *The Neuropsychology of Art: Neurological, Cognitive, and Evolutionary Perspectives.* Philadelphia: Psychology Press.

About the Author

Jeff Garton is a speaker and certified professional career coach living in Lincolnshire, Illinois. He is actively involved in managing the Campaign to Retire Job Dissatisfaction, which involves training and education on the subject of career contentment. His career before becoming an entrepreneur in 2000 included more than 20 years in human resources with the Philip Morris Companies, where he led the global recruiting and internal staffing functions for Kraft Foods and the Miller Brewing Company. He has devoted his entire career to recruiting and coaching people through transitions. Since August 2007, he has also been the host of a talk radio program, *Career Contentment Radio*, which is heard worldwide every Thursday at noon PST on the VoiceAmerica.com radio network.

Garton holds an MA in organizational communication and public personnel administration from the University of New Mexico and a BA in history and political science from Glenville State College in West Virginia. His coaching certification is with the Career Coach Institute. He is a recipient of two Employment Management Association best-in-class awards for recruitment marketing. He has been a contributing author to *Employment Management Today*, a former advisory board member of the National Society of Hispanic MBAs, and a volunteer facilitator for the Career Resource Center in Lake Forest, Illinois. He is a member of the International Coach Federation, the International Association of Career Management Professionals, the Society for Human Resources Management, and the Employment Management Association.

Index